S0-ADV-549

Praise for B. Marie Christian's
Belief in Dialogue

"The subject of religion and spirituality in Latina literature merits as insightful an analysis as Christian's. This book adds to the understanding of Latina literature and its significant place in U.S. letters."

—Norma E. Cantú, Professor of English,
University of Texas at San Antonio

"This work is unquestionably an excellent contribution to the study of Latina literature. Its nuanced reexamination of conventional understandings of Latina Catholicism is both timely and compelling. Teachers and scholars of multiethnic studies and postcolonial studies will want to equip themselves with the insights of this important text."

—Dr. Teresa Derrickson, Assistant Professor of English,
Gonzaga University

"B. Marie Christian offers an incisive interrogation of Latina spirituality and empowerment through formation of feminist belief systems. Spanning a range of ethnicities and styles, Christian's masterly inquiry connects close readings of Latina texts with their larger, more profound cultural and historic contexts. Bold in conception and broad in scope, this masterly study provides a fresh perspective on women's ways of believing within repressive religious and cultural structures."

—Susan I. Gatti, Indiana University of Pennsylvania

CULTURAL STUDIES

A series of books edited by Samir Dayal

Belief in Dialogue

U.S. Latina Writers Confront Their Religious Heritage

B. Marie Christian

From one literature enthusiast to another! B. Marie Christian September 2005

OTHER

Other Press
New York

Copyright © 2005 B. Marie Christian

Production Editor: Robert D. Hack

This book was set in 12 pt. Apollo by Alpha Graphics of Pittsfield, NH.

10 9 8 7 6 5 4 3 2 1

All rights reserved. No part of this publication may be reproduced or transmitted in any form or by any means, electronic or mechanical, including photocopying, recording, or by any information storage and retrieval system, without written permission from Other Press LLC, except in the case of brief quotations in reviews for inclusion in a magazine, newspaper, or broadcast. Printed in the United States of America on acid-free paper. For information write to Other Press LLC, 307 Seventh Avenue, Suite 1807, New York, NY 10001. Or visit our Web site: www.otherpress.com.

Library of Congress Cataloging-in-Publication Data
Christian, B. Marie.
  Belief in dialogue : U.S. Latina writers confront their religious heritage / by B. Marie Christian.
    p. cm.
  Includes bibliographical references and index.
  ISBN 1-59051-146-8 (pbk. : alk. paper) 1. American fiction–Hispanic American authors–History and criticism. 2. American fiction–Catholic authors–History and criticism. 3. American fiction–Women authors–History and criticism. 4. Catholic women–United States–Intellectual life. 5. Hispanic American women–Intellectual life. 6. Religion and literature–United States. 7. Women and literature–United States. 8. Hispanic American women–Religion. 9. Spiritual life in literature. 10. Religion in literature. I. Title.
  PS153.H56C465 2005
  813'.50938282–dc22

                                                              2004020958

For my parents and my husband,
three people whose love and support
have made all the difference

Contents

Series Editor's Introduction

Samir Dayal

Today "globalization" is a word on everyone's lips. But if globalization has brought us a new age of "empire"—a new regime of sovereignty—then paradoxically the importance of the local, the particular, has also grown for those who are subordinated within this new regime of globalization. But to cleave to the particular and the local is not necessarily an abject or nostalgic reflex, as if one were living in denial of the inevitable. Against the universalizations and homogenizations of culture as well as the economy, the turn to the particular is a defense of place, culture, history, and individual experience. This turn is among the major concerns of cultural studies at our contemporary historical conjuncture. Barbara Christian's book is, in this respect, a timely contribution, sensitive to the exigencies of an affirmative politics of location.

Christian's book also seeks to redress the problem of the narrowness of the canon of Latin American literature. Even as the interest in Central and Latin American literature has grown considerably, this canon tends to underestimate the contribution of Latina writers and the significance of the Catholic Church in Latino/a cultures. The author's concentration on a carefully limited selection of women writers with a Latina cultural background provides insights into their shared dimensions and common motivations, and shows how a coherent critique of Catholicism informs their work. The premise here is that these Latina writers can make a particular contribution to an understanding of *communal* experience.

Other writers have proceeded from similar premises. Adrianne Aron, for instance, wrote that in many Latin American communities "people with little preparation for public expression—most notably, women—have come forward . . . to challenge oppressive power structures and to reappropriate for themselves and their communities the moral standards and social order taken away by the repression" (p. 175). Aron was writing with reference to women's groups such as the Mothers and Grandmothers of the Plaza de Mayo in Argentina, the Co-Madres (the Committee of the Mothers and Relatives of the Disappeared, Political Prisoners and Assassinated) in El Salvador, and the Grupo de Apoyo Mutuo (Mutual Support Group) in Guatemala. And there has been a prodigious output, especially since the 1980s, of literary studies of *testimonio* by Latin American women by literary scholars such as John Beverley and Kathleen Logan. Some of the surge in *testimonio* scholarship was indeed motivated by the conviction, as George Yúdice puts it, that *testimonio* could allow the voiceless to speak without the mediating intervention of intellectuals (see Bueno, pp. 116–117). These *testimonio* happened to be largely authored by women, but if the academic fashion for *testimonio* has passed, Christian suggests that other types of Latina women's narratives have still not received the kind of attention they deserve. While Christian's focus is on the literary aspects of the narratives, her situating of literary analysis within religio-sociological contexts is a significant contribution to the field.

This important work performs a crucial function in reminding readers that Catholicism is an irreducible element of the lives of so many, including the authors discussed in *Belief in Dialogue*, even if they have disavowed Catholic ritual and formal observance in their personal lives. Latino life is suffused by Catholicism's presence as a way of being in the world. At the same time, the writers Christian considers are critical of the sexual, political, and sociological ramifications of Catholic doctrine, and of the effects of patriarchal, hierarchical power in even the intimate particulars of daily living.

It would be a mistake to characterize this as an account of the literature of the "native informant," or a way of washing the community's dirty linen in public. Christian is more concerned with showing what "may appear to be political polemic to outsiders is actually an inside view of a culture continuing to develop an alternate philosophy. Marginalized, they desire their voice." That is to say, she regards these well-known women writers as providing a particular internal critique, a specifically gendered perspective on an indispensable feature in the culture and the everyday experience of Latinas.

Christian's analysis is nuanced enough to acknowledge that the writers are not concerned so much with Catholicism's future, but with "its permanent presence in their history and heritage. They cannot write accurately without revealing its failures, its importance, and the efforts to improve it through additions from other spiritual systems." Interestingly, what emerges from the discussion of the literature, as in Christian's second chapter, is not merely an internal critique of Catholicism but a specific reluctance to *abandon* it. Such reluctance would hardly be an issue if Catholicism did not permeate and in some ways constrain the social behavior and life-chances of ordinary people, especially women, in Latino/a cultures.

Not all of the writers are so reluctant, however. Christian details the withering interrogation of Catholicism in works by Helena María Viramontes, Esmeralda Santiago, Judith Ortiz Cofer, and Ana Castillo (most powerfully in *So Far from God*): such writers seem far indeed from belief. Whether the writers remain close to their faith or far, Christian demonstrates the depth and variety of the *presence* of the spiritual in Latina/o consciousness even—or especially—where it emerges as counterposed to the resistance to the authoritarianism of organized religion. As Michel Foucault put it, "Where there is power there is resistance" (p. 71). But an adjunct insight emerges as a result of Christian's strategy: that where there is resistance to the Church, there is also something like reverence for spiritual community.

This strategy is not without risk. The author clarifies, invoking Gloria Anzaldúa's much-quoted term, that in foregrounding religion Latina writers tread in a borderland, an "energetic but dangerous zone where beliefs, attitudes, and practices rub against each other in dynamic friction" (p. xvii, this volume). But there is also a potential reward: "Whether through argument or peaceful exchange, new resources and new solutions become available." One could even argue that a new, *gendered* relation to modernity lies waiting in the wings for minority literatures—a modernity that might be imagined from the margins, through the kind of Latina cultural invention that Christian seeks to document in this book. And while these Latina writers may live between two worlds, their challenge is not so much the postmodern one described by Ramón Saldívar, to "remain modern, to keep in step, to be contemporary, to make of modernity an incomplete project" (p. 84), but rather to reimagine modernity from their specific location, putting Catholicism in dialogue with a *mujerista* ethos.

Such dialectics, as the book's title suggests, are characteristic of Christian's procedure, although she herself does not insist on being "dialectical." Witness other key themes that motivate Christian's discussion, including syncretism and hybridity. These terms circulate as almost generic ciphers in some versions of postcolonial theory or cultural analysis. But there is a specific inflection to Christian's recourse to terms such as syncretism or hybridity. For instance, Christian writes that for Latina women, hybridity and syncretism are not merely fashionable rhetoric: "survival" itself "lies in the persistent restructuring of ideas drawn from as many sources as possible." And it is the archaeology of this particular dialectical instantiation of terms such as "permeability," or indeed *mestizaje*, that drives the argument and the close readings the author provides. The author notes, for instance, that readers, reviewers, and teachers are not always alert to the melding of Mexican, Yoruban, or other ancient belief systems in the common culture. Nor do they always grasp the ways in which "Ortiz Cofer explains the Espiritismo (European spiritism) practiced by her Puerto Rican grandfather, [or] García describes the Santería (African spiritualism) of Cuba, or . . . Anzaldúa invokes Coatlicue, an earth goddess of ancient Mesoamerican tribes."

One of the key arguments made by Christian is that Catholicism is not a monolithic and one-dimensional set of beliefs and practices. "The 'Catholicism' in these works draws from two millennia of Mesoamerindian spiritual beliefs; from multiple centuries of official and popular versions practiced by the Spanish in the vast Americas; from centuries of the spiritism of Africa, Europe, and the Antillean Caribbean; from decades of Latin American liberation theology; and recently, from mujerista theology." The author points to other, more particular differences that may not be clear to those outside the Latino/a community. She notes, for instance, that "[w]hile many non-Latinas/os recognize the figure called the Virgin of Guadalupe, few have noted that she is *mestiza* and is pregnant. Even fewer would recognize the Black Virgin, the Virgin of Monserrat, Our Lady of Regla, or Our Lady of Charity of Copper. Most are unaware of European and East European icons of a dark-skinned Virgin, so they could not realize that some such pictures and statues must have arrived with the Spanish," or indeed that "the Virgin of Guadalupe is both a sympathizer and a fighter for the poor and oppressed, a chief deity sometimes more revered than the Holy Trinity or Jesus."

Christian carefully contextualizes her recourse to theory. For instance, her preference for the term "another" as opposed to "the other" is evidence of her astute avoidance of preciousness and jargon. In contrast to the carelessness with which "otherness" is used in so much contemporary cultural theory, Christian is admirably restrained. She writes in her preface, "'Anotherness' as a philosophy works in Latina literature when characters shrug off their differences to preserve the mutual good." Furthermore, Christian is committed to the struggle in which anotherness can yield ethnic solidarity; yet she does not permit herself facilely to wave the banner of "*la Raza.*" Neither does she reach for ready-made narratives of "the nation," or "*mi pueblo,*" my people. Her way of tying the theoretical to the particular, and the particular to the collective, is to perform close textual readings with an eye on religious and gender politics.

It is not as though Christian is averse to theory or cultural criticism. Theory for her is not an end in itself but a scaffolding that supports the careful analysis of the body of works Christian wishes to focus on. She does reference cultural critics who use the postcolonialist paradigm implicitly: for instance she cites "non-Latina theorists such as Toni Morrison in *Playing in the Dark* and Anne McClintock in *Imperial Leather* [who] have explored the manner in which Western writers employ the imagery of darkness as a writing tool—in the 'darkening' or 'blackening' of character." While she distinguishes her own conception of "anotherness" from, say, a Frantz Fanonian conceptualization of "otherness," she recognizes the relevance of the postcolonial paradigm, and invokes the work of Edward Said, Homi Bhabha, and others such as Barbara Harlow to draw parallels with attitudes toward those vanquished in the conquest of the New World, as she does in Chapter 4, for instance. In that chapter she points out that some U.S. Latina writers have explicitly reminded readers of the collusion between the Church and colonizing powers. The confluence of antiracist, antisexist, anticlassist, and anticolonial theory provides a critical framework for Christian's work. Yet her more telling insights come from her culturally specific lens on the works she writes about. While she may not attend to the specific differences among the particular varieties of colonization in Asia, Africa, the Middle East, and the New World, her reference to postcoloniality as frame is appropriate, given the sociopolitical conditions that produced the writers she examines. As she writes, "Critically, Latinas do acknowledge the combined power of their political and religious colonization by the Spanish." Yet she also notes that "A significant aspect of Latina writing is [the] triple burden it carries as literature, social criticism, and literary criticism," and that the "syncretic, postcolonial view" represented in that writing "questions an all-or-nothing purism in religion and culture."

If the colonization of territories by imperial powers is a preoccupation for postcolonialism, the colonization of women's minds is an even more pressing issue for Christian. In Chapter 3, she notes that the modern Roman Catholic leadership "persists in doubting woman's equality in grace." So the resistance of Latinas did not emerge from a vacuum. Christian elaborates on the Latina writers' access to liberation theology and *mujerista* theology to elaborate the richness of the tradition of Latina cultural critique in a way that is surely unsurpassed by any comparable study of recent years.

Usefully, Christian takes pains to disabuse outsiders of common misconceptions and assumptions, such as that all Latinos are Catholic and that outsiders, including the reader, will readily recognize any and all manifestations of Catholicism. Beyond that she also distinguishes among establishment (Church) Catholicism, folk Catholicism, liberation theology, and *mujerista* and communitarian Catholicism, providing a historical contextualization to make sense of the emergence of these varieties of religious commitment. For instance, she points out that at the Council of Trent (1545–1563), Church leaders reentrenched their doctrinal control but effectively left everyday practices open to interpretation by the people, and these day-to-day practices eventually condensed into a folk tradition. By the same token in the distant Americas, local traditions were amalgamated in a hybridized manner with the practices transmitted across the Atlantic in a variety of ways, including the Conquistador voyages. This offers further evidence that in Christian's account "hybridity" has a specific genealogy, and she is especially careful to highlight the diversity of even the hybrid forms of popular religion.

Today it is as crucial as ever to understand the resistance to authoritarian cultural formations of all kinds, including established religion and globalizing capitalism in Central and South America. Liberation theology seems to have receded from public view, but its forms of resistant spirituality, if leavened by a *mujerista* awareness, can continue to be relevant notwithstanding that the term itself may not seem to be worth recuperating. While writers such as Enrique Dussel, for instance, continue to write prominent works developing ideas thematized in a liberation theology perspective, they tend to underemphasize women's issues, and this is where Christian seeks to intervene. She traces strains of such issues in

Ana Castillo and Sylvana Paternostro as well as in works by Sandra Benítez and Helena María Viramontes, for instance their representations of the travails of coffee plantation laborers and migrant workers. She also identifies similar politicized consciousness in Julia Alvarez's novel about Rafael Leónidas Trujillo's regime in the Dominican Republic.

There are points at which the author is almost too anxious to avoid direct confrontation of the masculinist or patriarchal tendencies in the Catholic Church, though she herself brings up these sensitive issues. Or perhaps it is more that the writers themselves are balancing conflicting impulses: to criticize as well as maintain a reformed religious institution on which they depend and seek to preserve as an important cultural matrix in which they themselves are nurtured. As Christian observes, the furthest that Judith Cofer's female protagonist will venture is to withhold giving "credit" for the resolution to her problems in life to "the patriarchal Christian God or to the intercession of Catholic priests." This is in part because Christian wishes to show how the Latina writers do not simply reject or deny Catholicism, do not see it as merely an oppressive influence on their lives and freedoms. In discussing Edna Escamill's *Daughter of the Mountain*, for instance, the chapel of Our Lady of Guadalupe is a literal as well as figurative desert refuge for the protagonist. The fine line these female characters must tread is seeking refuge in the Church while underscoring the ways in which it ultimately fails women as members of the flock. While the author's focus is on a *mujerista* or woman-centered critique, her more general motivation is that, as she writes in her second chapter, "[s]tatistically, the Latina world includes a heavy share of suffering from poverty and from biases related to race, gender, and class."

Catholic ritual itself (such as the Communion or the washing of the feet), whether undergirded by a firm belief or not, permeates the social arrangements and relationships represented in the works of the writers, especially those discussed in Chapter 4. The appearance of ritual as a leitmotif in these works, rather than being an empty performance, actually anchors the indi-

vidual who otherwise might not find a shared horizon with her
community. In another context, T.S. Eliot too had been drawn
as much to the ritual of the Anglican Church as to its theology.
Ritual then is a performative act that, even when it is transmuted
into new forms, induces meaning into the lives of those Christian's
authors write about. Even when there is an underlying suspicion of ritual as a distraction from authentic faith, this feature
of Latina women's everyday lives emerges as a central concern
of Christian's analysis: the negotiated dialogue between daily life
and belief, not canceling each other but gesturing toward an
"expanded spirituality."

But again the negotiation of such a spirituality does not pre-
clude a political critique. Writers such as Julia Alvarez, Christian
shows, are not above engaging in a re-negotiation of social conditions and the religious and political status quo. In *The Other Side
/ El Otro Lado*, Christian points out, Alvarez articulates a sting-
ing rebuke against the Catholic Church in the historicized context of the current political regime in the Dominican Republic. She
chastises the Church for "promoting martyrdom as a model of
fulfillment instead of fighting for the people's right to life and
peace." Similarly, Christian discusses Ana Castillo's critique of the
misogyny of the Church in her *Massacre of the Dreamers*. It is this
range of engagements with an institution fundamental to Chicana
life that Christian seeks to capture, and she organizes her book
by different modes of engagement.

The authors discussed in Christian's book often narrate the
varieties of suffering of the ordinary people and of women in
particular. Yet the point of these narratives is not to wallow in
pain or the *jouissance* of victimization. Often the account of suffering is testimony to the passion of the people and an occasion
for ennobling or at least humanizing sympathy, or fellow feeling,
with them. This is evident, for instance, in Chapter 7, which examines how Judith Ortiz Cofer's *Silent Dancing* and *The Latin Deli*
express the frustrations of growing up Latina in fact and in religion: "Although as an adult she no longer tries to wash away
her heritage the way she once tried to wash the color from her

skin, she still protests the restrictions placed upon Latinas/os from within and without their increasingly mixed culture."

One of the most attractive features of Christian's method is that she offers such close readings of the texts and that the claims she ventures on the basis of these close readings are supported and clarified by the wealth of cultural detail she has at her command. In Chapter 5, for instance, she discusses Julia Alvarez's biographical novel *In the Time of the Butterflies* in a close reading that draws out some of the themes she develops in the earlier chapters. Yet this book goes beyond providing another detailed literary analysis of narratives with a common thread running through them. It is also an important intervention in the study of Latino/a culture. It suggests that there might be promising continuities between the secular and the spiritual, that organized Catholicism ought to be supplemented with a multifaceted and rhizomatic "catholicity" of consciousness, an openness to questions of class, gender, and modernity. This urgent agenda even today remains underexplored in cultural studies. This is one of the book's most intriguing, if subtextual, provocations, and it points to one of the central tensions of our time: the tension between secularism as reformulated in a time of postmodern reason—and religion, which seems to belong to an utterly different discursive universe.

WORKS CITED

Amireh, A., and Majaj L. S., eds. (2000). *Going Global: The Transnational Reception of Third World Women Writers*. New York: Garland.

Aron, A. (1992). Testimonio, a Bridge between Psychotherapy and Sociotherapy. *Women and Therapy: A Feminist Quarterly* 13.2, part II: 173–189.

Beverley, J. (1989). The Margin at the Center: On Testimonio: (Testimonial Narrative). *Modern Fiction Studies* 35.1: 11–28.

Bueno, E. P. (2000). Race, Gender, and the Politics of Reception of Latin American *Testimonios*. In *Going Global*, ed. A. Amireh and L. S. Majaj, pp. 115–147. New York: Garland.

Foucault, M. (1978). *The History of Sexuality. Vol. 1: An Introduction,* trans. R. Hurley. New York: Pantheon.

Logan, K. (1977). Personal Testimony: Latin American Women Telling Their Lives. *Latin American Research Review* 32(1): 199–211.

Palumbo-Liu, D. (1995). *The Ethnic Canon: Histories, Institutions, and Interventions.* Minneapolis, MN: University of Minnesota Press.

Saldívar, R. (1995). The Borders of Modernity: Américo Paredes's *Between Two Worlds* and the Chicano National Subject. In *The Ethnic Canon,* pp. 71–87. Minneapolis, MN: University of Minnesota Press.

Yúdice, G. (1991). *Testimonio* and Postmodernism. *Latin American Perspectives* 70.8, No. 3: 15–31.

A Note on Terminology

The authors discussed in *Belief in Dialogue* represent diverse cultural backgrounds. Julia Alvarez and her family fled from the Dominican Republic to the U.S. Northeast when she was a teenager. Edna Escamill grew up in both the U.S. Southwest and Baja California, Mexico; and Judith Ortiz Cofer's immediate family lived with extended family in Puerto Rico when her U.S. Navy father was at sea, and in a barrio apartment in Paterson, New Jersey, when he was on shore. Esmeralda Santiago, also born in rural Puerto Rico, offers a different view of Puerto Rican life there and in New York City. Rosario Ferré, Rosario Morales, and Aurora Levins Morales provide still different insights on island existence and Puerto Rican heritage. Cuban-American Cristina García comments on island conditions and on the complex loyalties of Cuban exiles in the U.S. Gloria Anzaldúa, Pat Mora, Ana Castillo, Sandra Benítez, Helena María Viramontes, and Graciela Limón present views from the Tex-Mex borderland and California.

This heterogeneity complicates the vocabulary used to discuss the writers. The term *Latina* is widely used, but it is not the only one that refers to women of Latin American descent. Indeed, *Latina* is problematic because the diverse peoples grouped together as *Latin* and said to be from *Latin America* have been given those generic labels by anthropologists, sociologists, academics, government officials, and religious leaders. More precise terms exist to describe individual groups: *Hispanic, Chicana/o, Nuyorican, Puertoriqueña/o, Dominican American, Cuban American*, and so on. Nonetheless,

Latina and *Latino* appear most often in literary discussions about the people and lands once colonized by the Spanish. In the following chapters, *Latin American* refers to people who live in the Spanish-speaking lands south of the United States. *U.S. Latina/o* refers to a woman/man who derives from the people of Latin America but lives in the U.S. The adjective *Latino* also describes factors common to the men and women alike, such as the larger culture with its many components. A writer's specific heritage is noted only if the writer herself names it.

The terms *Mexica*, *Mexico*, and *Mexican* also may cause confusion. The noun or adjective *Mexica* pertains to an ancient Mesoamerican tribe of the area now known as Mexico. In the same context, some writers prefer the term *Aztec*, which denotes the ruling culture at the time of the Spanish conquest, and that term appears in quotations taken from them. In all situations, the adjective *Mexican* pertains to the Spanish colony called Mexico or to the later, independent country of Mexico.

Throughout the book, the word *church* is capitalized when it refers to an organized religion. It is not capitalized when it refers to a building.

Belief in Dialogue includes a glossary for Spanish and Spanglish expressions as well as allusions to Catholic, Mesoamerindian, Mexica, or Yoruban beliefs, deities, or symbols. Details of the complex history of Latin America are limited to those pertinent to the literature, and these are explained at the time of usage. The same is true of the specific religious vocabulary and concepts of Catholicism, Amerindian religions, spiritism, and *Santería*.

Introduction

Writing about spirituality is a daunting exercise. Every statement can be questioned from multiple angles, and the definitive statement is always out of reach, spinning around somewhere, pieces of it here and there, but no two in the same place at the same time. The diverse particles of the overall don't add up to an overall, as if they have affinity but no desire to commit. Instead, they rub together, their friction throwing off possibilities like sparks.

The spirituality operating in the works of U.S. Latina writers likewise defies definition but implies a lively and changing philosophy. It is always present, always important, and always different, even though the works in which it appears are not overtly about religion. Often labeled "Catholic," it is both more and less than that; it embraces elements of ancient Mesoamerindian religions, African spiritualism, and regional secular customs as well as the medieval Catholicism brought to the Americas by the Spanish. This complex underlying spirituality operates in the psyche and motivation of the characters; its flaws and merits reveal themselves in the outcome of events; its tone contributes to the ambiance of the stories. It deserves discussion.

Although the heavy influence of official Catholicism in this spirituality is generally acknowledged, Latinos as well as Catholic theologians and specialists on Latino cultures recognize that Latino Catholicism differs from the mainstream U.S. version of the religion. Various terms have arisen to describe it: popular Catholicism, folk Catholicism, popular religion, spirituality. As dynamic as the Latino culture itself, this unofficial or even anti-official religious sensibility adjusts constantly to the tensions between formal religious ideals and the realities of Latino experience. An expression of hundreds of years of such dialogue, it demonstrates the same resistance and resilience that have kept the wider culture alive despite the devastating political and economic colonization of Mexico, Central and South America, and the Caribbean. It also exhibits an openness to the side-by-side acceptance of vastly different ideologies, and thus it preserves its capacity to surprise participants and observers alike.

All of the authors discussed in *Belief in Dialogue* cite Catholicism—official as well as popular—as an influence on their growing up and an element of their current consciousness. Many of them have abandoned the private practice of Catholicism, but they cannot eradicate it from their bloodlines, language, and conscience. They consistently record its impact on Latino life regardless of the extent to which their own individual families have practiced, ignored, or rejected the faith. Their comments invite readers to consider not only the cultural persistence of Catholicism but also the constant criticism and unofficial modification of it.

Most of these authors are old enough to have chafed under the official Catholicism of the mid-twentieth century. They may have been in the process of rejecting it in the mid 1960s, when two watershed Catholic conferences changed the direction of Church leadership. During that time, the Second Vatican Council met in Rome to address attitudes and practices that failed to meet the needs of the faithful worldwide; and then the Latin American bishops met at Medellín, Colombia, to examine the recommendations of Vatican II in the context of the Americas south of the U.S. Despite the gradual changes begun during this decade of Church history, Latina writers do not appear to have been drawn back into the Church of their birth. Although they rarely engage in anti-Catholic polemic, they do question that religious code for its failure to nurture their people.

The writers' awareness of official and popular forms of Catholicism lends reliability to their picture of Latino life in the second half of the twentieth century. Writers such as Julia Alvarez, Judith Ortiz Cofer, Edna Escamill, and Graciela Limón depict the decades before the Vatican II changes. Others, such as Pat Mora, Ana Castillo, Esmeralda Santiago, Aurora Levins Morales, and Rosario Ferré, describe times up to the present, but in doing so they reveal centuries-old practices and attitudes that have survived among the priests and congregations in rural areas. Yet others, such as Cristina García and Margarita Engle, reveal the tensions suffered by families that have been physically, religiously, and politically divided since Castro came to power in Cuba. Sandra Benítez and Helena María Viramontes expose similar tensions accompanying the strife in El Salvador. For all these writers, an awareness of the interplay of culture, religion, and politics adds integrity to the physical, social, and psychological details of their creations.

Still, Catholicism is not the main topic of their works, and the writers do not make specific comparisons between mid-twentieth and twenty-first-century Catholicism. They are not concerned with its future, but with its permanent presence in their history and heritage. They cannot write accurately without revealing its failures, its importance, and the people's efforts to improve it by combining it with other spiritual systems. The religion evident in their characters' lives is in the process of change, and the ones adapting it are the people themselves, particularly the women.

If the works reveal any consistent viewpoint, it is that the term "Catholicism" encompasses a far greater variety of beliefs and practices for Latinas than the uninitiated reader might expect. The "Catholicism" in these works draws from two millennia of Meso-amerindian spiritual beliefs; from multiple centuries of official and popular versions practiced by the Spanish in the vast Americas; from centuries of the spiritism of Africa, Europe, and the Antillean Caribbean; from decades of Latin American liberation theology; and recently, from mujerista theology. The works present a spiritual sensibility not covered by any of these formulas, a highly variable set of beliefs from which the official Church distances itself by adding the modifiers *folk* or *popular* to it. U.S. Latina writers seem to prefer the folk version to the official version because it holds comfort and value for the group with whom they identify, the one called "the common folk" or "the people." Consistencies among their stories create a general picture of the people's spiritual sensibility, and variations give the picture texture.

Unfortunately, the sometimes devastating accuracy of the picture leads some critics to define these works not as literature but as political or sociological didacticism. The argument that links accuracy with didacticism has been challenged for years by critics who comment specifically on matters of race, color, gender, and class. Well-known Chicana critic Norma Alarcón points out that Latina writers consider the personal and the political to be *mestiza*—mixed—just as they are. The situations they present and the words they put in their characters' mouths reveal a political, economic, social, and cultural reality that should not be considered less artistic simply because it questions the philosophies of the dominant group.

Indeed, the Latina truth is a feminist and postcolonial truth: the indigenous, the female, the weak, the poor, and the darker-skinned are oppressed, and the Church has often participated in this oppression instead of defending them from it. As a people colonized five hundred years ago and made independent less than two hundred years ago, they daily face questions of identity. Their bodies, their landscape, their political systems, their education, their very language bear the ineradicable imprint of colonization. They interrogate the condition constantly, but they avoid rejection because that would entail rejecting themselves and their culture. What may appear to be political polemic to outsiders is actually an inside view of a culture continuing to develop an alternate philosophy. Marginalized, they desire their voice. They know that art, religion, politics, and culture constantly interact, and each can influence all the others. Thus, through their art, through their mixed genres and their juxtaposed religious and cultural systems, they open a dialogue with religion, politics, and culture.

In other words, these writers do what literary writers have always done.

In the terminology of Latina criticism, authors who enter the discussion also enter the cultural borderland defined by Gloria Anzaldúa in *Borderlands/La Frontera*. Their readiness to renegotiate their cultural standing throws them into this energetic but dangerous zone where beliefs, attitudes, and practices rub against each other in dynamic friction. Anzaldúa and others admit that religion is one of the many aspects of culture in dialogue there. Voices represent precolonization goddess worship, Mesoamerindian spirit beliefs, Yoruban saints and deities from Africa, medicine women, Jews, nuns, priestesses, Muslims, and seekers. Whether through argument or peaceful exchange, new resources and new solutions become available. Participants may elect whichever elements are appropriate to the moment, regardless of their source, and leave the rest in place for other situations. Spiritual survival is possible when beliefs and practices stand side by side in equality rather than above or below one another in rank.

Latina writers do not deny the risks of the borderland. Julia Alvarez, a Dominican-American, tells of being marginalized with a hyphen in both of the countries she joins. When she visited the Dominican Republic, a Dominicana writer accused her of hypocrisy for living in the United States and writing in English. Alvarez (1998) later commented on the importance of claiming her hyphenated identity and the uncharted connecting points it offers. Although she wants to be honest about its threats and tensions, she respects its potential for giving a complete, balanced view of the contemporary world. Embracing this multiethnicity and valuing syncretism, she celebrates the Caribbean and her home island as "sponge[s] . . . absorbing those who come and go . . . permeable countries. It's in our genes to be a world made of many worlds" (p. 175).

Syncretism. Permeability. The words capture the sense of openness to information and experimentation that appears repeatedly in the literature of Alvarez and other Latina writers, inside and outside the United States, whether describing culture, art, or spirituality. They express not only the acceptance but also the enjoyment of change. They are brave.

Eighty years ago, Mikhail Bakhtin (1921) promoted a similar tolerance for uncertainty. In *Toward a Philosophy of the Act*, he describes an ideological space where different forms might be placed side by side, where connections might be revealed, and where all parties might recognize themselves as being "another"— that is, just one more among many. Indeed, the term *another* differs greatly from its sound-alike term *an Other*. *An Other* is a combative term that automatically opposes two sides, whereas *another* is a nonthreatening one that increases the number of related members. It can indicate equality or even kinship.

"Anotherness" as a philosophy works in Latina literature when characters shrug off their differences to preserve the mutual good. In *Song of the Hummingbird* (Limón 1996), it allows Huitzitzilin and Father Benito to compare theologies. In *Daughter of the Mountain* (Escamill 1991), it offers Maggie a bridge to the old ways through her ancient grandmother, Adela Sewa. In *House of Houses*, it helps Mora (1997) establish her genealogy through the complementary calendars of Western time, Catholic and Amerindian liturgical cycles, moon phases, and gardening seasons. In memoirs by Judith Ortiz Cofer, it shows in the respect for the white altar of Puerto Rican spiritism. Based upon two-way inclusion and acceptance rather than replacement, anotherness offers a less aggressive and backward-focused solution than the violence acceptable to postcolonial theorists such as Frantz Fanon (1961), for whom the total elimination of the colonizing force and its ways is the only sure way to overcome its influences. Whereas Fanon completely rejects Christianity, calling it a benevolent form of slaveholding, the Latinas choose to reject just the dehumanizing traditions of their inherited Catholicism. They wish to perpetuate its loving ideals and its long presence in their identity. Paradoxically, they preserve it through practices that are not technically Catholic, and sometimes, not Christian.

Critically, Latinas do acknowledge the combined power of their political and religious colonization by the Spanish. Gloria Anzaldúa, Ana Castillo, Cherríe Moraga, and Sonia Saldívar-Hull, among others, confirm Church influence on women's self-worth and thought patterns; and writers of fiction and nonfiction alike portray those effects, revealing how the mind and even the tongue have become colonized. That this present-day criticism actually belongs to a centuries-old pattern has been documented in recent sociological and historic studies by the U.S. Catholic Church. The Church, as well as Latina writers, describes the inseparability of religion and culture and the long entanglement of official Catholic practices with a multitude of other spiritual beliefs. However, what the Church views as an aberration to be eased out of existence, the writers view as a life-sustaining store of alternatives.

Those alternatives include a constant dialogue to increase understanding, promote inclusion, and encourage responsiveness to change. Rather than destroy everything colonial, including their very identity, they open the discussion. Although they offer sometimes harsh criticisms of their colonizing Church, they never deny the value of some of its ideals in their broader sense of spirituality. Where it is joyless and individualistic, they add festivity and community. Where it discriminates by color, race, and class, they celebrate their *mestizaje*, their abundance of inherited qualities. Where it undervalues the feminine, they redeem *La Malinche* and *La Llorona* as well as supply their own goddesses, priestesses, and female trinity. Where it overvalues humility and suffering, they engage the spiritual or even the political underground, as they do through liberation theology and mujerista theology. Certainly, the Church resists change, but they refuse not to change. Their own sense of physical and spiritual abundance keeps the dialogue going.

This dialogue permeates the testimonials, memoirs, nonfiction, fiction, poetry, and drama currently being produced by U.S. Latinas. One idea emerges repeatedly: survival lies in the persistent restructuring of ideas drawn from as many sources as possible. A leveling of the playing field, a readiness to negotiate, a continuous sense of exploration—these are the practices that promise a future. The goal of their spirituality matches what they believe a religion should do: it must listen to, nurture, and encourage the people.

1

CATHOLIC—WITH A DIFFERENCE

Among the tales in the oral tradition of the U.S. Southwest is a story called "*El indito de las cien vacas*" ("The Indian and the Hundred Cows"). It goes like this: A pious Indian decides to donate a cow to the Church after he hears the priest repeatedly say that generosity to the Church will be repaid a hundredfold. The priest accepts the cow, reaffirms God's promise, and sends the Indian home. The Indian waits patiently for some days before deciding that God must expect him to help himself, whereupon he locates the priest's large herd and drives a hundred cows home as his promised reward. When the priest tries to take the cows back, the Indian notches an arrow and threatens to send him to hell, where he may collect his hundredfold of arrows from the devil (Griego y Maestas and Anaya 1980).

With all the brevity and accessibility of a biblical parable, this *cuento* or folk story teaches about pride, greed, and incautious speech—and directs the message not at a congregation but at the priest, the local representative of the hierarchy of the Catholic Church. That the Indian man focuses his anger on the priest, rather than on the conceptual religion or its God, is significant. In doing so, he accentuates the difference between spirituality, which he values as a sincere reverence for the sacred mysteries of existence, and religion, which he associates with arbitrary and often misleading precepts and practices.

Folk tales like this one have long been cited as depositories of cultural history, experience, and truth; they are said to reveal a worldview or a solution for the unanswerable questions of existence. Certainly, for the descendants of the fifteenth-century Native Americans and their Spanish conquerors, the "truth" of their experience since colonization has included an ongoing relationship with the Catholic Church. Over the centuries, Church and culture have become intertwined in complex ways that continue to provoke comment from the institutional Church up to the present day. Likewise, this deep and often perplexing relationship appears as text or subtext in most works by Latinas writing in the U.S. today. The authors may openly discuss religion—particularly Catholicism—as a force in the action, or they may reveal it obliquely through their characters' ways of speaking, thinking, and acting. Regardless, the religion is almost always embedded, and the attitudes surrounding it may be fond, nostalgic, acid, or angry. It may appear with great subtlety in the imagery or metaphors chosen, but its shape and influence provide an inescapable background and motivation for any honest tale, any convincing action, and any accurate picture, fictional or not, of the life of Latinas/os in the United States.

Understanding this relationship requires an awareness that the Latino use of the label "Catholic" indicates something different from the usual expectations of mainstream readers, most of whom make two erroneous assumptions: first, that virtually all Latinos are Catholic; and second, that as readers they themselves possess sufficient knowledge about Catholicism to recognize its workings when they see them. Some, of course, have no information but hearsay about mainstream Catholic beliefs, attitudes, and practices. Those with minimal knowledge may assume that Latinos attend a Sunday celebration called the Mass, participate in rituals called sacraments, and strictly adhere to the laws and doctrines prescribed by official Catholic leaders in Rome. Mainstream U.S. Catholic readers may also suppose that Latinos believe the same doctrines and worship in the same manner as they do. All of these assumptions are faulty; all will diminish these readers' understanding of the literature. Although the majority of U.S. Latinas/os call themselves Catholic and indeed have been baptized into that

Church, their individual definitions and expectations of the religion vary greatly from those of U.S. Catholics as well as from those of other Latinos.

At the turn to the twenty-first century, Latinos made up approximately half the Catholic population of the U.S., and their numbers were expanding. According to Ana María Díaz-Stevens (1994), a professor at Union Theological Seminary who studies the numbers, ethnicity, and needs of U.S. Latinos, the Latino definition of "Catholic" includes all individuals who have been baptized into Catholicism, who continue to claim it as their religion, and who expect the attention of the official Church. Notably, this definition does not refer to specific doctrines and traditions. In Díaz-Stevens's opinion, the diverse beliefs of the group, taken together with a rapidly increasing Latino Catholic population, are already influencing mainstream Catholic practices in the U.S., and they are likely to continue to do so.

Church commentary generally agrees with Díaz-Stevens, though the description of Latino Catholicism varies depending on the individual consulted. Even the name of the belief system changes. Theologians and sociologists variously label these religions "popular Catholicism," "religión popular," "popular religiosity," or occasionally, "folk Catholicism." In addition to these older forms, "liberation theology," a widely recognized and more clearly defined twentieth-century philosophy, arose among the people and their sympathetic local clergy in South America, Central America, Mexico, and the Caribbean. It arrived in the U.S. through immigration and through increased political consciousness among Latino groups. More recently, some U.S. Latinas have accepted "mujerista theology," a more woman-centered and community-driven interpretation of Catholicism.

According to Church commentary, the forms labeled "popular" or "folk" were identified centuries ago as aberrations that the Church needed to correct before they spread further. Theologian Orlando O. Espín (1994), who is somewhat sympathetic to these popular variations, describes them as a reinterpretation that has resulted in the elimination of some doctrines or beliefs and the addition of others. Espín believes this process of translation began as soon as the Spanish conquered Mexico, for at that time the Catholic Church had not yet declared a difference between traditions that were unchangeable doctrine and traditions that were reformable practices. Their missionaries likewise could not separate the two. In addition, he believes, the highly educated theologians in the Spanish universities were so far from the colonies that the priests and their new congregations were left to create their own understanding of doctrine and celebration. The newly colonized peoples found every element of their home, family, work, and indigenous traditions influenced by this influx of new religious rules, rituals, and iconography. Their accommodations to it were learned and passed on as family or community traditions, not as written doctrine or rules.

According to Espín, the Council of Trent (1545–1563) marked a change in policy. Church leaders solidified their control of Tradition (doctrine) and left tradition (daily practices) open to modification by the people. The message had trouble taking root in the distant Americas, where clergymen were neither numerous nor necessarily well trained in Tradition, and the colonized peoples still practiced many of their old religious customs alongside the new ones. The hybrid religion that grew in this power gap welcomed those familial structures, community customs, and ancient sacred figures that were essential to indigenous cultural identity.

Espín's observations make sense on the secular plane as well if one accepts that culture and religion must adapt together to protect the philosophical and ceremonial needs of a people subjected to social, economic, and political change. Because they help protect the identity of the group, the resulting religious hybrids can resist outside direction and defy efforts to eradicate them, regardless of the desires of officialdom and the considerable pressure for assimilation. U.S. religious leaders, politicians, sociologists, anthropologists, readers, and literary critics who belong to the mainstream majority constantly find their contacts with Latinos nuanced by this religio-cultural worldview.

A description of the flexible beliefs and practices of popular Catholicism is difficult to render. In *Bridging Boundaries: The Pastoral Care of U.S. Hispanics*, coeditor Kenneth G. Davis (2000a) offers useful insights that could be summarized in four main points:

- The people accept their suffering and martyrdom as a sign of solidarity with Christ and the saints.
- The people ask the deity and saints to grant miracles against the trials of existence.
- The people value community over individuality.
- The people themselves, especially the older women among them, determine the rituals and symbols.

Other individuals engaged in the formal study of popular Catholicism reaffirm these characteristics or add others to them. Espín's 1994 description generally agrees with Davis's comments, but Espín stresses that popular Catholicism eludes easy definition. Instead he offers two guiding principles to this belief system: it has been developing constantly since its inception in colonial times, and it does not adhere to a predictable base line. While one generation might place great value on specific symbols, rites, or beliefs, another generation may discard, downplay, or alter them. Nevertheless, the presence of an identifiable popular Catholicism has remained constant in the Americas throughout the centuries since contact.

The changeability of folk beliefs and practices is further explained by Anneris Goris (2000), who describes the religious practices of Catholic Dominican immigrants to the U.S. Goris stresses that Dominicanas/os consider religion very important in all aspects of their life, but to them it is a community matter rather than a private pursuit because the Church is a huge family they are born into, not an organization they have joined and whose rules they must follow. Thus, they participate in Church routine when they feel the urge or need. Cuban-American Ada María Isasi-Díaz (2000) likewise affirms that "one of the key elements of Hispanic identity is religion, religion as manifested in *religión popular* and not necessarily church affiliation and participation" (p. ix). She further asserts that the people should be trusted for seeking "the ongoing revelation of God in our midst" (p. xi).

What emerges through these comments is a picture of a religion that changes its beliefs and rituals to accommodate new pressures. Its followers are also its inventors. To some, the religion is a matter of community or cultural identification, not a personal pursuit, and they can "lose" their religion no more easily than they can shed their origins. Attending church services is not the defining action. According to Eduardo C. Fernández (1997), in fact, a 1992 study by Rodolfo O. De la Garza and colleagues showed that that "63% of persons of Mexican origin said that they receive a great deal or quite a bit of guidance from religion" (p. 88) despite the fact that many of the respondents rarely attended church themselves.

These are the attitudes that underlie the secular fiction, non-fiction, and criticism produced by most Latinas writing in the U.S. today. In their works, the popular form of religion is a given, an unquestioned and usually unnamed element of daily existence. Sometimes these writers specifically challenge popular religiosity and/or the official Catholic Church, but they never deny the constant influence of both in their cultures. In the lives they describe, religious tension joins a multitude of other tensions faced daily. In fact, religion is implicated in the origins of much discrimination based upon race, class, and gender.

In addition to an awareness of the presence of diverse forms of popular religion, these writers often demonstrate an understanding of recent resistance movements that have grown out of religious dissatisfaction in Central and South America. One such movement that has been responsible for a significant change in the Latin American Catholic Church is liberation theology, a philosophy that originated amid political and social unrest in South America, where the devastation visited on the common peoples provoked some Church leaders to intervene in political, economic, and cultural matters, sometimes even through guerrilla violence. As a spiritual philosophy, liberation theology rejects the silent, humble acceptance of suffering that is often associated with popular Catholicism. It maintains that the kingdom of God cannot be perpetually delayed to an afterlife that is earned through misery in this life. Instead, it follows the advice of one of its early martyrs, Archbishop Oscar Romero of El Salvador, who called upon the Church to listen for the voice of God in the voice of the poor. Such liberators agree that because Christ charged his followers to love all people alike, the Church is duty bound to bring some realization of God's kingdom to all the people of this world, regardless of their economic level or religious affiliation.

Liberation theology is recognized as a positive force by some of the Latinas writing in the U.S., but they cannot give it their wholehearted support because of its failure to specifically attack the oppression of women, particularly among the poor. In their view, the philosophy doesn't address a destructive viewpoint that has been propagated politically, socially, and religiously since the colonization of the Americas: that woman at her best is less than man, and in most cases, is either so frivolous or so corrupt that she must be controlled throughout her life. Enrique Dussel, an early voice in liberation theology, wrote two volumes about it in the mid 1970s. In the combined works, however, he addresses women's issues in only one chapter in *Ethics and the Theology of Liberation* (1974), and that chapter ignores the role of women outside the women's religious orders in Latin America. Dussel criticizes the nuns, exhorting them to actualize their leadership potential instead of allowing themselves to be psychologically limited by traditional roles of service and silence.

Gustavo Gutiérrez (1973), in another definition of liberation theology, presents a "new" Church, but his focus remains upon a male leadership and agenda as well as on a Church of universal, unvarying doctrine. This ideology runs counter to the practices of gender equality, anti-essentialism, and reverence for life favored by poor women and current Latina writers. Whereas the liberation theology of Dussel and Gutiérrez seeks to make people alike through the reduction of differences and an assimilation to a common model, the broader view of the women writers seeks to recognize, value, and accept differences.

Liberation theology is only occasionally named in Latina stories and essays, but an underlying philosophy similar to it seems to guide them. Ana Castillo and Sylvana Paternostro address it directly in some of their essays, and its intent and underground nature are reflected in those works by Sandra Benítez and Helena María Viramontes that expose the dilemma of coffee plantation laborers, small growers, and migrant workers. The workings of liberation theology are noticeable in the Julia Alvarez novel *In the Time of the Butterflies* (1995a), a fictionalized history of four sisters who resist Rafael Leónidas Trujillo's regime in the Dominican Republic. Alvarez wrote the novel during a decade when Church-sanctioned rebellion had become familiar, but the era she depicts predates that broad awareness. The underground movement she describes is a grassroots resistance joined by militants, Catholic clergy, and individual citizens. To join the movement, each sister must risk her comfortable social status and her personal safety. Overcoming religious scruples, the cultural expectations of women, an ingrained admiration for powerful Church and political leaders, and the family's political lethargy, they side with the rebel priests and the poor. Their original religious structure crumbles, but they never abandon a spiritual awareness. By the end of their ordeal, they have forged new ideals that nurture the family, the community, and the country better than the old. These ideals substitute a righteous anger for the patient suffering traditionally preached by their Church.

Many Latina writers do not portray Mirabal-style armed resistance, but they consistently expose and condemn social and religious inequities based upon race, class, and gender. More community and life-centered, the spiritual sense in their stories somewhat resembles "*mujerista* [womanist] theology" or Hispanic Women's Liberation Theology, a movement by Latina women in the U.S. This philosophy, which was launched in the 1980s by theologian Ada María Isasi-Díaz and activist Yolanda Tarango, emphasizes the wisdom developed as a result of *lo cotidiano*, the daily lived experience of the common Latina. *Mujeristas* know the realities of being *mestiza* (mixed Spanish and Mesoamerindian blood) or *mulata* (mixed Spanish and African blood); they recognize the need for constant mediation between the nature of living and the definition of morality; and they appreciate the power of the poor to reject their tradition of humble suffering in favor of an effort to liberate themselves. Justice and reconciliation are its most important goals (Isasi-Díaz 2001). As described by Isasi-Díaz and Tarango (1988), *mujerista* theology promotes women's local action groups rather than military involvement. These groups labor for the preservation of the family and the community. In their religious philosophy, they honor scripture, but they consider the Bible secondary to the pursuit of justice in daily life. They support efforts to raise Latino consciousness and self-esteem, to exert a nonviolent pressure against sexism, racism, and classism, and to insist upon solutions that enable rather than coerce the people. *Mujeristas* restore honor to the attributes that have not been valued by the Euro-centered Catholic leadership: their mixed ethnic background and the richness of their syncretic religion. They celebrate a body of beliefs that reflect "the African traditions brought to Latin America by the slaves, and the Amerindian traditions bequeathed by the great Aztec, Maya, and Inca civilizations, as well as other Amerindian cultures such as Taíno, Siboney, Caribe, Aruacano, and others" (p. 64).

Elements of this mujerista theology are evident across the genres of U.S. Latina writing. Ana Castillo sides with *mujeristas* rather than with liberation theologians for reasons she states in her collected essays, *Massacre of the Dreamers* (1995a). In her opinion, liberation theology is just one more male-centered ideology that represses the interests of enlightened *mestiza* feminists, whereas *mujerista* theology, as envisioned by Isasi-Díaz and Tarango, allows women first to express their very different reality and then to actively engage in having their needs met. Sylvana

Paternostro (1999), writing about poor indigenous women in Brazil as well as about Latinas in the U.S., notes that many women may not hear the sociopolitical debates or even become aware of grassroots parish movements because they aren't allowed to leave their homes or because they race from family duties to job duties and back to family duties, excluding all else. Liberation theology will not reach them, but the highly personal *mujerista* approach, which allows them to speak out in safety, may lift their isolation and give them hope and purpose.

In many cases, U.S. Latina writers favor even greater flexibility than that offered by *mujerista* theology. Rejecting denominational labels and the restrictive term "theology," they merge Catholic practices with those of Mesoamerindian, Yoruban, and numerous other earth- and spirit-related philosophies. The difference is largely one of attitude: spirituality cannot be subjected to limits and codes. "Catholic" refers to a heritage, not to Church affiliation. It represents an inescapable aspect of their culture but is not their entire culture. Spiritually, they honor the deities and ceremonies for the comfort and diversion these offer to the people, but they do not consider deities and ceremonies unassailable or immutable. For an author such as Edna Escamill, a new approach to living may emerge in a blend of *curandera* beliefs, modern education, and multicultural wisdom, as it does for her character Maggie in *Daughter of the Mountain* (1991). For Pat Mora, a person may fill a spiritual need through an aggregate of earth religion, family history, and popular Catholicism, as she does in her memoir *House of Houses* (1997). For Ana Castillo, revitalization can lie in a combination of religious, political, and social activism based on the values of life and family, as it does in *So Far from God* (1993). Two concepts underlie the resolutions of such stories: the moment is ever-changing, and an unassimilated difference is not a source of dismay. Like *mujerista* theology, this spirituality arises naturally in response to *lo cotidiano*, the daily lived experience.

Consciously or not, and regardless of their personal reservations about theology and Catholicism, U.S. Latina writers frequently include details and motivations that could only come from a character's spiritual sensibility. Furthermore, they frequently use the simple designation "Catholic" when they name that spirituality. The label refers to a received heritage, an internal construct that comes of being born and raised in a culture steeped in that religion. In that usage, someone described as "very Catholic" typically complies with Church-approved beliefs and practices. Someone who is merely "Catholic" bears the marks of that colonial heritage. When the authors discuss their own beliefs in essays and memoirs, they generally describe an open-ended spiritual awareness drawn from popular Catholicism, liberation theology, *mujerista* theology, precontact religions, African spiritism, secular theories of gender and culture, and more.

Coming at religion from these angles, Latina secular writers give substance to the concept of popular Catholicism, even if they do not define it. Many of the authors—and the characters they create—have ceased the formal practice of their religion, but the depth of their familiarity with its folk rituals and beliefs is constantly apparent. Their references to the official, Rome-directed traditions of the Catholic Church abound, and the situations they or their characters face usually reveal the official Church to be less open, understanding, and protective than they think it should be. Despite their insistence that religious formulas can be too restrictive, however, they stop short of gratuitous faultfinding or ridicule. As Ana Castillo (1995a) has pointed out in regard to Chicano activism in the 1960s and 1970s, an assumption that the people had rejected Catholicism would be erroneous. What the movement did, she says, was act upon the difference between religion and spirituality.

Significantly, Castillo's assertions operate as underlying assumptions in recent U.S. Latina literature, some of which predates the Catholic commentary in *Hispanic Women, Hispanic Catholic Culture in the U.S.*, and *Bridging Boundaries*, respectively published in 1992, 1994 and 2000. The similarities tempt some critics to view the creative writing as sociological rather than literary, but that assessment misses the point. Latina writers' observations about spirituality resonate because the works are valid representations of Latina experience. In most cases, the spiritual details emerge as elements of physical setting, as psychological motivation, or as a character's way of perceiving. If these works are to be "true" in the sense of "true to life," the authors cannot ignore common moral and spiritual attitudes any more than they can ignore the gender, skin color, and socioeconomic realities their characters face. If the authors believe in the importance of preserving Latino cultural identities, they must also preserve the "Catholic" one—and show the reader that it is "Catholic" in a different way.

2
THE DIFFERENCES

The works of Latina writers in recent decades offer readers a different and provocative worldview. Statistically, the Latina world includes a heavy share of suffering from poverty and from biases related to race, gender, and class (Moore 1994, Tabares 2000). Stories that are faithful to that world must incorporate the people's practical and philosophical response to these pressures and the dilemmas resulting from them. Predictably, characters turn to their spiritual understanding for solace and guidance, and if that understanding is inadequate to the task, they must decide whether to abandon it, seek beyond it, or adjust it.

The modern Latina Catholic, as she is portrayed in Latina literature, will pursue one or more of these options. One might reject not only the Catholic Church but all Christian Churches. Another might investigate ancient indigenous beliefs, spiritism, or evangelical religions. Still others might modify traditional Catholic beliefs or practices to meet the new demands. Typical adjustments include a rejection of "Christlike" humility in the face of disaster or repression, a respect for the value and wisdom of women in the preservation of the people, and a restructuring of the Virgin Mary, the Catholic Church model of womanhood. Taken together, these adjustments offer the believers alternative, woman-centered forms of wisdom and leadership.

Traditionally, the Catholic Church has counseled the poor and oppressed to endure their hardship with humility so they may find comfort and happiness later in heaven. Much Latina literature exposes the strength of this programming and firmly rejects the practice. In her memoir *House of Houses*, Pat Mora (1997b) examines its impact upon her father Raul right up to his final days. In his life he has been a good, simple man who has made mistakes, sometimes with intention, but rarely with malice. He has responded in very human ways to a life plagued by war, displacement, economic upheaval, and discrimination. Still, for himself and for a family afraid of retribution in the afterlife, he pleads forgiveness from the very God he believes has assigned him those burdens. His frightened prayers torture the family. Even the priest's visit cannot bring him or them complete solace, for the holy oils and prayers of the Sacrament of the Dying emphasize that salvation and heaven are available but not guaranteed.

Despite her memories of events like this, however, Mora herself tells interviewer Karin Rosa Ikas (2002) that she retains fond memories of her Catholic upbringing. She also says she appreciates and admires the nuns for what they did to educate her, and she sees no reason to react to the official religion with anger. Nonetheless, her own view of religion has broadened, and now she describes her beliefs as catholic rather than Catholic. Some evidence of this ambivalence appears in her poem "To Big Mary from an Ex-Catholic," in which she wonders if Mary will reject or even punish her for no longer offering up penances or honoring her statue with rose petals. A similar reluctance to abandon ritual shows in *House of Houses* when Mora introduces her children to Catholic traditions at a family Christmas gathering even though she has consciously raised them outside of the Church. In all of her books, she makes frequent metaphorical use of religious terms such as *sacrament*, *host*, and *communion*.

Other writers find less forgiveness for a religion that has promoted abject humility. Ana Castillo and Helena María Viramontes criticize it in stories of the Texas and California borderland, and Esmeralda Santiago and Judith Ortiz Cofer show its negative workings among Puerto Ricans who have migrated from their island to the big cities of the U.S. Northeast. These stories are drawn from vastly different subcultures, one rural and Mexican-American, and the other urban and Puerto Rican-American; yet the pictures they offer bear resemblance. All four authors re-create an atmosphere in which poverty-stricken Latinos, particularly the women, deprive themselves of comforts and even essentials so they can donate money, goods, or labor to a Church that looks down on them. Judith Ortiz Cofer in particular writes about ordinary women who endure self-imposed suffering to strengthen their petitions to God, Mary, and the saints. This bargaining venture suggests that the deities require payment in advance because they don't trust the petitioner to continue in gratitude and good behavior afterward. For Ortiz Cofer and others—many of whom admit to having strayed from their family's practice of Catholicism—such humble actions provoke frustration, disgust, and even anger, but with great consistency, the writers direct their negativity at the Church that has traditionally glorified suffering, not at the people who continue to accept the message.

Latina writers often interrogate their religion directly. In *Under the Feet of Jesus* (1996), Viramontes's young character Estrella questions the power of a Jesus whose statue must be trundled around, its open hands frequently removed and packed because they are too delicate to share the hard migrant life that God has allotted to the family. To the feet of this symbol of power, Estrella's mother Petra consigns the family birth and sacramental certificates, the symbols of their belonging in the U.S. and the Church. Estrella watches her mother and is watched in return as she matures in an atmosphere of male impermanence, hard labor, deadly pesticides, inescapable poverty, and harassment by the immigration police. Finally losing confidence in the absolute power of God, Estrella strikes back at the migrant condition on her own. Later, when Petra's Jesus statue breaks and Petra pins her last hopes on a reluctant man, Estrella pulls herself high up on a barn roof in an affirmation of her own strength and resolve. However, even in these final actions, neither woman has abandoned God as much as she has decided she must look to additional sources for survival. Petra carries the head of the statue with her as she confronts her lover, and Estrella climbs toward the clarity of the heavens, where she is like "an angel standing on the verge of faith" (p. 176). The symbols and metaphors of their religious past are inescapable, too much a part of them to be left behind even as they pursue change.

A similar push-pull of religious sentiment preoccupies characters across the literature, whether the conflict is thematic, as it is in Ana Castillo's *So Far from God* (1993), or is an occasional eruption, an element of a larger motivation, as it is in Cristina García's novels. In *The Agüero Sisters* (1997), García's character, Dulce Fuerte, visits a stony, decaying little church and remembers taking refuge in the Havana cathedral as she fled from a violent boyfriend. Although she accuses priests and bishops of general corruption and bad faith toward their flocks, she admits that the building's "veneer of civility" may be the "greatest solace" it can offer (p. 207). In a similar gesture with a less cynical evaluation, Maggie, of Edna Escamill's *Daughter of the Mountain* (1991), finds refuge in a desert chapel of Our Lady of Guadalupe. There she begins to puzzle out her need for a religious philosophy more generous than the one offered by the village priest. The tonal difference between these two fictional experiences may be due to political differences in the characters' lives and to the specific presence of the Virgin of Guadalupe in *Daughter of the Mountain*. The Virgin, ubiquitous in many different forms throughout Latino cultures, is especially loved in Mexico, where she is seen as a champion of the poor and a rebel for good causes. Whereas Dulce Fuerte's church invokes the image of a decaying physical and official institution in a country where Catholicism is discouraged, Maggie's desert chapel invokes a sympathetic and familiar figure linked to daily culture and spirituality.

In most instances, including these last two, the characters seem unwilling to let discomfort with their Catholic heritage separate them from family and community. They cannot redefine and revalue themselves in isolation. However, if they reject the destructive elements of their religion and maintain the healthy ones, they protect themselves from the hatreds, including self-hatred, that accompany lost ideals. Through such a process, a writer such as Judith Ortiz Cofer may express an amazement bordering on hor-

ror when she describes the women of her family making pilgrimage on their knees or wearing abrasive clothing for penance, but
she also can recognize the paradox that through these subservient actions, the women receive peace and a sense of control in their
constant battle against physical, social, economic, and political
odds. Even when protesting such practices, Ortiz Cofer respects
the petitioner's courage and her need to believe in the power of
choosing a discomfort instead of having it imposed on her. When
a petition is answered or a miracle appears to occur, the woman
enjoys a sense of accomplishment, and the narrative voice refuses
to deprive her of that satisfaction. Rather, it opens the possibility
that a mother, a friend, the community, or an unknowable, unnamed earth/life power actually intervened, and it acknowledges
that these forces, too, are mysterious and wonderful. What Ortiz
Cofer will not do is credit the solution to the patriarchal Christian
God or to the intercession of Catholic priests.

Complaints about Catholic male leadership abound as U.S.
Latinas reflect on the role of Church and religion in the people's
lives. Some writers pen serious accusations of Catholic Church
failures to protect and understand its people, as Alvarez does in
In the Time of the Butterflies (1995a) when she identifies an unholy symbiosis between Church and state during Trujillo's brutal regime in the Dominican Republic. Likewise, Graciela Limón
focuses on the pride and biases of many of the priests who followed the Spanish conquistadors to Mexico. Even when the complicity of Church and state is not a main concern, the storytelling
exposes the sorrows of a life spent emulating the crucified Christ
and the tortured martyrs rather than celebrating the love, joy,
customs, and community of the living.

In investigating the identities of an immense but not yet identified Power, many authors foreground traditions from Mexica,
Yoruban, and other ancient belief systems that have become interwoven in the common culture. Their characters are comfortable with a syncretic spirituality that admits its Catholic elements
but equally values its non-Catholic and non-Christian practices.
As a whole, their spirituality echoes the home altars they describe,

regardless of country of ancestry: it belongs to the household and daily life, it honors a crowd of deities (and nondeities), and it invites the spirits of the dead because those spirits remain accessible to the living. Their spiritual sensibility finds echoes in the religious celebrations they describe: it strays from the sober and dignified rituals of the Euro-American Church, and it welcomes many different types of expression in noisy contradiction. The writers seem to believe that what belongs in the culture belongs in the religious philosophy and its proclamation.

Not unusual among the characters in these stories is someone like Escamill's Maggie, who reestablishes her spiritual balance by accepting the ancient Yaqui beliefs and practices preserved by her outcast grandmother. The characters recognize that their cultural religion has been multifaceted from times beyond memory, as when Ortiz Cofer explains the *Espiritismo* (European spiritism) practiced by her Puerto Rican grandfather, when García describes the *Santería* (African spiritism) of Cuba, or when Anzaldúa invokes Coatlicue, an earth goddess of ancient Mesoamerican tribes. As Anzaldúa states in an interview, these aspects of existence are essential, but they are seldom recognized by readers, reviewers, and teachers. She speaks of the act of writing as an immersion in the ancient Mexican *nahual*, a shamanlike, shape-changing spirit that possesses the ability to move among worlds. For her, the *nahual* state is the desirable place for the modern *mestiza* to reconnect the fragments of her existence and release the power of her rich inheritance. The awesome power of the ancient earth goddess Coatlicue resides in the shifting, in-between *nahual* experience (Reuman 2000).

For others, power resides in people who defend themselves instead of waiting meekly for a reward in the afterlife. Sometimes the gap left by Church leadership and understanding must be filled through more modern and concrete means. The history-based Mirabal sisters in Julia Alvarez's *In the Time of the Butterflies* must reach far beyond their Catholic training in order to reconcile armed resistance and the idealistic, submissive religion learned at their convent school. Their bishop ignores the murder of Haitians and dissidents; their faraway Pope does not invoke excommunication even when Trujillo oversteps into sacrilege; and the humility modeled in their Good Shepherd icons can't stop the killing or the loss of rights. However, the violent underground resistance by individual priests and peasants, neither meek nor silent, speaks and acts even in death.

Alternative wisdom and leadership also come from a source honored by ancient tribes but not by the modern Church or the U.S. culture as a whole: the women of the community, particularly the grandmothers. Cultural traditions and recent Catholic Church scholarship agree that Latino respect for the religious power of woman derives from the ancient indigenous custom of leaving the details of family worship to the women. Ana María Díaz-Stevens (1994) in particular provides an important discussion of the traditional role of Latin American women—grandmothers, mothers, healers, midwives, and community-identified holy women—in preserving and adjusting the faith life of the community. Even after colonization, these women remained especially influential in rural areas, where priests tended to be itinerant, relatively powerless in the church hierarchy, insufficiently trained, and not born of the indigenous people. In this leadership gap, the women absorbed the care of shrines and the planning of religious festivals because those functions fit with their cultural role of maintaining home, family, and community; and through these activities, Díaz-Stevens maintains, the women left discernible female influences on popular Catholicism. Possibly, this control of religious practice has proven useful to women in a Church that has always denied the priesthood to women with a religious calling.

The matriarchal core is a constant in Latina fiction and nonfiction. The women unite to protect and maintain the family, which frequently is a family of women. They are the sustaining element in a culture that loses its men to war, to prison, to despair, to drink, to wandering. Even with the men present, the women retain control of the home and its connection with extended family. They constitute community, and community is strength. In the presence of this female core and the statistics that show the Latino population to be more than half female, Latina spirituality represents a force in the culture. This "Catholic" spirituality influences the study of U.S. literature because its power has been transplanted to the United States as families have migrated north—or when they've been adopted along with the land when the United States has extended its borders southward, as it has in the territory of Puerto Rico and in the previously Mexican lands of the U.S. Southwest. Readers, as much as Church officials, need to be aware that *this* Catholicism may be very different from the religion they think it is.

This different religiosity manifests itself in subtle ways, such as the multiple manifestations of the Blessed Virgin Mary, none of them identical to the white European image familiar to mainstream American Catholics and even non-Catholics. While many non-Latinas/os recognize the figure called the Virgin of Guadalupe, few have noted that she is *mestiza* and is pregnant. Even fewer know of the Black Virgin, the Virgin of Monserrat, Our Lady of Regla, or Our Lady of Charity of Copper. Most are unaware of European and East European icons of a dark-skinned Virgin, so they could not realize how easily such pictures and statues could have arrived with the Spanish.

The variety of forms the Virgin may take is not the most unusual feature about her, however. That would be her aura of power. Unlike the Blessed Virgin Mary of European tradition, the Virgin of Guadalupe is both a sympathizer and a fighter for the poor and oppressed, a chief deity sometimes more revered than God the Father (Randall 1996). She is invoked in political rallies and union protests just as she is in church or in the home. Her image appears on blankets, lamps, protest posters, endless holy items, and countless trinkets. Some Latinas equate her with the Nahua goddess Tonantzin because her miraculous appearance to Juan Diego occurred on Tonantzin's sacred hill. Widely recognized in Church commentary on popular Catholicism as well as in secular studies of the peoples of the Americas, the Virgin of Guadalupe also receives mention in the majority of the fiction and nonfiction produced by U.S. Latinas. Her centrality to Latino life and spirituality is undisputed.

In part, Latina devotion to the Virgin of Guadalupe may be a response to the all-male godhead and all-male leadership in Catholicism. A lack of power in issues outside of homemaking, childcare, and family worship continues to plague the women of Latino cultures, and against these difficulties, the Church has little to offer. The U.S. Catholic Church has defined these women as "less"—less important, less powerful, less human, less deserving of salvation—just as it has defined the Virgin of Guadalupe as a lesser image of the Blessed Virgin Mary. Latina writers and critics don't hesitate to call attention to this discrimination in their inherited Church. In their fiction and nonfiction, they portray female leadership far beyond details of family worship, and they give an honest assessment of all that complicates it.

One example of the religious bias they face is the habit of the Church to counsel *la mujer*, woman, to be a faithful, enthusiastic wife and mother even as it denies her the guilt-free enjoyment of her sexuality, overlooks her husband's infidelity, and ignores a father's failure to help support and rear his children. As Viramontes demonstrates in several of the stories in *The Moths and Other Stories* (1995), disaffected relationships and even violence can result from such unreal expectations. In the story "Growing," she re-creates the confusion and resentment experienced by fourteen-year-old Naomi, who reaches puberty and suddenly loses her personal freedom and her father's trust. Her father's philosophy, cultural as well as religious, tells him that because Naomi is now a woman, she is both the tempted and the temptress, and she must be watched every moment. "*TU ERES MUJER*" ("You are a woman"), he shouts at her when she wants to leave the house without a chaperone, and Naomi hears the words "not as a truth, but as a verdict" (p. 36).

In another story, Viramontes suggests that even marriage can't redeem a woman because virginity and fidelity continue to be the sole measure of female worth. In "The Broken Web," two people marry even though the woman is pregnant by another lover, and in their effort to preserve their social images, they each sacrifice their own self-image. Significantly, the wife loses more status than the husband. Throughout the story she has no name other than "the wife of Tomás"; for in marriage, even though it is a sacramental state thought to bring God's blessings, this woman "no longer owned herself" (p. 60). The resentful union ends when Tomás justifies his marital infidelity on the basis of her premarital affair, and she shoots him to death in the despair of her nonbeing. Their tragedy is a cultural tragedy; readers know that the couple's daughters, Martha and Yreina, will enter the culture just as vulnerable to its dualistic mores as Tomás and his wife have been. The Church cannot save these children. When Martha seeks solace from religion in the aftermath of the murder, her priest lacks both the insight and the desire to help her unravel her nightmares. Recurrent in these terrible dreams is an image of her mother's bullet shattering the family's statue of Christ. Martha is too young to untangle the triple conflation of the powerful cultural "fathers" in her life: the Latino man of the house/father who owned her family's lives and should have been their provider and protector; the all-powerful, loving Christ who should have been present and sympathetic to them; and the priest who should have placed himself second to the service of his flock. All three ideals shatter in one devastating blow. Along with them goes the idealized mother, who in Martha's culture is charged with keeping the family together regardless of her own personal suffering.

The tragedy of double standards receives more in-depth examination in Graciela Limón's *Song of the Hummingbird* (1996). Set in the early years of the Spanish conquest of Mexico, this novel presents Huitzitzilin, a former Mexica concubine who cannot return to her people because the Spanish have massacred the entire city. She cannot find a place with the Spanish, either, because she is considered too old-to warm their beds and too Indian to be allowed to do anything else. She wanders the desert. She loses all her children. In her final years, she finds refuge among the nuns, who are duty-bound to take her in, but she will find their acceptance—not to mention the salvation they believe they can help her attain—only if she declares herself depraved and rejects her birth culture. Like *La Malinche*, despised forever because she was given as consort to Cortés, and like *La Llorona*, condemned to wander forever in search of her murdered children, Huitzitzilin is the victim of colonial politics, racism, and gender bias accepted by the Church. Only through subterfuge does she obtain a chance to speak out at last.

Huitzitzilin retains her respect for pre-Aztec goddesses to the very end, finding them a more positive presence than the distant, male godhead of Catholicism. In a similar manner, the protagonists of stories set in more recent times respect these powerful female deities of the earth, of life, and of woman. The women drawn by Ana Castillo, Denise Chávez, Cristina García, Sandra Benítez, and others also find spiritual guidance through *curanderas* (medicine women), through the solidarity of female family and friends, or even through an earthly trinity composed of three generations of women. They reject the long-imposed image of woman as either virgin or whore, preferring to describe themselves as encompassing all the gradations between those violent extremes, whether as individuals or as a gender. They redefine goodness as well, declaring it an openness to new ideas, a loving concern for the well-being of the people, and a willingness to accept and even enjoy differences.

In the midst of these adjustments, many writers and characters continue to identify themselves as "catholic," referring more to their heritage than to their beliefs and practices. They seem confident that their *spirituality* is an altogether different attribute that allows them to adjust the inherited religion to meet their own needs and the needs of the people. As a group, they recommend openness and an ability to entertain alternatives. Often, the *curanderas* and grandmothers join forces with other generations of women to meet the challenges of an ever-changing society, and together, the women knead their rigid Catholic culture not to destroy it but to activate it, to create something *un*formed, something affirming, responsive, and open-ended. While their works do reveal the presence of what the Catholic Church variously identifies as popular Catholicism, liberation theology, and *mujerista* theology, they also push into the free spaces beyond these formulas. Their spirituality mediates between religion and culture to foster a strong sense of community, a matriarchal control of religious practice, an openness to multiple deities, a disapproval of martyrdom, an acceptance of home altars and rituals, and much more. Flexible and open, it adapts to the needs of the people instead of requiring them to adapt to it, and thus it preserves its ability to comfort the people and nurture their hope long after the institutional Church has failed. These Latinas respect and encourage dialogue. When they dialogue with their spiritual sides, they become aware that they are, after all, catholic—and much more.

3

COLONIZED BY CATHOLICISM

Although they don't necessary follow the philosophies and dictates of the U.S. Catholic Church, Latinas/os daily face other people's assumption that they do. Statistically, this stereotype would seem supportable, for Latinos constitute nearly one-half of the U.S. Catholic population. As is often the case, however, stereotypes mislead and statistics tell an incomplete story. In reality, Latino religious attitudes, beliefs, and practices may differ significantly from both mainstream U.S. Catholicism and the Catholicism of Rome, and individuals may criticize or even reject their inherited Catholicism. Some of this religious ambivalence proceeds from a perception of the Church as a vestige of Spanish colonial domination, a lingering influence that continues to burden the people even though their political connection with Spain ended many generations ago.

Postcolonial critics insist that colonization forces a reinvention of country, society, and self. Furthermore, this new perception remains in the structure of life and in the collective memory of the subjects forever. Even after a successful move for independence, the people's attempt to forget involves an identification of the material to be discarded, and that process gives it life again. Moreover, political, social, and religious structures remain entrenched as the successors of the colonial leaders move into the power positions that are vacated. The groups who were most oppressed under colonial rule tend to remain oppressed unless they seek ways to subvert the system, forge new ways, and regain their voice and dignity.

Since the 1970s, literature and literary comment by U.S. Latinas have examined the Catholic Church as a colonizing agent. They define the Catholic religion as patriarchal in its leadership and teachings, they deplore that the Spanish imposed it ruthlessly upon the indigenous peoples, they assert that it has worked with the state to benefit the upper class, and they claim that its precepts continue to promote the negative attitudes they face daily.

In 2000, Ralph Rodriguez credited Chicana writers since 1984 with creating a literature that overtly challenges all oppressions based upon race, class, gender, or sexual preference. In his opinion, this opposition is peaceful in nature, favoring discussion and negotiation rather than armed resistance or revolution. It seeks to draw attention to a problem in the hope of precipitating responsible solutions. While his evaluation recognizes the Latina push for dialogue, however, it doesn't honor the forthright grittiness of their literature.

With the exception of the Mirabal participation in armed underground resistance, it is true that only a small portion of Latina literature concerns itself with violence returned for violence. However, the writers consistently promote not only dialogue but also unified action in response to the dangerous realities of their existence. In stories such as Helena María Viramontes's "The Cariboo Cafe" (1995) and Sandra Benítez's *Bitter Grounds* (1997), accusations of high-level U.S. complicity with Salvadoran death squads and corrupt political regimes throughout Latin America emerge clearly. The exposure of racially biased and religiously hypocritical treatment of Mesoamerindians and *mestizos* is central to Graciela Limón's 1996 novel *Song of the Hummingbird* and Estela Portillo Trambley's 1983 plays *Sor Juana* and *Puente Negro*. Affirmations of the need for Latino cultures to assert themselves are frequent in novels by Ana Castillo and Denise Chávez. Castillo (1995a) in particular insists upon both the need to become *Xicanista* (a socially and politically aware Chicana feminist) and the importance of *con-*

scientización (the raised political and social consciousness prerequisite to being *Xicanista*).

Through edgy poetry and storytelling rather than through polemic, Latinas uncover the ongoing effects of their centuries-old political colonization as well as their current social and economic colonization by the U.S. Of particular concern is the resulting three-way lock composed of race, class, and gender discrimination. Among the populations the Latinas describe, to be born poor, dark-skinned, and female is to remain poor unless an outside force undoes the lock. As Debra Castillo points out in *Talking Back* (1992), the poor woman of color is likely to have limited education. She might find work as a domestic, taking care of someone else's home and children during the day and nurturing her own family in the evening. Her life reinforces her stereotype. The one who employs her, on the other hand, gains the time to pursue more education or training, to accept a higher-profile job, to travel, to get involved in politics, or to otherwise act against color, class, and gender barriers. The situation holds true whether the servant works for a white woman or another woman of color. Even within a group, the class system constantly renews itself.

As much Latina storytelling shows, the institutional Catholic Church has exacerbated this situation for five hundred years by urging the poor to endure their lot with humility and await the rewards of the afterlife. In the opinion of Latina writers, this same Church has offered immediate and earthly rewards to the powerful and has helped them maintain their position. Some record the Church bias that once encouraged Amerindian or *mestiza* women to work in the convent but denied them the right to join women's religious orders. Others, such as poet-novelists Julia Alvarez and Judith Ortiz Cofer, as well as social scientist Ana María Díaz-Stevens, affirm the twentieth-century existence of class discrimination in Church-sponsored education. For them, "parochial school" is often synonymous with "private school," and private schools serve those who can afford transportation, tuition, and uniforms. In these writers' experience, poor families further the problem by accepting their implied unworthiness: they impoverish themselves to send their children to the very schools that perpetuate the division, hoping to somehow overcome it.

Even the languages spoken by these women serve to maintain color, race, class, and gender lines. Whether in English or Spanish, terms like "dark" and "female" exert strong but subtle control over thought and behavior. Non-Latina theorists such as Toni Morrison in *Playing in the Dark* (1992) and Anne McClintock in *Imperial Leather* (1995) have explored the manner in which Western writers employ the imagery of darkness as a writing tool: in the "darkening" or "blackening" of character, for example; or in references to "dark" crimes, "murky" pasts, and "swarthy" villains; or in the degradation associated with work commonly done by darker-skinned servants. Morrison notes that until recently, both the white writer and the writer of color have perceived the reader as white, and both have used the metaphor accordingly. Thus, literature has promoted the association of darkness with all things evil, depraved, mysterious, threatening, sinful, and dirty, and by extension, these characteristics have attached to people with dark skin. From long training, readers with a white, Western perspective accept this social and religious metaphor without thought, but readers of color find its implications confusing and insulting. They cannot speak without discriminating against themselves.

The language and iconography of Catholicism, of course, have constantly reinforced this metaphor. The medieval Spanish invoked all the pejorative adjectives of darkness against the tribes they encountered in the New World. They also transplanted the medieval perception of woman as a dusky, mysterious force that is incomprehensible, vaguely corrupt, and dangerous. Gloria Anzaldúa (1987) examines this collusion of culture and religion when she links the negative connotations of darkness to the biblical creation story, which banishes darkness and declares the light "good." The biblical story of the creation of woman fits Anzaldúa's model as well, for Adam was created from earth illuminated by the light of God, but Eve came from the darkness of the inner body during the darkness of sleep. Freudian theory reinforces this linguistic color and gender discrimination when it identifies woman as a "lack" and categorizes the wild, irresponsible id as "female." Bonnie Zimmerman (1981) accuses anti-lesbian commentary of employing this "dark side" imagery when it labels lesbianism monstrous, evil, and unnatural. Edward Said (1978) makes a similar point about perceptions of the darker-skinned peoples of the East, a place already defined as mysterious and marginal by its peripheral placement on Euro-centered maps. These people are thought of as exotic, sensuous, depraved, and greatly in need of civilization and Christian conversion. Henry Louis Gates, Jr. (1985) protests that dark-skinned peoples either are portrayed as threatening or are set aside as inferior, childlike, silent, and sufficiently strange to require anthropological, sociological, or psychological study. According to critics of Church participation in Spanish colonization, all of these derogatory attitudes were applied in the New World. After all, Spain had just completed eight centuries of war to drive the "infidel" Moors from Spanish soil. That campaign had barely finished when Spain happened upon the Americas, a place so peripheral that it was not even on their maps, a place inhabited by additional dark-skinned, "pagan" people to be converted or driven off.

The association of skin color with depravity is of central importance in Latina writing. Ana Castillo (1995a), like Anzaldúa, complains that the *mestiza* is immediately suspect simply because of her color. Julia Alvarez (1995b) reveals the influence of this bias in her poem "Mamí and Gauguin," in which a painting of barebreasted Tahitian girls embarrasses a dark-skinned maid. The maid, who would prefer a picture of the Virgin, finds herself linked by color with women that the artist and the family consider too exotic, untaught, or pagan to behave morally.

The religious stereotype reaches far beyond the naughtiness or hypocrisy of a painting, of course. Its more sinister manifestations link all women with the biblical figures of Lilith, Eve, and the snake of Eden. Ana Castillo locates Lilith's unpardonable sin in her refusal to be subject to Adam and to accept a permanent role of motherhood. Borrowing upon several sources in *Massacre of the Dreamers* (1995a), Castillo suggests that Hebrew beliefs required woman to be inferior. Since Lilith was created at the same time as Adam, she was an equal and therefore had to be banished (or remove herself) to make room for Eve, who was clearly derived from man and should be subject to him.

Castillo believes that subsequent Catholic interpretations of Lilith transformed her into a night demon responsible for crib deaths and wet dreams. In this role, Lilith could be conflated with *La Llorona*, the crying woman who wanders the night looking for children to replace the ones she has lost or killed. *La Llorona* is also linked to the ancient goddess Cihuacoatl, who in turn is one aspect of the great goddess Coatlicue. The interconnections among these four figures derive from their individual degree of association with snake imagery and/or moaning in the night. Lilith, in the prepatristic traditions of Europe and the Middle East, is drawn as a snake with wings, a symbol associated with woman and her power of regeneration. Likewise, the powerful Coatlicue is depicted with a skirt of writhing serpents, for snakes symbolized the power of earth and the womb for pre-Columbian and pre-Aztec Mesoamericans. Cihuacoatl is linked to snakes by her association with Coatlicue, and she is linked to *La Llorona* because she wails in the night for women whose lives wash away in the waters of childbirth. Before the Christian era in the Americas, these images of the snake, the water, and the night indicated awe and even sympathy toward women, not distrust.

Castillo goes on to explain that the demise of the serpent image coincided with the coming of the Judeo-Christian tradition and its Old Testament story of Eden, the story that would shift the religious power in the New World to a single male deity. In that tradition, Eve accepts her role as a subservient being, thereby allowing men to declare Lilith a wrongdoer rather than an alternative voice. Later, when Eve listens to Lilith's advice coming from the snake of Eden, she can be accused of courting evil and of going on to corrupt the innocent Adam. Of course, both Lilith and Eve will end up damned: Lilith for refusing the secondary, passive role as mother of the human race, and Eve for accepting this reproductive imperative without which humankind and all the earth would perish. The emerging Judeo-Christian tradition will eventually declare sex and offspring to be the *right* of the man but the *duty* of the woman, and the woman will bear the burden of guilt for sexual activity and reproduction outside the sanction of marriage. In addition, she will be lessened (that is, made less than the Virgin) by sexual contact even within the bonds of marriage. In Castillo's opinion, modern woman continues to be a victim of this double bind.

Modern Roman Catholic leadership does little to dispel this notion, for it persists in doubting woman's equality in grace. A Catholic News Service article (Norton 2001) about women in the clergy provides an interesting insight into the modern Church's continuing disregard for the female half of their flock: females may not become deacons (ordained ministers who possess significantly fewer sacramental powers than a priest). One spokesperson for this ban admits that a women diaconate did exist in the early Church, but even then it was not equal to the male diaconate. The women served only to perform services the men considered improper for themselves, such as touching women during the administration of a sacrament. This Church stand against granting even minor holy orders to women suggests not only patriarchal privilege but also misogyny, if the leaders truly believe a man to be corrupted by merely touching a woman.

Numerous Latinas note the self-disgust or even self-hatred generated by a persistent religious message that women are tainted. Admitting that pre-Conquest indigenous societies also held women in disregard, they don't blame the Church exclusively for gender discrimination. However, they do accuse the colonial Church of perpetuating the beliefs that women are corrupt or at least easily corrupted, that dark skin links a person more closely with depravity, and that poverty is an appropriate condition for people of color.

This recognition of the self-hatred generated by colonization and oppression links the authors with postcolonialist theorists. As early as 1952, theorist Frantz Fanon (*Black Skin, White Masks*) recorded the experience of the native islanders of Martinique who internalized French language and values, only to discover that they still were not—and never would be—considered equals. These natives discovered that the pairing of blackness with sin, savagery, inferiority, and dependence was not an innocent metaphoric device but rather a reflection of the way whites actually perceived blacks. In their shock and frustration, they came to despise their skin color, and thus, themselves. Since their accomplishments were tainted by their blackness, they came to desire to be white and to attain all that whiteness offered: intelligence, power, freedom of action, superiority, desirability, and sanctity.

In the opinion of many U.S. Latina writers, the situation in Spanish-dominated lands is no less severe. The biases they find embedded in Church traditions and doctrine drive them to label Catholicism a hostile remnant of colonization. Gloria Anzaldúa, Pat Mora, and Sandra Cisneros are among those who exhort women to speak out against their negative image. So is playwright Maria Irene Fornes, whose title character in *Fefu and Her Friends* (1977) responds in startling ways to her husband's assertion that women are hateful and repulsive. At first appearing to agree with him, Fefu gradually reveals her real meaning: women *are* as hateful and depraved as men perceive them to be *if they don't close ranks and fight back.* Fefu's rifle shots at her husband are always blanks, but they make the point that she can shoot and can choose whether to kill. Marital peace is scarcely the result, of course, but it's not intended to be. Her unpredictable behavior levels but does not reverse the long-established inequality between the genders. It reinforces the idea that the oppressed can regain their self-worth through wholehearted thought and action. Murder isn't necessary, but confrontation is. In the end Fefu inspires herself as well as the less timid of her friends. Only the fragile Julia succumbs to psychological paralysis and then death in her unwillingness to oppose the sexual stereotype that is her own particular obsession.

Fefu is a survivor in the gender war, a woman willing to employ the tools of power, a woman willing to agree when her friend theorizes that angels grade people on sexual performance and admit only the good lovers to heaven. So are Ana Castillo and many of her characters. Castillo's (1995a) view is that Eve was the first human, not Adam, and Eve gave nothing away when she bit into the apple. In her lusty poem "Después de probar (la manzana)" ["After trying (the apple)"], Castillo (1995b) argues that Eve's "fall" gave every one of her female descendants the opportunity to enjoy the sweetness of sex. In her opinion, tradition is wrong about the origins of the human race, wrong about the goodness of women, wrong about the sinfulness of sex, and wrong about its interpretation of skin color.

The power and persistence of these errors cannot be laid wholesale upon the Catholic Church, of course, even though it has associated evil with darkness and woman. Feminist and postcolonial critics such as Anne McClintock (1995) and Andrée Nicola McLaughlin (1990) investigate how secular use of the metaphor works in conjunction with the terms "female" and "lower class." These two agree that being female and darker-skinned automatically relegates a woman to poverty and low cultural status. In most cultures, they claim, the woman was of secondary importance even before colonization, for she was subject to the males of her group. During colonization, she underwent the same political and social stresses as her male counterpart and was often sexually mistreated as well, and as a result, she became "less than" the conquering male, his racial mate, and the men of her own race. If she was also poor, uneducated, and among the darkest-skinned of her own people, she continued her social descent. When such a woman was raped, or even if she consented to sex with a male of the dominant culture, she became the lowest of the low. The mixed-blood children of the union were acceptable to neither group, and as their mother, she shared their fate. In addition, she received the displaced anger of the males of her race, who often turned their frustration against the only individuals lower than they in status: the women and children of their own culture.

In the colonial Americas, certainly, the official religion reinforced this misogyny. Numerous U.S. Latina critics have commented on the influence of Christian beliefs in defining the cultural demons known as *La Malinche* and *La Llorona* as well as the European Catholic icon known as the Blessed Virgin Mary. This female trio continues to complicate Latina self-identity. They appear in the grandmother stories told to children and in the gossip, criticisms, religious practices, and superstitions of daily life. They provide the pattern for numerous characters in fiction and nonfiction alike. The fates of brown-skinned *La Malinche* and *La Llorona* threaten Latinas daily, and the only alternative provided is the unattainable purity of the Spanish Blessed Virgin Mary, who—not coincidentally—is usually portrayed as white-skinned, blue-eyed, and honey-haired.

The unfortunate *La Malinche* figure grew from the historic Indian woman the conquistadors renamed Doña Marina. As a young woman, Marina was taken as an interpreter and mistress by the Spanish conqueror Cortés. Although she may well have been either a gift given to Cortés or a prize seized by him, she came to be perceived as a willing mistress and a traitor of the people. Though surely she could not have been the only Indian to inform Cortés of the warring factions that would help him overcome Moctezuma, she bears this burden of guilt. Likewise, being caught between two cultures in which celibacy and marriage were the only two acceptable sexual roles for women, her relationship with Cortés rendered her an outcast in both cultures. She became *La Chingada* (the fucked one), the source of an epithet still used by Mexicans to indicate voluntary sexual degradation. Even today, even in the supposedly more sexually liberated Latino communities in the U.S., lost virginity seriously decreases a woman's reputation and marriageability, and thus her personal worth. The taint follows any loss of virginity, whether through consent, rape, or even marriage. Sobering evidence of this comes from Silvana Paternostro's 1999 revelations of New York City hymen reconstruction clinics frequented by Latinas who wish to restore the hymen and/or tighten the vagina. Some of these women want to fool a husband on their wedding night, but many others, like the clinic professional contacted by Paternostro, submit to the surgery to please a husband or to prevent one from wandering. The accessibility of such painful and secretive surgery gives credence to Paternostro's claim that Latina immigrants don't receive the full benefit of Northern freedom because their traditions follow them north. Culturally and religiously, they continue to interpret the hymen itself as a mark of inferiority—whether it is intact or not. Paternostro lays the blame on male attitudes that the hymen represents woman's moral weakness and that a woman is "used" once she has surrendered it, regardless of the circumstances.

Ana Castillo (1995a) finds the Catholic Church guilty of perpetuating this degradation of women through the story of Eve's disobedience. The forced choice between lifelong virginity or the unfortunate but forgivable loss of virginity in marriage, she says, constitutes oppressive control of the female body. Even lifelong virginity is only considered pure if it is pursued in dedication to the religious ideal of the Virgin Mary. Virginity in order to reject the role of motherhood, à la Lilith, is sinful and perverse.

In Latino religio-cultural logic, the damnation incurred by Doña Marina compounded itself when she mothered the first *mestizo* children, the first of many who would bear the blood of two or more races but would not be fully accepted by any of them. Eventually, Cortés would be allowed to hand off Marina and the children to a lesser officer. A similar pattern of abandonment is not unfamiliar in Latino culture today. Latina mothers and their children still are at the mercy of the fathers, who may elect not to "recognize" and support their children conceived out of wedlock, who may cease to support the children from a marriage that has ended, and who may refuse to support the stepchildren gained through his other marriages. The implication is that intercourse and conception are the sin of the woman, and a man is generous indeed to assume responsibility for either her or their offspring. Thus, with the continuing sanction of the Church, the story of Doña Marina becomes a cautionary tale for women alone. It teaches them that Marina was cast out as a traitor not just to the people as a whole, but to the men in particular, for she made the Aztec men feel inadequate when they could neither control her nor protect her from Cortés.

The desperate fear of social rejection and abandonment provides a link between *La Malinche* and another cultural figure of darkness and loss, *La Llorona*, the woman who haunts the watercourses at night, wailing and looking for replacements for her own children, whom she killed in grief and vengeance against her unfaithful lover. Mortal families fear that she will seize their children—especially their male children. More recent interpretations of these two women suggest that *La Malinche* and *La Llorona* may actually have had their children taken from them against their will (Carbonell 1999, Cypress 1991). Possibly, *La Llorona* killed her children to prevent their being seized by the Spanish women, who found Indian children very beautiful. Other explanations might be that the children were stolen by her own people to be raised in traditional ways, especially if they were not of mixed blood; or that they were stolen by their Spanish father for European upbringing if they were *mestizo*; or that either the Spanish family or the Indian family killed them *because* they were *mestizo*. In each of these situations, the mother would be a victim, not a villain. She and the children could also have been victimized in the common scenario of abandonment. The woman Huitzitzilin in *Song of the Hummingbird* (Limón 1996) experiences all of these losses, having to abort one child to save her life, relinquish her love child to be raised by his Mexica father, wander abandoned in the desert with her *mestizo* children, and finally lose her *mestizo* boy to schooling in Spain and her *mestiza* girl to Spanish colonial society. Helena María Viramontes offers a modern-day version of child theft in her story "The Cariboo Cafe" (1995), in which an old woman grieves over a son who was "disappeared" by death squads in El Salvador. She accuses the American government not only of condoning these death squads, but also of allowing American immigration agents to persecute Latino children who have escaped to the U.S. The old woman in the story fails in her attempt to prevent the deportation of two resident Latino children who have become separated from their parents, and thus from their citizenship papers.

Even among present-day U.S. Latino communities that escape the daily threat of deportation, *La Llorona* survives as a potent reminder that the mother is the child's last defense, whether the enemy be armed forces, border patrols, child social services, or religio-cultural attitudes. If she is to avoid becoming *La Llorona*, this woman must preserve the lives of the children, with or without the assistance of the father(s). She is not helped emotionally by clergy who offer her social programs but still view her single parenthood as embarrassing or even sinful. In such circumstances, wailing may indeed be her only resort.

What the Catholic Church has traditionally offered as an alternative to these dark-skinned and desolate *La Malinche* and *La Llorona* figures is the European Blessed Virgin Mary, who is presented to the Latina as a white and impossibly pure model: the only human ever born without original sin and the only one to bear a child without sacrificing her chastity. Mary receives constant male protection/domination: first by God, through her election to bear the Son of God; then through Joseph, Jesus, and Jesus' disciples; and finally through the hand of God once again as she is taken up to heaven. In a religion centered on a three-faced male deity, she is a model of trust and subservience, but she is hardly one whose life resembles the lives of most Latinas, except that her child was despised and murdered by political and religious zealots.

The *La Malinche, La Llorona,* and Blessed Virgin Mary figures may well reinforce the often-discussed cultural definition of a Latina as either a virgin or a whore. Debra Castillo (1992) in particular examines the effect these three models have on Latina self-identity. She notes that the role of the Blessed Virgin is clearly impossible to imitate in real life, where simultaneous virginity and pregnancy are unachievable. *La Llorona* is no model, for she is both an unmarried mother and a murderer. *La Malinche* is a mother, but she is a traitor twice over for betraying her people and for bearing the first *mestizos*. Latinas are thus left without a model. If a Latin woman has chosen to remain a virgin, she is considered incomplete in a family-centered, male-dominated culture, and if she has chosen to become a married mother, she has diminished her value through her accompanying loss of virginity. If she is an unwed or abandoned mother, she edges closer to being seen as a whore, a traitor, an insane woman, or a murderer. Nowhere except in "darkness" is there a definition for the sexually active woman who doesn't marry, or the one who marries but doesn't have children, or the one who has children but doesn't marry.

Castillo's list of unacceptable women becomes long indeed if expanded to include women who have taken a female lover, women who have been raped, or women who have had an abortion. Even the virginal and much-revered Sor Juana Inés de la Cruz fares badly against this cultural measure. A Hieronymite nun in seventeenth-century colonial Mexico, Sor Juana would seem to have modeled herself after the Virgin Mary. However, she presided over intellectual gatherings reminiscent of the *salons* of Enlightenment France, and she dared to write in favor of female participation in learned life. In the end, she was pushed into the darkness of silence by the bishops of the neophyte Catholic Church of Mexico because they believed she lacked proper female humility. They convinced her that her behavior had caused the disastrous crop failures of 1692, and she died of the plague after humbly and quietly exhausting herself in service to the ill (Trueblood 1988). Respected as she is today, she is known for her opposition to, not her success against, a colonial religious system with impossible expectations of womanhood. Unlike the bellowing Felice of Cisneros's "Woman Hollering Creek" (1991) or the Fefu of Fornes's play, Sor Juana ultimately emulated the heaven-dwelling woman martyrs, those models of humble acquiescence.

It is real-life, earthly women—divorced or abandoned mothers, mothers of *mestizo* children, unwed mothers, career women, lesbians, abortive mothers, rape victims, rebellious nuns—who are represented by character after character in U.S. Latina creative works. As a way to understand and write about the religio-cultural prejudice against them, some U.S. Latinas have turned to additional feminist and postcolonialist theories. Cordelia Chávez Candelaria (1997) echoes Elaine Showalter and Hélène Cixous when she recommends that Latinas leave behind the literary patterns and hierarchies of men so they can explore their own ways of writing. She agrees that women have been developing patterns, metaphors, and topics for centuries, but because men haven't followed women's writing and don't understand it, male critics still consider it a literary subculture or footnote. Candelaria considers this female writing an unfettered place where color, class, and gender coexist, a place of multiple consciousness, multivocality, and mixed genres. In it, women of all races and experiences may find positive ways to regard themselves. This productive and promising region bears resemblance to the "borderland" area of dangerous but abundant connectivity and information described by Anzaldúa. It also suggests the buffer space Homi Bhabha (1988) believes exists between cultures in contact, a zone of floating meanings where mutually beneficial exchanges may occur.

Such open spaces invite the exploration of alternative and expanded spiritual systems. According to multiculturalist Ilán Stavans (1995), that kind of openness, flexibility, and reciprocity in culture and religion is the goal of many U.S. Latinas/os who have rejected the colonial model of assimilation in favor of syncretism. He describes the Hispanic view as comfortable with contradictions, reversals, and the hazy space between dream and reality, and he thinks U.S. Anglo culture would benefit from embracing it. Latina writers seem to support this goal as they maintain certain literary characteristics despite the possibility of being categorized and marginalized by their use: the simple voice of a family storyteller, even when the message is life-shattering; the occasional flight into magical realism; the incorporation of *Santería*, *Espiritismo*, and ancient Aztec references; the multivocality; the facile switches between English and Spanish; the mixing of genres; and the exploration of their conflicted relationship with the Catholic Church.

Religious, cultural, and literary commentary find common ground in this resistance to assimilation. Isasi-Díaz and other Church scholars insist that Latinos in the U.S. do not necessarily reject citizenship in the U.S., the Catholic Church, or Christian Churches in general. Rather, they reject the attitude that their culture and religious expression are somehow backward or inappropriate. Postcolonialists would certainly agree that a colonizing power is ill equipped to determine which parts of an indigenous culture should be preserved in practice and artifact, and which must be discarded as unworthy or sinful.

This same message permeates secular works produced by U.S. Latinas since the middle of the twentieth century. Where the theological works focus on Catholicism more than on the daily lived experience of the people, the secular writers focus on daily life, including Catholicism as just one aspect of the whole. While readers may not be able to determine how much the storytelling of five hundred years has affected the theology, or how much the theology has affected the literature, they can recognize that art and life—literature and culture—reflect and influence one another in a continuous reciprocity. In five hundred years, the people's need to interrogate their imposed religion has not abated.

4

THE COLONIZED TONGUE

In their book *Hispanic Women: Prophetic Voice in the Church*, Ada María Isasi-Díaz and Yolando Tarango (1988) sometimes record the storytelling of the Latina women they organize into action groups in Catholic parishes. In these stories, religious references pervade the language, regardless of the main topic of the story or the level of a women's dedication to the official Church. Such complete penetration—a colonization of the mind and tongue—gives credence to the view that colonization has not yet been overcome.

The colonial Catholic past is also inextricably woven into the language of published Latinas and the people about whom they write. Catholic practices insinuate themselves into story action even when the storyline has nothing to do with religion. Catholic metaphors and half-prayerful exclamations to saints and deities color the narrative voices and the dialogue as if permanently embedded in Latino thought and expression. Rosaries, altars, and Catholic iconography texture the settings of most family scenes, and churches dot the landscape. Even where religious practices and churches are missing, both are paradoxically present, for their absence is specifically mentioned, sometimes with irony or satisfaction, sometimes with nostalgia or guilt, and sometimes with unsettled emotions. Rarely will Catholic actions and artifacts be ignored to the degree they are ignored in non-Latina U.S. literature of the same era.

Latina writers pry at these colonial bonds on their thought and expression. One such writer, Esmeralda Santiago, discovers that

Catholicism influences her even though she has never practiced the religion. Her memoir *When I Was Puerto Rican* (1993) includes perplexing encounters between the faith practiced by her relatives and friends, but not by her immediate family. In one such incident, Santiago asks her father whether saying "*Ay Dios Mío*" and not attending church are sinful. He agrees that both practices are sinful for the very good, religious Catholics, but seems unconcerned because he, Esmeralda, and the rest of their family are not good Catholics. She is left with an unsettled religious identity that continues to preoccupy her. Sometimes she wishes she could ask God for an answer, but she can't do that because her mother ignores religion, and her father, who is familiar with prayers and the Bible, doesn't share that knowledge with his family. Most of the time, however, Santiago doesn't miss Catholicism; she is merely curious about its absence. Attending Mass with her grandmother, a practicing Catholic, she concentrates more on the difficult act of behaving herself in church than she does on the mysteries of Catholic communion, and the entire episode reads as an amusing anecdote about being Catholic-but-not-Catholic. However, a later experience provokes more serious thought. A neighborhood infant dies, and Esmeralda, as the only available young virgin, must perform the solemn ritual of closing its eyes. For her, the spiritual power suddenly placed in her hands does not compensate for her terror at performing the rite.

Similar observations about the push and pull of Catholicism texture Santiago's later memoir, *Almost a Woman* (1998). One persistent conflict surrounds her mother's desire to see her daughters married in white dresses, in a church, with a priest, even though she herself avoids religious observances. She has not insisted that Esmeralda's father marry her even though he has fathered eight of her children as well as several other children by other women before and after her. Another contradiction surfaces when Esmeralda's grandmother moves in with a lover and sees no incongruity in immediately rebuilding her home altar in the new place. Perplexed, Santiago remembers how violently the women of her family have opposed birth control pills as a moral disgrace even though almost all of them have engaged in sex without marriage. Santiago never understands the complexities of her family's spirituality, but she also never doubts their belief in the mysterious power of the deities and saints. She decides her family interprets strict morality as an unattainable goal that must be attempted but should not cause distress if not achieved. Esmeralda refuses to part ways with her confusing family, and eventually they all accept their right to differ on religion.

Characters in Santiago's fiction must seek this balance, as well. In *América's Dream* (1996), the title character leaves her religious village on a Puerto Rican island to care for the home and children of a wealthy New York family. Among the many differences between their lifestyle and her former one, she notices one set of habits they absolutely lack: they don't keep statues, pray, exclaim to the deities and saints, or petition and complain to God. Because América has always been amid but not involved in Catholicism, she remains curious about this complete absence of the language and artifacts of religion. The explanation, for her, is that the poor need God but the rich don't. However, these rich people do need someone to show them how to be a family, and América starts by getting them to eat healthful meals at the same table at the same time. She doesn't realize that by offering them this pseudocommunion, she enacts the religion she claims she doesn't have.

Current leaders of Catholic Church ministries for U.S. Latinos acknowledge this persistence of Catholic identity even in the absence of regular Catholic practice. Kenneth G. Davis in particular finds this tenacity akin to the concept of *mestizo*, or mixed blood, and relates it to the "exuberant acceptance of ambiguity" (2000c, p. 112) that he identifies in Latino expression. Describing Latinos as a *raza cósmica*, a race that "embraces the bloodlines of virtually every continent" (2000b p. xiii), Davis enumerates the interior and exterior borders that they have straddled for centuries: multiple ethnicities, fluctuating gender roles, pressures for and against acculturation, and hierarchies of color. To these tensions must be added the friction of widely varying religious practices.

In the creative works of U.S. Latinas, inclusion of these practices is far more than a technique for establishing setting or a writerly effort at verisimilitude. Rather, it underscores the inescapability of Catholicism in the history, culture, blood, and upbringing of Latinas, real or fictional. Chicana writer and critic Ana Castillo acknowledges its perpetual presence and influence to an interviewer (Navarro 1991, p. 119), and her admission is borne out by author after author. This complex heritage is particularly apparent in the books by Pat Mora, whose family has dwelt on both sides of the Río Grande. In *House of Houses* (1997b), Mora demonstrates the degree to which religious metaphors are embedded in her consciousness. The title of the memoir reflects its concern with her commingled heritage, but it also plays upon Christ's assertion that his Father's house has many houses in it, a suggestion of a similar commingling (John 14:2). Mora echoes the Bible again when she writes that her Aunt Lobo "longed to dwell in the house my siblings and I grew up in all the days of her life" (p. 14), and her words imitate the phrasing of Psalm 27 as it appears in the *New American Bible* (Confraternity of Christian Doctrine 1970):

. . . I seek
To dwell in the house of the LORD
all the days of my life.

Throughout the memoir, she investigates the idea of "house" as a living source of identity and sustenance. Eventually she writes her way to an appreciation of her spiritual heritage and the variations she and her family have worked upon it.

One of these subtle but significant variations is the parallel Mora creates between her own connection to family spirits and the Catholic spiritual connection known as the Communion of Saints. The Catholic concept describes a mutually beneficial alliance among the living, the dead who may be caught in the intermediate punishments of purgatory, and the sanctified souls in heaven. Through the Communion of Saints, the faithful on earth offer prayer and sacrifice for the souls of their deceased dear ones, thereby begging the powers in heaven to diminish the time those souls must spend in purgatory. When the souls released from purgatory ascend to paradise, they are able to return the favor by petitioning heavenly intercessions for the faithful on earth. In this symbiotic relationship, the holy ones receive praise, the dead advance toward holiness, and the faithful are blessed for their devotion.

When Mora builds her house of houses, she imitates this pattern by seeking the attention of the family's favorite saints and deities as well as the ghosts of her family, including some who probably have not yet entered heaven. Offering contemplation, food, and praise, she ritually opens the paths of forgiveness, heals her family's wounds, and enables herself to embrace the past that created her. Notably, her communion of Mora saints wears an overwhelmingly female face, a face that repeats the modern-day Latina reality of female heads of families. The original Catholic pattern, God-centered and focused on suffering as a route to heaven, may still be visible to generations raised under the old Catholic tradition, but the updated version offers to the religious and the nonreligious alike an encouraging and practicable solution of community-building. Through it, women foster awareness and forgiveness within the family and the self.

Another Catholic symbol, Holy Communion, underlies the emphasis that Mora and other writers place upon gathering and feeding the family. In *House of Houses* and elsewhere, Mora often employs the preparation and sharing of food as a metaphor for the preservation of family and community. Religious terms such as *sacrament* or *host* appear often.

Through its sacred rite of Holy Communion, the Church renews its dedication to Christ by sharing his body and blood in the form of bread and wine. Family food rituals likewise reinforce unity and continued life. They feature traditional foods drawn from the land, imitating the link to culture and place provided by the Church's focus on wheat and wine. A chief celebrant is in charge, but the gender of the celebrant differs significantly from the Church model, which allows only an ordained male priest to sanctify the food. Holy Communion itself follows the model of the Last Supper, a ritual celebration arranged by male disciples and presided over by Christ. In contrast, the family meals that are so prominent in Latina literature are usually held at the insistence of a woman elder and jointly produced by the women of the family. These meals occur for many reasons, but one will always be arranged when the family faces separation, as when the father leaves the area to find work or the children embark on new lives. This Last Family Supper reaffirms family ties and promises spiritual support during the coming absence. The woman elder retains great power at the meal, for the home is her realm.

Another biblical ritual, the washing of feet, also occasionally emerges in a new form. In the story of Christ's Passion, Christ humbles himself before his disciples by washing their feet, and in another New Testament story, Mary Magdalene honors Christ by washing his feet and drying them with her hair. Foot washing as a meaningful service appears with differing impacts in stories by Denise Chávez and Sandra Cisneros. In the Chávez novel *Face of an Angel* (1994), Soveida's reaction to having her feet soaked and massaged resembles the resistance the disciples offered to Christ's ministrations. Both she and they consider such a service to be demeaning to the one performing it. Like the disciples, who learn they not only must practice humility themselves but also must learn to accept it in another, Soveida discovers that an earthly angel must accept comforting as well as provide it. This intimate human connection allows understanding and forgiveness to flow in both directions. In *Face of an Angel*, it eases Soveida's distress over personal disasters and increases her awareness of the holiness of ordinary humans.

A reference to foot washing also appears in the Cisneros story "*La Fabulosa*: A Texas Operetta" (1991), but there it operates as a protest rather than a parallel. The narrator alludes to Mary Magdalene's demonstration of humility before Christ, but she uses it to criticize Latino male expectations: "But you know how men are. Unless you're washing their feet and drying them with your hair, they just can't take it" (p. 61). She rejects not the humble service but rather the ingratitude and self-centeredness of those who expect it. In her view, Christ degrades Mary Magdalene's loving act by neither resisting it nor thanking her for it. Where Chávez has recast the event to stress reciprocity among women, Cisneros lets it stand to stress Church support for male domination.

To varying degrees, religious references appear in most works by U.S. Latinas. An underlying theme in *Face of an Angel* is the need for Soveida to redefine her value in her people's religious system at the same time as she redefines herself. The many assumptions she discards or reinterprets along the way include Catholic concepts. Even though Catholicism has ceased to help her deal with life as she must live it, she maintains an analytical but tolerant attitude toward the religion. Her grudging fondness for it echoes her family's fondness for their feisty, elderly friend Oralia, a woman who scolds and fusses, but whose critical attention is essential to their sense of home. Like Oralia, Soveida's embedded religious training aggravates her with moral prodding, but its very persistence gives her a touchstone in her pursuit of the proper way to live. She and her religious sense remain in constant dialogue, and rather than dismiss each other completely, they negotiate an expanded spirituality. She ends her reevaluation of angels, service, and self with a side trip to witness a folk miracle in which an image of Christ's face has appeared on a tortilla being browned in an ordinary woman's kitchen. The stunned family creates a shrine in their living room so the faithful may honor the miraculous bread. Visiting that shrine with a touch of smug superiority, Soveida suddenly discovers herself refreshed by the love and hope the people derive from their humble miracle. Even though she has spent many years discarding or reinterpreting her own beliefs, she continues to honor the positive effects of faith.

Other Latina writers, of course, are less accepting of a Catholic heritage that they find tainted with the hubris of the colonizers who brought it. Among these is Julia Alvarez, who defines herself as Dominican-American. While Alvarez generally incorporates the impact of Catholicism on the daily lives of her characters, her novel

In the Time of the Butterflies (1995a) clearly investigates its more damaging effects. In this novel, she accuses the Trujillo-era Catholic Church leadership of failing to live by their stated ideals when they tolerate the dictator instead of protesting his repression and ethnic cleansing.

Alvarez's other prose and poetry interrogate the lingering effects of colonial religion in more incidental ways. In her novel *¡Yo!* (1997), for example, she briefly recalls the superior attitude of colonial priests who established themselves in a relatively comfortable settlement and then counseled the starving people in remote mountain villages to accept their hard lives with humility and wait for a better afterlife. Alvarez voices other complaints in *The Other Side/El Otro Lado* (1995b) as she records the emotional experience of visiting her former country. She accuses the Dominican Catholic Church of promoting martyrdom as a model of fulfillment instead of fighting for the people's right to life and peace. In her opinion, the idealization of suffering and death is itself a murderous act because it creates "history's selfless heroes—men and women who died by the truths that they believed in" (p. 115). In particular, she laments the naming of newborns via an almanac that "each day lists saints born, virgins raped, apostles martyred" (p. 114). Where, she seems to ask between the lines, does this model promote the sense of individual worth that Christ offered his followers?

The voice most critical of the Church belongs to Ana Castillo. Her considerable body of fiction varies in its attention to Catholic influences, sometimes foregrounding them in reference and metaphor, as she does in *So Far from God* (1993), and sometimes relegating them to deep background, as she does in *Loverboys* (1996) and *Peel My Love Like an Onion* (1999). However, she takes the topic head-on in her collection of essays, *Massacre of the Dreamers* (1995a). There, she specifically condemns the cold superiority of the colonizing Catholics who continued to doubt that Amerindians had souls even after they learned that the indigenous peoples believed in the soul and philosophized about life after death. Her observations bring to mind the comments of Isasi-Díaz

(2000), who accuses the modern-day Church of trying to wean the people from their popular religion instead of appreciating that a person may be Catholic in a number of different ways. To both writers, Church behavior indicates a leadership from the top down, not a caring response to grassroots expressions of need, and both writers recognize a five-hundred-year-old rejection of that mode of operation. Indeed, in *Hispanic Women: Prophetic Voice in the Church* (1988), coauthors Isasi-Díaz and Tarango strongly suggest that popular Catholicism originated as firm but quiet resistance to the colonizing forces of Spanish Catholicism. Any countermovement against forces that could put an army behind their rules of morality would have to be subtle if the people are to survive the encounter at all.

Other writers and experts suggest that the flexibility inherent in Latino popular Catholicism is less an attack on the Church than a result of the ongoing, necessary negotiation among the many belief systems present in the Americas: ancient indigenous religions, Catholicism old and new, African slave religions, western-European spiritism, and non-Catholic Christian religions brought by immigrants and missionaries. The parallel practice of elements from two or more systems allowed the people to forge a group identity instead of allowing themselves to be divided and conquered completely.

As social scientist Díaz-Stevens (1994) suggests, the indigenous people may have responded to the pressure to convert by adopting the official prayers and motions in public, but in their internal lives and in the sanctity of their homes, they may have maintained their traditional practices, perhaps by camouflaging them with Catholic trappings or by practicing the old and new religions alongside one another. Similar subversive efforts to preserve pre-contact identities have been noted in other colonized areas, and the similarity seems entirely appropriate if the Catholic Church is viewed as a colonial partner with the Spanish conquistadors who began to subdue the Americas at the end of the fifteenth century. The records of the discovery and subjugation of the Americas reveal that the Spanish and their accompanying clergy often viewed the indigenous people with benevolent superiority, at best seeing them as children to be raised above their misguided practices, and at worst, deploring them as fiendish pagans to be annihilated if they could not be swiftly converted. Just as the conquistadors substituted their political, economic, and social systems for Aztec ways that they considered primitive or even barbaric, the missionary priests sought to completely supplant the gods and rituals they considered blasphemous. State and Church were paternalistic rulers, and not always kind ones. Resentment toward these destructive attitudes has persisted into the present and is reflected in Latina fiction and nonfiction.

The religio-cultural domination of the Latina is also recognized by Norma Alarcón, another established Chicana critic. Alarcón (1990) comments on the illogic of well-meaning non-Latina feminists who assume that a program of consciousness-raising should suffice to enable Latinas to improve their self-confidence and overall status. She explains that the U.S. Latina lags too far behind the Euro-American feminist for any such quick fix; that is, she has great difficulty viewing herself as a valuable and free individual because the many discriminations in her daily life continue to destroy her self-concept. Alarcón's view is supported by theologian Isasi-Díaz, who notes that the daily experiences of many Latinas do not include models in the form of powerful and educated women (2001). Even the nuns that many Latinas encounter during their schooling cannot inspire them to freedom because the nuns themselves hold very humble status in the overall hierarchy of Catholic religious orders. According to the memoirs of writers such as Judith Ortiz Cofer, Julia Alvarez, and Pat Mora, the greatest attraction offered by convent life was its aura of privacy, order, and peace. Mora recalls being attracted to "that sweet habit, smelling of purity" (1997b, p. 245).

Not all Latinas have had the advantage of exposure to nuns living a convent life, however. As Díaz-Stevens points out, the common Latina lives a disadvantaged, undereducated, isolated existence—and has lived it for a very long time. Thus, she needs different models and different solutions. Perhaps, as the *mujerista* theology of Isasi-Díaz suggests, spiritual encouragement for this woman comes not from a study of Catholic doctrine but from a local Church effort to help her identify and ameliorate the frustrations of her daily life.

Exploring the nonreligious elements of day-to-day Latina experience, activist critics Barbara Harlow (1991) and Yvonne Yarbro-Bejarano (1991) separately stress that most employed Latinas endure and have always endured poor wages and work conditions. Furthermore, Latinas in general suffer and have always suffered from the *machismo* of their men in their homes and their culture. In addition to that, significant numbers of them live as exiles in the U.S., commonly facing racial violence and political deportation. Harlow, Yarbro-Bejarano, and others insist that U.S. Latinas must create their own practical and spiritual paradigms instead of trying to follow traditional, male-oriented patterns of social, religious, or literary thought. They suggest that if Latina writers are to step into the postcolonial breach to inspire their people, and if non-Latina readers are to comprehend and appreciate them, their works will have to reveal the lingering religious and cultural colonialism that diminishes Latina self-worth from inside the culture just as much as mainstream U.S. discrimination against race, color, and gender erodes it from without. Norma Alarcón (1990) maintains that the U.S. Latinas who have achieved stature in the literary world—albeit a small number—may be providing that insight, for they consistently interrogate the influences of class, employment, politics, religion, race, gender, and sexual orientation upon the people for whom and about whom they are writing.

Paradoxically, the resistance offered by these women may not be something new at all, but rather the recovery and adaptation of beliefs and attitudes backgrounded after colonization but preserved in the spoken wisdom and stories of grandmothers and *curanderas*. Long dismissed as the nattering of women, and thus allowed to proceed for centuries under the very noses of Church and government, these views have most likely remained fluid and responsive to changing needs. Following a largely oral tradition, the women have been able to eliminate what is no longer effective and replace it with useful discoveries. The tradition covers religious matters, as well. According to Díaz-Stevens, women have had control of family religious practices since precontact times, and since contact, they have actively cared for the Spanish mission churches and commanded the social details of celebrations. She believes that this core of females sought to meet the demands of the colonial Church without sacrificing their old communal faith life. Thus, they have had a significant role in shaping popular Catholicism.

The attitude embedded in the works of contemporary U.S. Latina writers reaffirms this female power over religious practice. They and their characters seem to believe that the Church has tried to change them too much, that the Church itself needs change, and that they are the ones to change it by pushing the backgrounded female role to the fore. Whether or not the writing deals overtly with religious topics, the women seem to automatically assume leadership in ethical and spiritual matters, and regardless of the spiritual pathway chosen, they consistently work for the betterment of the people. Furthermore, the other characters look to the women for guidance. The trusted *curandera* is a recurrent figure. So is the grandmother or godmother who urges life onward despite the abuses, poverty, deportations, abandonments, street violence, revolutions, and natural disasters faced by her family. Sisters, mothers, and daughters may struggle against one another, but they do so with the hope of reconciliation. The resulting impression is that community and family are indeed valuable, but that the community of family itself has the greatest importance, and all these matters are in the hands of the women. Named or not, the *mujerista* theology identified by Isasi-Díaz (2001) operates in the stories: "family" reflects the family of God, an ever-changing and responsive "*kin*dom" as opposed to official Catholicism's God-centered "*King*dom."

The salvaged family tradition noticeably follows the pattern described by Díaz-Stevens in her analysis of the female "genius" evident in popular Catholicism: they relate to rites of birth and death, to the in-home observance of religion, to healing, and to the comfort and preservation of the people. One prominent aspect is the maintenance of home altars. Another is the care of family graves in the communal cemetery, a ritual tradition that employs the kitchen and garden arts and includes the children, the neighbors, and the town pathways, as well. Its importance is clear in Escamill's *Daughter of the Mountain* (1991) when the entire village makes an arduous, priest-led trek to a dim grotto dedicated to the suffering mother of Jesus. On this forced march, the women assume the duty of encouraging and sustaining the people during the journey. Besides packing food and drink, they preserve the true spirit of the journey so it may be released after the required Catholic worship, when the people are free to share food and companionship amid the graves in their old cemetery near the grotto. A readiness to enjoy the company of their family spirits permeates this scene, just as it runs through Day of the Dead celebrations described in numerous other Latina stories. Typically, these celebrations do not involve the church building.

Spirits are present in the home on a daily basis, as well. Mora's ancestors willingly shuffle through her ethereal *House*. When alive, they themselves invited the spirits, as Mamá Cleta does when she throws a party for her favorite saints and the Virgin of Guadalupe. A similar confidence in the good will of the spirits inspires the main character in Edit Villarreal's 1989 play, *My Visits with MGM (My Grandmother Marta)*: she engages in daily, lively consultations with her dead grandmother, the only person who ever understood her free-wheeling gusto for life. At a more somber level, Graciela Limón's (1996) Mexica woman Huitzitzilin finds solace among the spirits who inhabit the convent courtyard built over the remains of her shattered village. Guidance flows from these ancients into the women who listen, the women who pass the wise and hopeful messages to their people.

This "passing on" is both an important role for women and a prominent aspect of their resistance to colonization. If the people's cultural identity is to survive, it must do so within the very fabric of the community. In themselves, old family stories and a respect for tradition are curative only to a small and somewhat selfish degree, for information hoarded in exclusive groups does not weave the community into an enduring unit. Only if the women's stories and remembered interconnections are shared may they nurture the identity and self-worth needed to resist political and cultural domination.

At times the effort to preserve this sense of connection and belonging takes a character beyond the point of legality and safety. For her play *Puente Negro* (1983a), Estela Portillo Trambley creates a tough, resourceful *coyote* (border guide) named Chaparra. This woman sustains herself and her clients by means of her grit, her familiarity with ancient pathways and hiding places in the desert, her practical distrust of human nature, and her balancing trust in the guidance and protection of a sympathetic rebel, the Virgin of Guadalupe. Most important, she trusts the identity she inherited from her ancestors. Chaparra is a businesswoman when it comes to easing Mexicans illegally into the U.S. She takes no chances and holds herself emotionally apart from the sad stories that have driven her charges to leave their country. She is not motivated by profit, however, but by the desire to keep her people and their hopes alive. She tries to protect her charges not only from *la Migra*, but also from unscrupulous Americans waiting to enslave them at the end of their journey. For this, she accepts the appearance of being a traitor in her own country and a criminal in the U.S.

Chaparra has a safer counterpart in the liberated woman Felice in *Woman Hollering Creek*, a Sandra Cisneros (1991) story about an abused and betrayed wife who mentally and physically escapes her marriage through the help of other women. The wife, Cleófilas, has been taken from her native Mexico to the U.S. and installed beside a creek called La Gritona, or "woman hollering." The townspeople dismiss the name as a reference to some old Indian fancy, but Cleófilas gradually realizes that the ancient story applies to her. As she sits alone with one baby and another on the way, she learns the lament of *La Llorona*, the betrayed and abandoned woman condemned to wander along waterways, wailing for the children she has drowned. She ponders that fate, her own desperate loneliness, and her despair over a philandering husband, finally asking herself if "something as quiet as this drives a woman to the darkness under the trees" (p. 51), and she wonders whether La Gritona cried out more from rage than from sorrow. Tempted to drown herself in the creek but finally committed to life and family, Cleófilas elects to face the shame of starting over at her father's house in Mexico. To do so, she needs the help of the female network, but it must be a new network that has remembered the ancient power and freedom of woman. Help cannot come from her abandoned and widowed neighbors, allegorically named Soledad (loneliness) and Dolores (pain). It must be the gift of the independent woman Felice (cheer), who possesses a truck and a sense of self. Felice drives Cleófilas across La Gritona, letting out "a yell as loud as any mariachi" (p. 55) in tribute to this one local landmark named for a woman other than the Virgin. Her holler shows Cleófilas the way out of pain and rage, loneliness and sorrow: a journey in the company of women who can transform wailing into shouts of solidarity and resistance. Although Cleófilas faces a long road to any kind of independence, she does so with a brand new model of independent womanhood.

Pat Mora proclaims a similar message with her poem "Llantos de La Llorona: Warnings from the Wailer" in her 1995 poetry collection *Agua Santa/Holy Water*. A celebration of the power and resourcefulness of women, the poem blesses women's tears and La Llorona's pathways. To Mora, both are holy water: pure, sustaining, and essential. Life cannot proceed without water, without woman. When a woman raises her voice, even if only to wail, she cannot be ignored.

Such models of resistance and of reliance on the female voice hold a prominent place in nonfiction, memoir, and fiction by other U.S. Latinas. Gloria Anzaldúa celebrates both the voice and the mixed language of "The New Mestiza" in her widely read *Borderlands* (1987). Her essays and memoirs leave little doubt about the potency of being *mestiza/o*. Through the wisdom gained from negotiating multiple languages and cultures in conflict, she says, comes the power to claim one's space and assure one's survival. The journalist Sylvana Paternostro (1999) likewise argues that women must find and use their voices, but she warns that many Latinas within and outside of the U.S. have yet to learn to speak. She partially blames the Catholic Church for silencing their voices, particularly in matters of sexuality, virginity, birth control, abortion, and divorce. She also recognizes the role that a male-dominated society plays in encouraging this deafness to the complaints of women. However, she insists that Latinas contribute to their own oppression when they accept the social model of woman as an attractive and acquiescent appendage. Citing the extraordinary willingness of some Latinas to undergo hymen reconstruction and tightening of the vaginal walls, Paternostro insists that Latinas will not achieve self-respect as long as they measure their worth by their ability to attract and hold a husband—or failing to do that, by their success in attracting a sexual partner who will "recognize" their children as his own.

A significant aspect of Latina writing is this triple burden it carries as literature, social criticism, and literary criticism. Viramontes (1989) refers to both her literary and her social habits when she admits to using her creative writing to "sabotage the stereotypes with whatever words are necessary" (p. 38). Denise Chávez (1989) also acknowledges a political motive when she calls her plays a "prayer for peace" (p. 32) because her casts include everyone, regardless of race, age, class, or sexual identity. That stance is reinforced by others: Debra Castillo, who insists in *Talking Back* (1992) that writing is active and meaningful work that should precede theorizing about writing; Judith Ortiz Cofer, who tells interviewer Rafael Ocasio (1994) that writers must pay attention to each other's works; and Julia Alvarez (1998), who declares that she and others are "forging a tradition and creating a literature" (p. 170). In this willingness to enter the dialogue, the secular writers echo religious commentators such as Isasi-Díaz, the prominent voice in *mujerista* theology. Both groups promote an ongoing creative interaction rather than a search for finality.

In their insistence upon dialogue, Latina writers do not advocate female dominance. They do not suggest a return to the beliefs of precontact Mesoamerica—a time that was hardly ideal for women—nor a complete rejection of beliefs based in the Catholic Church. Rather, they suggest that the ancient goddesses, the voice of *La Llorona*, and the constant presence of the Virgin of Guadalupe offer pathways to a balance in power and a recognition of the female's equal claim to wisdom. Their syncretic, postcolonial view questions an all-or-nothing purism in religion and culture. It rejects the continuing U.S. and Catholic Church pressures to assimilate, preferring a revitalization of historical identities, and it allows for a process in which religio-cultural elements are not discarded as much as gathered and preserved.

5
DEPROGRAMMING THE COLONIZED

Recovering one's sense of heritage, identity, and self-worth is an ideal that is far easier to state than to accomplish. The colonized mind and tongue do not free themselves without personal anguish and physical danger. Where Church, military, and government have joined forces, an opponent of the ruling power risks persecution as a rebel and a heretic.

Women accused of rebellion and heresy appear frequently in Latina literature. Their message is particularly strong in Julia Alvarez's biographical novel *In the Time of the Butterflies* (1995a), in which four sisters in the Dominican Republic oppose justice-by-color as it is administered by the dictator Rafael Leónidas Trujillo (1930 to 1961). During the latter two decades of his regime, these women of the Mirabal family gradually shed the religious and political complacency they have learned as members of the privileged class. Slowly they recognize that Trujillo promotes the "whitening" of Dominican society through the murder of Haitians in the country, through the oppression of the poor mixed-blood population, and through the brutal repression of voices raised against his policies. As the Mirabals reject his regime, they discover they must also reject the official Catholic leadership in their country because it fails to oppose Trujillo. Three of them join political rebels and rebel priests in a violent underground movement against the government, and the fourth maintains the family. Although their efforts predate the Latin American Catholic Church convocation at Medellín, their actions and attitudes typify the grassroots, Church-backed philosophy that would become known as liberation theology.

Well after the brave actions of the Mirabal sisters, and after the publication of *In the Time of the Butterflies*, Paulo Freire's *Pedagogy of the Oppressed* (1997) would supply a description for such activities. Like the earlier writer Gustavo Gutiérrez (1973), he would focus on ways to rehumanize the victims of colonial oppression, even to the point of confrontation. Freire and Gutiérrez agree that the first showdown must occur within the colonized population itself, with enlightened members taking on the long task of raising the people's self-image, for only when the people believe in their own innate worth can they be inspired to believe in their united power and their ability to manage their own lives. All three discoveries must occur before the people can build the righteous fervor needed to sustain a revolution.

Once the ire of the oppressed turns to insistence, Freire (1997) says, the conflict broadens. The group in power reinforces its psychological hold by sowing self-doubt in the agitators, labeling them ungrateful, misguided, immoral, and destructive; and the rebel leaders must return to convincing the people that militancy is just. The best argument for rebel leaders is that vocal and even physical resistance are actually acts of love, for they are corrective measures aimed not at the oppressors but at the "lovelessness" (p. 27) that leads them to oppress others. Rebel resistance, on the other hand, expresses love, for it seeks to liberate the dominant group from its moral blindness. Gustavo Gutiérrez, although he moderates his stand in later books, likewise states that the people's Church should be actively involved in raising and sustaining a sense of wronged dignity among the subjugated. He, too, promotes the idea that both the oppressed and the oppressor must be freed from the negative situation that binds them.

Some late-twentieth-century Latina voices echo these religiopolitical goals, but at the same time they find the progress toward them inadequate. Silvana Paternostro (1999) agrees with the goals of liberation theology, but she finds its current efforts less than satisfactory, particularly in the hope it offers to women. Writing about the inequities in Brazil, Paternostro reports that individual priests and parish groups have had some local success in protecting women and children, but overall, women's lives have not improved even where neighborhood-based liberation efforts have relied heavily upon the time and financial sacrifices of women. Isasi-Díaz, Tarango, and Díaz-Stevens echo her as they exhort their Church to greater action in the oppressed communities of the United States, sometimes using the voice of the ordinary Latina parishioner to do so. Among the many concerned women quoted in *Hispanic Women: Prophetic Voice in the Church* (1988), Isasi-Díaz and Tarango include study group members who continue to work for change within the Church even though the progress they see is only on a personal level. According to the terms of the liberation process set down by Freire, these women have been left stranded at the level of consciousness raising.

For the Mirabal sisters as depicted by Alvarez in *In the Time of the Butterflies*, the simultaneous rejection of government and Church is remarkable because of their position in Dominican society. Descended from Spanish bloodlines, protected within the strictly controlled family unit, and accepted in social and economic circles that bring them into contact with Trujillo himself, they are insulated from daily political violence and from the unrelenting poverty of the *campesinos*. Furthermore, they are dependents; for them, there is no survival outside the structure of family, Church, and government. The trust and obedience they have learned through these systems prepare them not only to trust Trujillo and the bishop, but also to obey and defend them. However, the very ideals promoted by Church and government eventually open the girls' eyes to hypocrisy in both organizations. Once that happens, they elect solidarity with the masses. The ideals they salvage are those associated with popular rather than official religion: a secular and spiritual consciousness that loves and preserves the community, the family, and the common culture.

Minerva Mirabal is the most political of the sisters, the one who seldom minces words about the evils of the Trujillo government. Largely through her efforts, her sisters Patria and María

Teresa join a rebel cell, but each woman is active in a different way and for different reasons. The regime finally falls, but not before Minerva, Patria, María Teresa, and the government driver assigned to them during their house arrest are shot as they return from visiting their imprisoned husbands. *In the Time of the Butterflies* details the resistance efforts, imprisonment, and murder of these three women, who were known to their cell—and eventually to the world—by the code name *Mariposas*, or Butterflies. Alvarez employs the narrative voice of a biographer who has interviewed the surviving sister Dedé, who didn't join the others but supported them from outside the movement.

Although the story is not primarily about religion, reading between the lines of the events and dialogue reveals a persistent spiritual element in each woman's decision to join the militants. All four girls become aware of corruption in the Dominican government, but Minerva is the first to accuse the Church of complicity through silence. For years, the other three continue to view Trujillo as a positive force because he is building schools, paying down debts, and remaining visibly connected with Church leaders. Furthermore, their cultural and social conditioning has convinced them their own political and theological views are naïve and inadequate, and this certainty is reinforced each time the Church or government rewards those Dominicans who accept its policies. Such powerful programming isolates them from Minerva's logic. She must let each sister recognize and resolve the religio-political dilemma on her own.

Minerva's awakening begins at age fourteen when she notices that her pet rabbit has grown so comfortable in its cage that it will not run away even when she tries to chase it off. The incident starts her thinking about the physical and mental cages that people in power have built around her and her family by offering them prestige, safety, and approval. Employing the folk wisdom that "until the nail is hit, it doesn't believe in the hammer" (p. 20), she reviews what she knows of Trujillo's methods. An obvious victim of his hammer is her schoolmate, Sinita Perozo, a girl so poor that only the unusual generosity of the nuns keeps her in the private convent school. Sinita tells Minerva that all the men in her family—father, brother, and five uncles—have been assassinated for opposing Trujillo. The brother was knifed by a dwarf whom Minerva recognizes as the amusing vendor of the lottery tickets her father buys as "a good investment" (p. 19). Upon hearing Sinita's story, Minerva's psychological ground shifts. Until this time, she has thought Trujillo a great leader, her father a cheerful, teasing man, her mother a killjoy, and the nuns an alliance beyond reproach. Suddenly, accusations form in her mind: If not Trujillo, who has the political power to murder the Perozos? If not Trujillo's guilt, what is funding the unusual generosity of the nuns? If not knowledge of Trujillo's murderous politics, what encourages her father's payments to the dwarf?

Amid her concern about family, school, adolescence, and the general political news of the country, Minerva includes another Church–government collusion in the drama of the beautiful Lina Lovatón, an unassuming schoolmate who has become the sexual target of the married Trujillo. His presents, private audiences, and outings with Lina trouble the nuns, but they suppress their objections as more and more benefits and gifts accrue at the convent and church. When Trujillo finally takes Lina away for good, Minerva doesn't miss the irony that both her Church and her upper-class society blame the illicit relationship on Lina, not on the powerful Trujillo or the complicitous nuns. She abruptly knows that she has not escaped anything by getting permission to leave home for Catholic boarding school. That school has a new gym named for Lina Lovatón and a new history text that presents Trujillo as a Dominican savior of biblical proportions. Rather than escape her cage, Minerva has merely entered "a bigger one, the size of our whole country" (p. 13).

Naïve and idealistic, Minerva and Sinita draw Trujillo's anger with a skit about the lost Dominican ideal of liberty. When Sor Asunción, their advisor, scolds them for their behavior, Minerva derives her own lesson from the incident. The nuns, the most powerful women she knows, have no voice, and neither does she. She will make no more frivolous protests, but behind a mask of female submission, she will bypass Catholic leadership and will plan nothing less than the overthrow of the government. Unlike the other rabbits in Trujillo's cage, she has chosen to bolt.

Minerva's sudden awareness of her potential for hiding subversion beneath a demure femininity may explain why she condemns the nuns less than she does the official male leadership of the Church. Perhaps she accepts that the nuns must work small deceptions within the constraints of their vows of poverty and obedience. Certainly, she notes their subtle efforts to slow Lina's progress toward Trujillo, and she admires the courage and finesse with which they later protect a political refugee by disguising her as a nun. Still, she believes the nuns should do more, and so should her Church, which is in a position to influence the masses with its bibles and its ceremonies, its imposing churches and schools, and its awesome power to withhold salvation. Minerva accuses the entire local organization of having sold out to Trujillo for new history books and a gymnasium named for a sacrificed daughter.

Alone among the Mirabal sisters, Minerva completely abandons her faith, but she doesn't do it painlessly. Her laughter is bitter when she calls Trujillo and Christ a matched pair of deceivers. She frets over a similar pairing of Trujillo and the Virgin on opposite sides of a party fan. Still, she means every word of her scornful accusation that the Church will never stand up for the oppressed, or even for itself, and she is proven right one day when the drunken Trujillo oversteps himself by taking over the distribution of communion at Mass. The Pope himself fumbles this opportunity for sanction: he talks about excommunication but fails to act.

What distresses Minerva far more than the loss of her religion is the new necessity to act in defiance of her family. In this, she is typical of many Latina characters, fictional and not. For them, religious observance and family tradition are inextricably linked. Rejecting one involves an excruciating dismantling and reconstruction of self to preserve what still has value. Minerva never relinquishes her unity with her family and the Dominican people. Her new vision diminishes her respect for her father, whom she mentally accuses of the general cowardice that has helped keep Trujillo in power; it causes her to view her mother as hopelessly naïve and sheltered; and it opens her eyes to the many oppressions that prevent the people from acting. Rather than betray or reject her people, however, she accepts the challenge to stand apart psychologically and politically but not personally or physically. Although she pushes her sisters to join her, she doesn't intrude on their right to decide.

Minerva thus becomes the first Mirabal to work from both within and without the system. If she is to die, she will not go as a martyr humbly baring her neck to the ax. Well before the date of the first official Catholic Church statement against Trujillo, Minerva has already taken steps against him. Much later, still loyal to her family but impatient with God at the moment of her murder on the mountainside, she joins Patria in prayer only as a reflex action, one she immediately—but silently—ridicules as counterfeit.

The other Mirabal sisters turn from the Church less easily and decisively, and so they are slower to act. María Teresa (Mate), the youngest by nine years, focuses her early resistance on the joyless life of the convent school, not on the questionable policies or politics of her Church. When the Mirabal family gathers to bury Patria's miscarried infant, however, Mate's thoughts begin to turn away from schoolgirl concerns. She sorrows over the baby "dead in a box like it doesn't have a soul at all" (p. 42), perhaps thinking of the Church's relegation of unbaptized infants to the forever-separate region of Limbo. She questions the platitudes about the Lord knowing best in matters so damaging to life and salvation.

Gradually, Mate realizes that great numbers of Dominicanas, even the privileged, remain weak and oppressed under their imposed beliefs. At the opening ceremonies of a new Catholic school term, she notes the Church–state partnership that requires the students first to sign an oath of political loyalty and then to parade before Trujillo, "women all together, in white dresses like we were his brides" (p. 131). She ponders their similarity to Nazi troops goose-stepping for Hitler. Starting her revolt in small ways that nonetheless make her feel guilty, she helps Minerva clear their home of materials that might reveal their connection with the rebels. To protect her sisters and their widowed Mamá, she helps Mamá write a letter assuring El Jefe that the Mirabal women remain loyal to the government.

Mate eventually joins the underground effort to transport and conceal weapons, and she is imprisoned along with Minerva. In the absence of Church intervention against police-state tactics, she must endure torture in the chambers of *La Cuarenta*, then risk further pain or death by smuggling a written account of prison abuses to the visiting investigators from the Organization of American States. In the absence of Church ministrations at the prison, she and Minerva take spiritual leadership upon themselves through morale-boosting measures like the "Crucifix Plot," during which they smuggle in enough small crosses to allow every prisoner, male or female, naked or clothed, to wear one around the neck. In a maneuver typical of popular adjustments to Catholicism, their action allows them to identify with the unjustly punished Christ but rejects the Church teaching that the meek will inherit the earth. The prisoners wear the crucifixes not in silent, humble endurance of their lot but as a defiant accusation against the conscience of Trujillo and their jailers. Like Minerva, Mate never relinquishes her dedication to family and population, but different from her, she remains more attached to a modified form of Catholicism.

Among the Mirabal sisters, Minerva and Mate join the resistance much more easily than Patria, the eldest and most devout, who reluctantly and incompletely gives up her submission to Church and government. A devout woman who believes she had a religious calling before she chose to marry, she pursues the culturally and religiously correct ideals of humility, obedience, and service. She focuses on caring for her extended family and leaves leadership to men like Monsignor Pittini and Trujillo. For many years, she believes her interior religious life will protect her and her loved ones from the exterior political reality.

Fittingly, Patria's devotion to family eventually brings her to the rebel fold. Because she loves and respects Minerva, she listens when Minerva challenges the logic of some Church teachings. Still, it is years before she sheds the guilt that has made her believe she miscarried a baby because she didn't become a nun. She begins to doubt that the Church knows best or speaks for the Lord. Finally she admits she cannot join Church and state in overlooking Trujillo's 1937 massacre of the thousands of Haitians who were living in the Dominican Republic, or his more recent murder of the men of the Perozo family. When Minerva points out the similarities in the family's side-by-side portraits of Trujillo and Christ, Patria suddenly sees the two male faces merge into one. Realizing she has been viewing the world through a lens given her by the very people she is examining, she begins to reinterpret everything she sees. She is ready to act.

Patria, however, has many layers of programming to peel away. For the rest of her life, Trujillo and Christ remain conflated for her, even to the extent that she finally maintains a home altar to each. When her son, Nelson, threatens to join the liberators, the balance of her devotion tips toward Christ and the Church, and she asks Padre de Jesús to get Nelson into a seminary school, for service to the Church is still the only sure protection from Trujillo's spies and assassins. She also strengthens her devotion to the *mestiza* counterpart of the Blessed Virgin Mary, *La Virgencita*, whom the people cherish as a sympathetic and willing intercessor. On a pilgrimage to Higüey, she studies a European-style portrait of the Holy Family and suddenly sees that the jeweled frame detracts from the truth of the image: the people pictured, the poor couple tending their infant, could have been any of the lighter-skinned *campesinos* of her island. Inspired to turn and adopt the Virgin's view of the pilgrims, Patria momentarily transcends the superficial elements of her beliefs and sees her fellow Dominicans in need.

Patria finally joins the rebels on June 14, 1959, the final day of a mountain prayer retreat with Padre de Jesús. That day, she witnesses a betrayed rebel invasion that leaves the underground forces decimated and their few survivors cast to the torturers of *La Cuarenta*. Watching young men being slaughtered on the slopes below her, Patria renounces the tradition of silent, humble suffering. Seeking God's face but not finding it in mountaintops obscured by the smoke of Trujillo's attack, she prays a rebel prayer: "I'm not going to sit back and watch my babies die, Lord, even if that's what You in Your great wisdom decide" (p. 162). Behind her homemaker facade, she becomes active in the Padre's rebel cell, where she finds that "something had changed in the way the Lord Jesus would be among us. . . . That room was silent with the fury of avenging angels sharpening their radiance before they strike" (p. 163). Within days, she helps unite Padre's splinter group with Minerva's resistance cell. The combined group calls itself the Fourteenth of June Movement.

But Patria's journey toward a new sense of self, country, and spirituality isn't over. Trujillo's forces burn her home and imprison her husband, Pedrito, and son, Nelson, then seize Mate, Minerva, and Minerva's husband, Manolo. All the revolutionary fervor drained out of her, she withdraws from political action but continues to offer comfort and support to her imprisoned family. On the day the Church publishes its first pastoral letter condemning the government's acts against its people, she prays to her conflated Trujillo/Christ, begging for Nelson's release and offering herself as a sacrifice in his place. Ironically, the prayer is answered by Trujillo, who calls to announce Nelson's freedom, and it is also Trujillo who orders the final sacrifice of Patria's life. Facing death with her sisters some months later, Patria offers one last prayer, a petition to San Marco de León for delivery from catastrophes. It is the prayer echoed and rejected by Minerva.

The religious journey of Dedé, the fourth Mirabal sister, differs from the others, a point that is doubly made by the change in point of view used for her chapters of the novel. Whereas Alvarez allows Minerva, Mate, and Patria to tell their own stories in the first person, she tells the story of the still-living Dedé from the third-person point of view of a biographer. The change in person reminds the reader that the other voices are spirit voices, voices from beyond the grave. The change also imitates the inner separation Dedé suffers as she questions her own inaction during her sisters' resistance. Not until the epilogue does Dedé speak in the first person as a unified self.

The combined chapters about and by Dedé reveal that although she sees through the Church and state deceptions and recognizes the restrictive definition they've imposed on women, she accepts the mask and remains officially outside the movement because of fears for herself, her sisters, and the extended family. At one time, nearly ready to leave her husband and join the movement, she visits a trusted priest, secretly hoping to be talked back into the Church-sanctioned role of humble submission, but she comes upon this priest hiding weapons for the resistance. At that point, she faces the reality that her fear is simply too great to overcome. She returns to her husband and limits her resistance to helping her sisters in domestic matters. Always available to look after their children, she becomes the survivor who will raise the children, preserve the story, and forever question herself for not acting with the others. Alvarez leaves Dedé in the position of the common citizen in the aftermath of civil war: conflicted, battered by losses, aware she fought the only way she could to preserve the continuity of Dominican life, and duty-bound to the future. Perhaps she was once among those unable to do anything for the revolution, but now everything is hers to do. She must restructure spirituality itself in her quest to nurture community, family, and self.

The years that Dedé faces after the Mirabal murders are tumultuous ones for the Dominican Republic. The nation suffers through the assassination of Trujillo, the overthrow of the "popular" dictatorship of his successor, Juan Bosch, another civil war, and another period of U.S. intervention that ends with Dominican control falling to former Trujillo aide Joacquín Balaguer (Burns 1972). It is a time that Alvarez (1997) describes elsewhere as full of death, "as if we couldn't kick the habit of murdering each other even after our dictator was gone" (p. 38). During this era, Dedé has to decide how much she should tell the children about their mothers and how firmly she should encourage their loyalty to state and Church. Although she tolerates the official Dominican valorization of her sisters, and although she maintains a religious pretense for her aging mother, who still brings all family crises to the feet of the Virgin, Dedé distrusts the government and finds ever-decreasing comfort in her religion. The religious pretense is even more difficult to preserve when facing Minerva's liberated daughter, Minou, who knows of her mother's spiritual attitudes and who crosses religious boundaries by visiting a *santera* to try to contact the spirits of her mother and aunts. To preserve Minou from harm, even Mamá makes a religious concession: she and Dedé drape the young woman with protective symbols drawn from both Catholicism and *Santería*.

Dedé's epilogue reveals the continuing human costs of the revolution. People are gone but things religious and secular remain: a scapular, a receipt, a missal, the rings that belonged to the women and their driver. These crop up to remind her that the spiritual and the daily can't be separated. Uninvited visitors call with scraps of her sisters' stories, especially the progress of their last day, and Dedé assumes the priestly role of confessor, forced to listen and absolve even as her heart aches. Hearing Manolo's story of the way he and the other imprisoned husbands were tortured with the news of their wives' deaths, she thinks, "it was as if Manolo had to say it and I had to hear it—so that it could be human, so that we could begin to forgive it" (Alvarez 1995a, p. 309).

The visits renew her guilt over her own past. The best she has been able to do is keep the remaining family together and a form of its faith alive to see a new era, whether the era is better or not. In that effort, Dedé joins the women described by Isasi-Díaz, Tarango, Paternostro, Díaz-Stevens, and others. Unable to sustain the family and the larger community without preserving the Catholic aspect of its identity, she negotiates a separate spirituality. She retains that which offers unity and hope, and she leaves the rest in abeyance. Surviving Trujillo's efforts to reduce the resistance movement to a society of women and children without men, she strengthens the remaining members. Unable to wait for a liberated Church to free the neglected women and children of the Dominican Republic, she raises children with all the information she can give them. Such may be the route to a sustaining spirituality for people who, like the Mirabals, live in the chaos of great change. They must discover who is wearing what face, and how the face got there. They must bring to the foreground those elements of heritage, identity, and self that will help them negotiate the still-dangerous zone between warring positions.

6

DEPROGRAMMING
THE COLONIZER

Although both novels record resistance to an oppressive government and its accompanying religion, Graciela Limón's novel *Song of the Hummingbird* (1996) presents a very different story from Alvarez's *In the Time of the Butterflies* (1995a). Set in the first century of colonization, *Song of the Hummingbird* records the aftermath of defeat rather than the birth of a movement to remove a tyrant. Like the Mirabals and the rebels they join, however, the main character, Huitzitzilin, must overcome her own doubts, hatreds, and failings before she can work to expose the hubris of the Spanish Catholic clergy who followed Cortés into her world. Separated by four hundred years of Catholic influence, the Mirabals and Huitzitzilin say the same thing: the existing Catholic Church leadership does not value its people, particularly those who are poor and darker-skinned, and that failure slowly destroys the people. Like Dedé Mirabal, Huitzitzilin must reveal the human impact of the Conquest before she and her confessor may embark on real understanding and forgiveness.

Much more than setting separates these two stories. Whereas the Mirabals belong to the upper levels of Dominican society, Huitzitzilin lies at the very bottom of post-Conquest social structure. The last living member of the Aztecs of the city of Tenochtitlan, she is old, destitute, female, and Indian. Her name is the Nahuatl word for Hummingbird, but the invaders long ago baptized her under the name María de Belén. She has become all but invisible, but in that lack of social, religious, and political existence lies her advantage. The powerful do not consider her capable of subversive thinking.

Though a fictional character, Huitzitzilin is not an impossible one. Social scientist Díaz-Stevens (1994) comments on the presence of such quiet revolutionaries as she examines the role women have taken in shaping the Catholic religion over the centuries since contact. Among her examples of ordinary but influential women is the late-nineteenth-century Mexican *curandera* Teresa Urrea. A peasant woman eventually exiled to the U.S. Southwest for opposing the iron rule of the Mexican dictator Porfirio Díaz, Urrea continued a simple, spiritual life and became known as a great healer. Her powerful and unassailable impact, according to Díaz-Stevens, typifies the religious and political impact of many unobtrusive women who have placed the spiritual comfort and physical needs of the people above their own need for official approval. That their ministrations remain necessary in the religio-cultural borderland today is further suggested by the constant presence of popular religiosity in Latina writing.

Graciela Limón's story of Huitzitzilin pushes the origin of this conflict all the way back to the early years of the Christian conversion of the Americas. The dying Mexica woman operates at personal and cultural levels while official Churchmen, scholars, and monarchs debate policy for the New World. She tells her story under the guise of a confession to Father Benito Lara, a dedicated young missionary who arrives in Mexico in 1583. Poor and silenced because she is Indian, additionally hampered by an ambivalence toward her old Aztec beliefs, she must tell her story in a manner that allows Father Benito to draw the conclusions she dare not state. A reader likewise has to delve below the events of her story to witness the multifaceted spiritual confrontation she seeks to provoke.

Huitzitzilin has struggled to survive the burden of womanhood under both systems. Born of a noble Aztec family, she is the product of a culture devoted to the war god Huitzilopochtli rather than the gods and goddesses of earlier Mexica cultures. Huitzitzilin's role as a young woman is to remain a virgin until her family can offer her as a concubine to a powerful man, but she defies them through a love affair with her cousin Zintle, with pregnancy as a result. To avoid detection and execution by Tetla, the government official to whom she is promised, she aborts the child, but Tetla discovers her lost virginity and beats her nearly to death on their ceremonial first night. Soon after, when Tetla leaves to investigate an astounding report about white gods come from the sea, Huitzitzilin returns to Zintle, later bearing him a son she calls Wing of a Bird.

Soon the Spanish Captain Cortés is welcomed into Tenochtitlan by Moctezuma, who believes the Spanish to be the gods of Aztec prophecy. Huitzitzilin sees Tetla and others who resist Cortés burned at the stake, and in despair and fear, she takes the Spanish Captain Baltazar Ovando as a lover, eventually bearing him boy and girl twins. She loves these two children with difficulty because they bear *mestizo* features. When organized Aztec resistance finally erupts, the Aztec warriors are massacred by the hundreds in a betrayed rebellion. Other battles and European sicknesses kill more of her people. When Wing of a Bird dies from smallpox, Huitzitzilin claws out one of her eyes in grief and wanders the countryside with the twins until starvation drives her to beg for work at Ovando's estate. When Ovando suddenly sends the twins to be raised in Spain, Huitzitzilin murders him in secret and abandons the city until old age forces her to seek care in the convent built on the land where her family home once stood.

Huitzitzilin's story is dramatic, but that's not her reason for telling it, and its drama need not be the greatest benefit of reading it. Equally with Father Benito, readers have an opportunity to understand the spiritual devastation that accompanies cultural and political upheaval. Huitzitzilin wants her say before she dies, not to evoke pity, not to rage at a representative of the Spanish, not to beg forgiveness for personal actions offensive to the Church, but to demand an audience for a culture she fears will die with her. She wants to engender and exchange a different kind of forgiveness, a two-way forgiveness built on mutual understanding between members of different cultures. She wants to assure the possibility of a more accommodating, nurturing spiritual system in the future.

For Huitzitzilin, finding an audience for her story is not easy, for she is scarcely considered human even by the nuns of the convent where she submits to colonial Church routine. Only her veneer of Catholicism makes her acceptable. A clever woman, she speaks through this mask to demand the Catholic sacrament for the forgiveness of sins. She knows the demand must be met and knows the priest who meets it will assume she has become penitent. Her skepticism about religion and her desire to keep it from further separating the Mexica and Spanish people need not show to anyone but the priest; and the priest, by the commands of his ordination, may not deny her a hearing, no matter how appalling the details of her life may sound to him. He also may not tell anyone about forbidden actions she admits under the seal of the confessional. Her personal mission is to open his eyes to another view of history and religion before he discovers she isn't seeking pastoral forgiveness.

For Father Benito, listening to her story is difficult not only because Aztec sexual practices offend his ideals of moral behavior, but also because the Catholic directives of the time forbid even listening to information about pagan gods and ceremonies. As his superior warns him at one point, even the faithful in the New World are not safe from the arm of the Inquisition. Thus, much of what Huitzitzilin wants to tell Father Benito puts him at risk, and the two seem headed for an impasse. If he insists on hearing only what his religion defines as sins, and if he wants those things stated as facts such as "I aborted my child" or "I killed a man," then Huitzitzilin's pose of a Catholic making a confession will not serve her at all. The deeds she wants to confess are measured against a complex personal code that transcends Catholic and Aztec beliefs alike. She needs to explain the code itself.

The impasse breaks under the influence of another phenomenon of intercultural communication, the behavior that Min-Zhan Lu (1996) has called "cultural tourism" (p. 118). Cultural tourists are so blinded by ethnocentrism and fear that they experience the rub of cultures without ever questioning their own sense of cultural and moral superiority. They continue to see the Other as an oddity to be studied, a kind of acquisition whose existence can be used to improve their own status or expertise. Ironically, it is this use of the Other as a means of self-advancement that causes Father Benito to continue listening to Huitzitzilin. The priest, appalled by her revelations during their first encounter, is also appalled by his own driving interest in her story. He wants to learn about her people, but he doesn't want to appear to encourage her in her unholy ways. He continues with the sessions because they are his priestly duty, but he develops an ulterior motive of recording information that might be as valuable as the impressions recorded by the first explorers and clergy in the New World. The thought of this useful and prestigious work keeps him going even when Huitzitzilin's history contradicts the accepted Spanish record. At one point, incensed over her insistence that Cortés ordered the death of Moctezuma, he refrains from walking away only because of the historic potential of such information. Other times, he is so morally offended that he is held in place only by his priestly duty to accept and forgive. To maintain his personal balance, he separates his two functions according to the symbols at hand: paper, pen, and ink for scholarly listening, and the ceremonial stole for sacramental listening. When Huitzitzilin thinks he is listening for his book rather than her message, she tells him to come without his papers.

Enthralled as he becomes with Huitzitzilin's story, Father Benito is so nervous about the dangers of listening that he repeatedly consults his superior, Father Anselmo Cano. The older priest counsels him to record the new historical data but to keep a safe distance from this strange woman who may work the devil's magic upon him: "Don't eat or drink anything she offers you. . . . Don't allow her to seduce you into believing that her ways were in any manner proper or virtuous. . . . [Don't trust her] merely because she is aged. Remember . . . Satan knows so much not because he is the devil but because he is old" (p. 127). Unfortunately for Father Benito's peace of mind, trust is exactly what develops. Early in his visits with Huitzitzilin, he already worries about her ability to provoke him to unorthodox thoughts.

Huitzitzilin does consciously manipulate the man she calls only "young priest," as if to stress the combined blessing and curse of youth: its lack of certainty. She is aggressive and conciliatory by turns as she promotes a broader spirituality. The accusations she wishes to make against both the old and the new religions must emerge together, intermingled in the story to reveal that neither system fully meets the needs of the people. Although she insists on this presentation from the start, reminding Father Benito that he must listen to her confession and that she can make it no other way, she avoids details that will distress him unnecessarily. She doesn't force him to listen to the words of "pagan" prayers. However, she does insist that he hear her reason for aborting her first child: "It meant my life" (p. 31). Her statement creates a dilemma for the priest. His training tells him to forgive a sin only if the sinner is repentant; he doesn't know what he is to do if the sinner regrets not the act but the fact that she was forced to perform it. He finds personal peace by deciding to differentiate "between Huitzitzilin's sins and the customs of her people. The first he was to absolve and forget; the second he was to commit to paper" (p. 34).

His solution is easier to imagine than to carry out. When Father Benito first finds himself flinging down his pen to scramble for his stole, Huitzitzilin mocks him, asking him if she should repeat herself now that he's in the right frame of mind. But she pities him as well, and she goes out of her way to warn him when she has something shocking to relate. Through her long coaching, the priest begins to appreciate the parallels she sees between their separate spiritual systems: both seek answers through their priests, both have statues representing what is sacred, both practice atrocities in war and treacheries in recording history. He admits that people cannot describe their own faith life if they can't mention the name of their god or the content and reasons for their prayers. Eventually he accepts that Huitzitzilin can commune with the spirits of the dead because she believes they are present and accessible rather than gathered in some distant place. With more difficulty, he understands that she considers her one-time prayers to the Goddess of Hell to be wrong not because they were blasphemy or goddess worship but because they were said in hatred.

Over time, Huitzitzilin also reveals the way in which both religions put themselves at the mercy of their prophecies. She says Moctezuma failed to fight the invaders because he believed an ancient prophecy that the gods of the new time would be white and would come from the sea. Through his trust in prophets, she implies, her powerful king/priest Moctezuma eventually lost his throne and his people to the Spanish. For his own part, Father Benito cannot ignore that he and the Spanish are also directed by prophecies. They believe themselves to be part of a sacred mission to prepare for a Second Coming of Christ that will be unannounced and may occur at any time. Besides increasing the power of their country by claiming new lands, they are bringing new souls to salvation in the Church. Furthermore, they are extending a mission recently completed in Spain, where they have finally freed their land from a thousand-year occupation by Moorish "infidels." The years of this Reconquest have conditioned them to offer only death, retreat, or conversion to those who believe differently from them. Each of these options creates silence, the silence Father Benito cannot detect even when Huitzitzilin describes it: "It is the silence of our spirit, of our tongues that have dried up. It is the silence . . . that has wrapped itself around our bodies and faces, stopping the air from entering our nostrils . . . that smells of hollowness and nothingness. It is a silence of the living that are dead" (p. 96).

For a long time, Father Benito doesn't realize he is hearing a warning about the prophecies that guide his own life. All he knows is that something in Huitzitzilin's testimony threatens him. Only after her death does he realize she was teaching him that both their religions have driven away the gods of peace and love: hers in its long-past capitulation to the war god who demanded human sacrifice, and his through its partnership with European political powers.

From the start, Huitzitzilin tries to reveal colonial Catholicism's lack of a sustaining mercy and respect. She protests the priest's haste during their first meeting, suggesting that perhaps he should first learn her name. In translating her Nahuatl name for him, she gives him the opportunity to learn the significance of the hummingbird to her people, but he fails to ask this, as well. Thus, he never realizes that the hummingbird, like the numerous Spanish-Indian children of Mexico, is a *mestizo*, a bird formed specially from the colorful scraps left from creation. He doesn't hear the story that its feathers may have been the ones that engendered the war god Huitzilopochtli in Coatlicue's womb, or that a hummingbird saved the unborn god by warning him of his sister's plan to kill their mother before he can be born. He never recognizes that the names Huitzilopochtli and Huitzitzilin share the root word for hummingbird. Thus, he doesn't see that Huitzitzilin is the *mestiza* bringing news to his God, the new god in the land. As if in revenge for his lack of interest, she never calls Father Benito by his name, using only the title "priest" or "young priest." She imitates the lack of respect for her Nahuatl name when she spits out the name María, the "real" name given her in baptism, or when she calls her twins Little Boy and Little Girl rather than use their baptismal names.

Huitzitzilin does draw the parallel between the Spanish lack of respect toward Nahuatl names and the Spanish condescension toward the *Indios*. Father Benito is surprised to discover that she has feelings and suffers psychological pain from this treatment. He is not far himself from the doubts about Indian humanity that have triggered Spanish university debates for several generations. He is blind to the negative effects of arranged marriages and wife killing because both practices occur in his own culture as well as among the Aztecs. Nor does he see anything wrong with purifying nonbelievers by burning them at the stake. He willingly accepts Father Anselmo's evaluation of the Indians as human-but-less because they are in need of salvation. Also accepting Father Anselmo's fear that the people will return to their old beliefs, he cautions Huitzitzilin to forget her old beliefs except when her memory of them expands his historical record. Eventually, Father Benito's psychological journey will require stepping away from such belittling colonial logic. Even when he insists that the indigenous people are among God's children, he betrays his view of them as simple, naïve, and immature. More unkind than his trivialization of the *Indios* is his interpretation of their darker skin as physical evidence of spiritual and sexual depravity. He is trapped within the European metaphor for evil. Ironically, and unnoticed by Father Benito, Huitzitzilin applies an opposite metaphor embedded in her own culture: the association of whiteness with absence, death, or evil. To her, the Spanish are "white"; they are a heartless, arrogant, blinding, and silencing apparition. Her tradition and her colonial experience mesh when she attributes the death of Wing of a Bird to the "white beast" (p. 149).

The priest often behaves in this "white" or "silencing" manner. He frequently wants to jump forward to absolution so he can avoid the religious or sexual details of her confession. Unable to conceive of the snake as a symbol of creation, regeneration, and female power, he insists that the Aztec snake dance had to be eradicated because it constituted devil-worship. Much time passes before he notices that Huitzitzilin tells Aztec history "in terms of war and peace, not demons and gods" (p. 74) and even more must pass before he grasps the importance of that. When Huitzitzilin describes the religious celebration/war dance that preceded the massacre of the Indians in the plaza, he accuses the Aztec priests of being agents of the devil for being able to raise such great fervor. He does not consider the equally religious fervor that allowed Catholic Spaniards to slaughter the Aztecs.

Everywhere the priest looks, he sees but does not comprehend that even though the Spanish have imposed their order and values on Mexico, the old Mexico continues to show through, attesting to the possibility that a broader culture and spirituality could result from contact. To the priest, Huitzitzilin looks "as if carved in stone, she seemed so ancient" (p. 67), and Huitzitzilin herself remarks several times that the stones of current Spanish buildings came from dismantled Aztec temples. The courtyard where she meets the priest covers the ground where her family home once stood, and a bloody massacre occurred where the Spanish have built their church. Her story shows through the gaps of the Spanish version of the conquest, and her people are present in the *mestizo* population. In her own person, she embodies both *La Llorona*, the woman weeping over traitorous love and sacrificed children, and *La Malinche*, the Indian woman suffering for having mothered the *mestizo* race. The old times haven't disappeared. Like the spirits of the dead she senses all around her, they communicate with her daily.

Huitzitzilin not only sees these dual Mexicos but also believes they hold the better fruits of a new world. Under her pretense of confession, what she offers the priest is a new understanding of sin, mercy, and forgiveness. Perhaps, she suggests, sexual contact shouldn't condemn lovers to hell or force a woman to choose between abortion and death. Perhaps Catholic statues and Aztec idols fulfill the same spiritual purpose, and God and the gods represent the same awesome force. Perhaps dances belong in religious devotions. Perhaps the realm of the dead need not be far away and always invisible. Perhaps both Catholic and Aztec priests have behaved hatefully, and both Conquistadors and Aztecs have overreacted out of fear. In Huitzitzilin's opinion, Father Benito must be made to doubt so he can think properly. Only doubt can lead him toward a different understanding of the spiritual concepts of sin and forgiveness.

From the start, Huitzitzilin has interpreted the act of confession differently from the priest, not coming to it as a guilty penitent, but as one who needs to tell "how it was that I and my people came to what we are now" (p. 19). To her, a "confession," like an "apology," may be defined as an explanation. As she tells her story, she endures Father Benito's absolution, but she alters the rules and refuses to repent, for her definition of sin differs from his. In addition, she unsettles Father Benito by asking for his personal forgiveness, a request that forces him to examine his own reactions and to answer as a human being rather than a functionary. In watching the collapse of her own religion, she has learned

the danger of priests murmuring at a distance and people recit-
ing responses only because they'll be punished if they don't. The
Catholics and the Aztecs have not entered a fruitful discussion.
Rather, the Church has dragged the Aztecs across the borderland
and into the Spanish world—and the people have come in body
only.

The alternate behavior that Huitzitzilin describes to Father
Benito parallels that of the missionary Motolinía, an historic figure officially known as Father Toribio de Benavente. Motolinía,
whose name means "the poor one" in Nahuatl, believed he should
be among the people, living as they did, rather than ministering
comfortably in a settlement. Traveling barefoot and possessing
even less than the Indians, he became a much beloved and successful evangelist. Motolinía appears several times in Huitzitzilin's
narrative, always in his role of roving minister to the oppressed.
His personal humility and goodness, rather than his Catholic
preaching, persuade Huitzitzilin to allow him to baptize her and
her *mestizo* twins.

Huitzitzilin's challenges affect Father Benito deeply, particularly because the secrecy of the confessional precludes his seeking guidance from his superior on those details that are matters
of the stole rather than of the manuscript. In his religious dilemma,
waiting to feel certain of God's pardon by experiencing it in his
own mind and soul, Father Benito takes the path of humility.
Approaching the dilemma on a human rather than a priestly level,
he forgives Huitzitzilin as a fellow being, leaves ultimate forgiveness to God, and begs heavenly mercy for himself as well as her.
Approaching her again with a sense of personal progress and sanctity, he discovers her unwilling to grant him superiority for his
forgiveness. She will agree neither that the gods of the Mexica
have been driven from the land nor that the new religion holds
all the necessary answers.

Father Benito doesn't understand Huitzitzilin's true needs
until after her death, when suddenly he realizes "it was not absolution or even mercy that she had expected of him, but understanding of her life, of her people, and of their beliefs" (p. 217).

He had thought she was confessing the adoration of false gods, the abortion of a baby, the bearing of children out of wedlock, the murder of a master, the incomplete conversion to Catholicism. But those weren't the sins troubling Huitzitzilin. The transgressions she regretted were those she had committed against life. She'd lived by two codes, both of which had failed her, and she'd seen history only half recorded, but she hadn't spoken out until her final days. She had prayed against fertility with Tetla, she had betrayed her people by accepting Baltazar Ovando as a lover, and she had despised the *mestizo* looks of her children and let them be lost to Spain. The sins of Huitzitzilin, in her own words, were "I put aside the truth that [Ovando] was the enemy. I forgot that I loved Zintle and that I had a child. I forgot myself as well" (p. 116).

Unfortunately, Limón doesn't allow Huitzitzilin an answer to Father Benito's double-edged question about her murder of Ovando: "What would we do if all the mothers deprived of their children murdered the men responsible?" (p. 195). Perhaps Huitzitzilin would echo Patria Mirabal's declaration of war against despots: "*I'm not going to sit back and watch my babies die, Lord, even if that's what You in Your great wisdom decide*" (Alvarez 1995a, p. 162). Certainly, Huitzitzilin experiences the need to speak out against both the Spanish and the Aztec religions. Begging for dialogue, she decries the spiritual and physical death of her people and predicts similar losses for Spain. Her own history is her evidence: she lost her first child to misogyny when she lived by the Aztec code; she lost the son born in defiance of the Aztec code to a disease brought by the Europeans; and she lost her *mestizo* son to an accidental death in Spain and her *mestiza* daughter to Spanish social arrogance. She, Tetla, and Zintle die childless, and Ovando dies without male issue. If Father Benito keeps his vow of celibacy, he also will leave no children. Where, she seems to ask, is the future in such religious and cultural politics?

Unable to settle for mere tolerance for the Other or from the Other, Huitzitzilin insists that both sides must examine their prophecies; both must give up the notion that they can rule, absolve, or save the other; and both must be willing to examine beliefs that may be parallel and still be mistaken. For Huitzitzilin, rehumanization is possible through shared information and the admission that knowledge is dynamic and open-ended. Catholic pastoral guidance offers nothing to the people if it does not endorse their worth and listen to their voices.

From within their vastly different experiences, Huitzitzilin and the Mirabal sisters offer a similar message about the need for spiritual alternatives. Neither the fictional Aztec nor the fictionalized Dominicanas define their personal practice of Catholicism as blasphemous, folkloric, comfortable, or convenient. Rather, they live by a complicated set of beliefs that define and sustain them. In both *Song of the Hummingbird* and *In the Time of the Butterflies*, the alternative beliefs endure because the official religion has failed to preserve human freedom and dignity, particularly among the poor, the darker-skinned, and the female.

7

A Failure of Joy

In *Song of the Hummingbird*, Huitzitzilin questions Father Benito's certainty that the Catholic Church of the conquistadors answers all the needs of all the people in Mexico. Each of the Mirabal sisters in the novel *In the Time of the Butterflies* raises the same question about the twentieth-century Catholic Church in the Dominican Republic. The activism of such women leads them beyond home and community, finally placing them in direct conflict with religious and political authorities at the national level.

While Alvarez and Limón focus on the present-day political and military fallout from colonization, many other writers emphasize the lingering influences of colonial Church attitudes in the daily lives of ordinary Latino families and communities in the United States. In their view, the asceticism of sixteenth-century Catholicism still penetrates their lives, for it altered the weave of culture in ways that cannot be undone. Nearly five hundred years later, even the simpler joys of living, those pleasures such as food, companionship, physical love, or community celebrations, are diminished by a focus on sin, penance, and the general unworthiness of humans, particularly those humans who are poor, female, *india*, or *mestiza*. Their complaints are varied and far-reaching: adolescent frustration over religio-cultural controls, suicidal depression over disregard and discrimination, and a persistent longing for a belief system that preserves life and hope.

One of the authors who renders these complaints from adolescent and young adult viewpoints is Judith Ortiz Cofer, known for her poetry, novels, and the two cross-genre memoirs *Silent Dancing* (1990) and *The Latin Deli* (1993). In her memoirs, Ortiz Cofer reviews the years she spent shuttling between the small Puerto Rican village of Hormigueros and the crowded apartment buildings in her Puerto Rican neighborhood in Paterson, New Jersey. Inseparable from those experiences are daily Catholic observances at home and at school. Through her own experiences, those of her family, and those of composite characters, she describes a religious sensibility that glorifies suffering, fears sexuality, and discourages diversity in appearance and expression. For her, this religion of feast days, processions, and elaborate iconography fails to live up to its own grand message of jubilation. She is likewise frustrated with her faithful family and neighbors, and although she eventually understands their need to maintain a religion that is part of their identity, she reaches only an uneasy acceptance of it. The tone of her poetry and prose is that of a child or teenager still immersed in self-pity and denial: more anger than love, more rejection than understanding, and more complaint about the problem than commitment to a solution.

Ortiz Cofer is intimately familiar with ingrained Catholic rituals and viewpoints. Remembering her years in Paterson, she tells interviewer Edna Acosta-Bélen (1993) that her family continued their Catholic devotions even though they were far from the influence of their extended family and the religious culture in Puerto Rico. So many religious icons filled her home that she felt constantly under the eyes of God and the Virgin. Sometimes she remembers this constant indoctrination with irony, as she does in her poem "La Fé" (1995), which reveals the futility of trying to escape religious rituals. Other poems employ a sharper tone. In her *Terms of Survival* (1995) poem "Latin Women Pray," she plays upon the idea that a God who bears white European features may not be sympathetic to a people with brown skin. In fact, he may not even understand their language. In this poem, "women pray in Spanish to an Anglo God / With a Jewish heritage"; and this God "Looks down upon his brown daughters / . . . / Unmoved by their persistent prayers" (p. 14). The dual implication of "looks down upon" cannot be missed: this God is a superior who casts his glances with discrimination more than with benevolence.

Like this God, Ortiz Cofer says, her religious culture doesn't care to hear what women think or feel. Apparent female invisibility, along with the religious training that urges humble acceptance of their lot in life, may be factors in the women's attraction to suffering. One of her characters in *Silent Dancing* is Mamá Nanda, her paternal grandmother, who endures and even invites suffering in the belief that it will replace or prevent suffering in a loved one. Every week, on her knees, Mamá Nanda climbs one hundred rough-hewn stone steps to a hilltop shrine to the Black Virgin, the defender of the poor and the dark-skinned of Puerto Rico. Other village women climb with her to honor their own *promesas* to the Virgin. They all believe their silent, willing suffering will earn the Virgin's intervention, and she will return their sons safely from Vietnam. The demands of such *promesas* are set by the woman herself. They might be as simple as wearing a saint's favorite color, or as harsh as enduring the tropical heat with sackcloth beneath one's clothing. Mamá Nanda, who wore only the black of *luto* after losing six children and her husband, offered numerous such sacrifices to God. Ortiz Cofer reports her to have been a sad individual who was frequently disappointed, but who never gave up on God or the power of voluntary suffering.

Ortiz Cofer writes that she now understands the solace these women receive from taking action against their sorrows. The angry tone of her stories and poems, however, suggests rejection of the system and pity for the women driven to such behavior by a destructive and often double religious standard. She remembers the blissful smiles on the faces of women in religious paintings, even on the face of St. Agnes as she offers her head on the chopping block. This Latino Church emphasis on self-imposed suffering and even abuse is likewise recognized by theology professor Orlando O. Espín (1994), who also comments on the presence of such elements in religious art. Espín suggests that such willingness to suffer is strong because the conquering Church and state conditioned the indigenous peoples to believe that sanctity lay in declaring themselves subhuman and inconsequential. The Guatemalan writer-activist Rigoberta Menchú (1984) makes a similar observation and applies it in the present day when she claims that the glorification of humble suffering not only has allowed the Catholic Church to maintain its power, but also has prepared Latino peoples to accept dictatorial governments such as those in Central America. Despite this comment, however, Menchú sometimes defends the more recent Catholic practice of liberation theology in Guatemala, crediting the Church with leadership in dangerous conditions. She also comments on the parallel plight of Guatemalan men and women in the oppressive and discriminatory sociopolitical climate.

Such generosity toward the Church and such concern for men is more typical of Latinas writing in Central and South America than of those in the U.S. However, Ortiz Cofer does recognize a variety of suffering among the poor males of Puerto Rico. In *Silent Dancing* (1990), she describes the plight of numerous men who have been relegated to harsh, dangerous work in the cane fields. In the whimsy of childhood, she compared their synchronized chopping to a lovely ballet, but as she matured, she recognized their rhythms as "survival choreography," a defense measure to keep themselves alive and whole in fields that held "enough body parts . . . to put one whole man together" (p. 77). Neither the Church nor the state intervened against the physical and economic abuses perpetuated by the rich owners. The fields themselves lay beneath the hilltop shrine of the dark Virgin of Monserrate, long revered as a champion of the poor and dark of skin.

Elsewhere in *Silent Dancing*, Ortiz Cofer comments on the weight placed on Puerto Rican men by their religion and culture. She writes that her grandfather, a sensitive man who practiced as an *espiritista* or spiritist healer, led those who consulted him along the same humble path indicated by the Church. He focused them on a heaven-to-come, a place where their dedication to God would no longer be tested through suffering. This sense of life as a just trial influences Ortiz Cofer's father, as well: he accepts that the only way to advance his family is to join the U.S. Navy and leave his loved ones behind.

Eventually, his cold war experiences make him a sad and distant man even when he is in the bosom of the family.

Although she does recognize the plight of men, Ortiz Cofer centers her attention on the suffering of women. In exposing the ongoing social and political domination of Latinas, she places heavy blame on the tight integration of religion and culture. In her *Terms of Survival* poem "La Fé," she speaks as a woman who wants to overcome her automatic religious responses. She wants candles, litanies, saints, and rituals to recede, but the only way she can think to fight them is through humble supplication before the crucifix. For the speaker of "La Fé," the religion and culture are integrated, and the composite is permanently ingrained in her. In *The Latin Deli* (1993), other characters find themselves controlled by ritual and suffering. The poem "Orar: To Pray" reveals a girl's confusion as she hears her mother pray for an end to her father's philandering. Trained to never accuse God or men of injustice, the mother sounds as if she is offering praise even as she petitions. This female resignation to suffering is even more pronounced in the poem "Saint Rose of Lima," which exposes the horrors of self-punishment. The extreme penitential actions undertaken by the saint continue to shock and disgust Ortiz Cofer even though she is not surprised at the saint's popularity as a model. Saint Rose eats bitter food, makes a crown of thorns from roses, and burns her skin, first with pepper and then with an iron poker. The poet speculates that God has made Rose the butt of a joke for the amusement of the angels. The saint's very name suggests she has been programmed for worship. The rose, particularly the red rose, is favored in Latino cultures as well as in Latino Church iconography, particularly that associated with the Virgin of Guadalupe. Furthermore, the name of the flower calls to mind the rosary, an often decorative string of beads traditionally used for counting devotions to the Blessed Virgin Mary. Ortiz Cofer elsewhere comments on the penitent posture held by those who pray on these pretty beads.

Ortiz Cofer is not alone in her response to St. Rose of Lima. Pat Mora includes this saint among the many holy figures addressed in her collection *Aunt Carmen's Book of Practical Saints* (1997a). Whereas Mora approaches most of the saints with love, bemusement, respect, or sudden understanding, she is perplexed by Saint Rose, who is presented as a model to women from birth onward. Women don't know if Christ, the Virgin, or the saints pitied or even spoke to Rose. Mora offers that comfort, urging Rose to forgive herself for being human. Her intermittent refrain, however, questions how Rose came to be so stubborn, and the pivotal stanza admits that heaven sends no explanations. Even for the sincere seeker, the saints cannot or will not explain why joy must be subjugated to suffering.

In the world reflected in Latina works, the dangerous influence of a model like Saint Rose is compounded by cultural beliefs that women are inferior, worthless, or even corrupt. Taken to an extreme, such thinking yields stories like that of Doña Ernestina, the main character in Ortiz Cofer's (1993) *Latin Deli* story "Nada." Displaced from her Puerto Rican village to an apartment in Paterson, New Jersey, Doña Ernestina feels her powerlessness as a traditional wife and mother, a being who has no separate identity, income, or mobility. Already left a widow by the man who brought her to this foreign setting, she becomes childless when her son dies in Vietnam. Her neighbors, also floundering in a new place with new rules, are not yet able to comprehend the despair of a lone woman far from her extended family and her land. Their old rituals don't work to solace her. Eventually she conducts a *velorio* dedicated not just to her son but to all of her lost loved ones, but the women who attend fail to recognize her embedded plea for a new position in the apartment community. They themselves are trapped in the idea that a woman without a man is nothing and has nothing, and they hear only the common lament when Doña Ernestina wails that she has lost her own life. Her words express more than loneliness or the loss of her last chance to be taken back to her beloved Puerto Rico. Doña Ernestina has realized that in her mainland U.S. exile, she not only has nothing but *is* nothing: not a wife or mother; not a daughter, aunt, sister, or grandmother; not a *curandera* or *partera*. No existence, no new identity for her will result from her son's medal from the government, the token visit from the priest, or the ritual funeral. Even the women who would like to comfort her cannot truly see her. Frozen in the logic of their familiar phrase *Así es la vida*, even the younger ones do not interfere with her mourning, and their failure to affirm her personal worth opens her way to suicide. Over the course of some days, she gets rid of all her belongings, including the very clothes on her body. Possessing nothing, she proceeds to be nothing. Her death by tranquilizers is an eloquent surrender. She leaves life via the modern solution offered to the wailing woman: a pill to make one quiet.

Although Doña Ernestina's story is extreme, it is not unique, even among the works by Ortiz Cofer. Numerous other stories reveal the ways in which the glorification of humility diminishes the joy of daily living. Certainly, it underlies the feelings of guilt that accompany simple pleasures such as colorful clothing, energetic music, dancing, or even optimism. Numerous characters continue to wear black and avoid music and laughter long after the accepted period of mourning. Nearly all of them allow the terrifying torture of Christ on the cross literally to hang over their heads and around their necks in the form of a crucifix. Even the priest who tries to comfort Doña Ernestina seems to droop under the weight of the cross hung round his neck. Images of sorrow permeate the women's thinking and explode in exclamations like *"¡Dios mío!"* and *"¡Madre de Dios!"*—half prayer and half acknowledgment of the terrible power of the deities. Even an ordinary sight like an avocado pit being encouraged to sprout can provoke Ortiz Cofer to a gloomy reference to the heart of Jesus pierced by swords.

Frightening iconography is one of Ortiz Cofer's frequent targets. Her *Latin Deli* poem "Guard Duty" deconstructs the image of the Guardian Angel, questioning the actual comfort in this shining, armed personal protector. The angel she describes is more alien than reassuring as he glows above two terrified, barefoot children on a bridge over an also glowing abyss. The poem frets over a God or a parent who could place this smiling apparition in the room where children confront their fears alone in the dark. Other *Latin Deli* poems also place unsympathetic angels in league with a questionable God. In "Saint Rose of Lima," the angels laugh at Saint Rose's pathological pursuit of holiness, and in "Women Who Love Angels," the admiration for angels prevents women from seeking physical pleasures such as marriage. Isolated and esoteric, these misguided women never complain about giving up the color, productivity, and satisfaction of Latino living. In cultural terms, their sin is *el olvido*, a personal forgetting of one's roots and one's place in the culture.

Ortiz Cofer once explained the horror of *el olvido* in an interview, relating her mother's story about a child who forgot his very own mother. To her as a young girl, the sin seemed a trap as real as a deep hole in the ground (1997). She may be returning to that sensation of falling away from God and family when she writes "El Olvido," a *Silent Dancing* poem about a daughter who admits the danger she invites by living without religious pictures and statues, without the necessary devotions to assure protection, and without participating in the daily joys and sorrows of her community. She knows her actions worry her mother, who fears the girl will die alone among strangers, lost in the great pit of the non-Latino world.

Paired with the sin of forgetting one's culture is the punishment of becoming a *fulana*, a nameless woman or even a whore whose generic label is mentioned by good women only as a warning against temptation. A *fulana*, according to a poem by that title in *Silent Dancing*, might be a girl who dreams of trading her clothes for yellow feathers so she can soar above her friends. She might succeed for a while, but eventually life would bring her back to level ground, and there her sole purpose would be to keep others from seeking a world away from mothers, schools, and churches.

Ortiz Cofer questions the validity of this cautionary *fulana* figure. Among her vignettes in *Silent Dancing*, she introduces the welfare mother Providencia, a voluptuous earth mother with numerous children by just as many different fathers. The married women in her apartment building resent Providencia because her apparent happiness prevents them from using her as a negative model. Providencia fails to demonstrate that virginity is a woman's bargaining chip for the two things she should most desire: a husband and a way to heaven. Indiscriminate and cheerful, she prospers, delighted with her brood and adequately supported by the state. Worse yet, her enthusiasm for her parade of lovers provokes the girls to wonder if men might offer more pleasures than their mothers are willing to admit. The girls have probably been given the standard advice: they can have both fun and heaven, but they must be careful to follow the rules and rituals. Providencia leads them to ask which rules and rituals, how often, and how diligently.

Resolving such contradictions between a lively lifestyle and a subdued religion preoccupies Ortiz Cofer, often emerging in comments about her religious schooling. In Puerto Rico, she studied under American nuns, and on the mainland she belonged to the growing number of Latino children whose parents wanted them in Catholic schools. According to Díaz-Stevens (1994), whose studies focus on New York City parochial schools, parents who opted for a Catholic education during that era (the 1960s) underwent significant financial sacrifices to set aside the tuition. Due to the expense, the percentage of students of Latin American descent was so small that the schools expended little effort to make their curriculum relevant to children growing up Latino.

In *Silent Dancing* and *The Latin Deli*, Ortiz Cofer verifies that Catholic schools did little to accommodate students who straddled two cultures. She complains about elements as mundane as the lackluster uniforms and as weighty as the repression of mind and body. Describing a brown Puerto Rican uniform, she claims it made the children look like Mussolini's troops. The required outfits of successive years likewise failed to please her love of variety or her desire to be an individual. She attacks uniforms far more often than do the other U.S. Latinas who wore them as part of their Catholic school experience. For her, they are defined by their rigid design and fabric. Worse than that, they represent the powerlessness of a child placed under the thumb of adult authority. Each fall the new uniforms served to subdue the cheerful, summer-wild children with discomfort and lack of individuality. In a way, the uniforms oppress and disguise the students in the same way that Church and state have long suppressed and obscured the people's cultural expression. Both uniforms and laws are imposed to make the subjects more acceptable in appearance, more difficult to see as individuals, and more demoralized over their level of power.

In Ortiz Cofer's memoirs, the yearly recolonization of her body extends even to her tongue, for she has to curb both her voice and her imagination. She also has to match her language to the one spoken wherever she happens to be at the time. She never fits in linguistically because her constant travel between the island and the mainland has colored her Spanish with New Jersey English and her English with Puerto Rican Spanish. Despite the corrections she suffers from teachers and the ridicule she gets from classmates, however, she doesn't criticize the nuns. Although she recoils at their stern clothing and at their joyless demeanor, she refuses to hate them. Perhaps, like Julia Alvarez, she sees them as fellow prisoners who can only work quietly from within the system. As she describes them in *Silent Dancing* (1990), the nuns do protect their students and believe in them. Along with the rigor they impose, they offer her "order, quiet, respect for logic, and . . . the information I was always hungry for. I liked reading books, and I took immense pleasure in the praise of the teachers" (p. 126). Likewise, in *The Latin Deli* she includes the poem "The Purpose of Nuns," which expresses further appreciation for these quiet women who invited the girls to retreats at their large, tidy convent. In that spiritual atmosphere, she writes, the girls found refuge from the violence and uncertainty of their daily physical lives. Despite this appreciation, however, Ortiz Cofer doesn't find the nuns militant enough against life's inequities. Similar to other U.S. Latinas, notably Sandra Cisneros, Julia Alvarez, Denise Chávez, and Ana Castillo, she finds their quiet resistance ineffectual, and she rejects the idea of retreating from battle by wrapping herself in the system's habit.

Another stultifying cultural and religious habit that Ortiz Cofer rejects is that of a "young woman." This role is assumed at the age of fifteen and is initiated with a *quinceañera*, a sometimes elaborate observance which involves a church ceremony and a family *fiesta*. As an announcement of a girl's physical maturity and her eligibility for marriage, the celebration marks an increase in female status, but it also imposes restrictions stemming from the desire to preserve a girl's virginity until she marries or enters a religious order. In *Silent Dancing*, Ortiz Cofer says that a girl approaching her *quinceañera* is simply being broken in for her eventual roles as a Catholic wife and mother, and she paints the demands of the occasion in unhappy terms. Recalling her own rite of passage in the *Silent Dancing* poem "*Quinceañera*," she writes that her mother "nailed back" her hair so tightly it "stretched my eyes open," and she records the truths her wide-open eyes saw:

> . . . I am to wash my own clothes
> and sheets from this day on, as if
> the fluids of my body were poison . . .
> . . . Is not the blood of saints and
> men in battle beautiful? Do Christ's hands
> not bleed into your eyes from His cross? [p. 50]

This religio-cultural attention to a girl's physical maturation encourages young Latinas to contemplate virginity and its religious underpinning, which is the teaching that the Blessed Virgin Mary conceived Jesus through divine intervention, not through human sexual contact, and that she remained a virgin all of her life. To Ortiz Cofer, the dogma of the Virgin Birth became questionable when she began to study human biology. She argued vehemently about it with her mother, but her questions remained unanswered and the issue unresolved. The next year she was sent to a Catholic high school where the technicalities of human reproduction received little attention.

Ortiz Cofer's evaluations of Catholic sex education are verified by Díaz-Stevens, who admits that the Catholic Church did not handle such things well. During Ortiz Cofer's adolescent years, the Latin American Church inside and outside the United States upheld the chaperone system and continued to offer separate activities for young men and women. Díaz-Stevens suspects that such policies helped determine whether adult Latinas/os today feel comfortable in the U.S. Catholic Church or view it as an unresponsive, alien institution. In her opinion, the impact has been negative because such strict measures are inappropriate for an immigrant population in which children as young as eight or nine years old often experience the adult world in their role as translators and intermediaries. Because their language skills generally outstrip those of their parents, they participate in adult negotiations that cannot help but age them more quickly. In *Silent Dancing*, Ortiz Cofer specifically mentions the feelings of power and maturity her linguistic superiority gave her when her mother refused to learn English. She filled in as "interpreter and buffer . . . to face landlords, doctors, store clerks, and other 'strangers' whose services we needed" (p. 103), thereby gaining a sense of control that was sometimes difficult to relinquish when her father returned from sea duty.

The importance of this language issue repeats itself in other Latina works. Esmeralda Santiago, in *Almost a Woman* (1998), remembers missing school in order to fill out paperwork for her mother. She and other child translators not only have to brave the forms and clerks of the public assistance office, but they must do so with inadequate English spoken in the culturally acceptable, downward-gazing attitude of a child. The experience galvanizes Santiago to learn English so well she will never again have to fumble between languages, but her rapidly improving language skills don't improve her status. As a girl child, she remains undervalued by the family and the social services personnel.

Still, such brief escapes from abject dependence may enable young Latinas to at least dream of challenging the rituals and viewpoints they have inherited. Ortiz Cofer tells Edna Acosta-Bélen (1993) that she consciously textures her writing with the types of moments that once helped her define herself. Certainly, her stories, vignettes, and poems in *Silent Dancing* and *The Latin Deli* admit the repressive elements of Latino culture, including those embedded by its close link with Catholicism, but they also recognize the people's undefeated spontaneity and inventiveness. She has also said that as a writer she prefers to record life as it is: a mixture of good and bad experiences that are met with feelings ranging from sorrow to elation (Ocasio 1995). To accomplish this, she refuses to stick to one genre if she thinks a mixture would more accurately reveal the reality of living. Indeed, hinting that genre is a type of national literary uniform, she says that the term belongs more to the United States than to Latin America, and as a person used to crossing ethnic and geographical boundaries, she sees no reason to remain within literary ones (Ocasio and Ganey 1992). She also objects to having her writing classified as history or sociology just because it has factual or cultural content. She isn't writing to record fact, but to transmit truth. In her preface to *Silent Dancing*, she sides with Virginia Woolf in contending that truth resides in what a story means rather than in the veracity of its details. She insists that a good poem is truthful because it is honest about life, whether the contents are historically accurate or not. Like her grandmother's stories, which made the family laugh but always had a moral, her own stories and poems have an ulterior purpose (Ocasio 1994). By using a folk form that is often dismissed as quaint and harmless by the people in power, she and her grandmother have engaged in a subversive activity. Their storytelling mask is transparent to other rebels, but only after the revolution will it be transparent to all.

The skill of subtle manipulation, Ortiz Cofer says, also came to her and her brother as a result of their constant shift between the vibrant beauty of the tropics and the gray cement of Paterson. They learned to adapt their clothing, their cultural behaviors, their language, and even their noise level. In dull Paterson, they lived quietly to avoid disturbing the other tenants in the apartment building, but at their grandmother's home on the Island, they leapt into the energetic jumble of neighborhood and family doings. Still, in either place, their unavoidable, noticeable difference from the other children plagued them (Ocasio 1994). In her *Latin Deli* poem "The Chameleon," her speaker reveals a moment of painful discovery that may well have been one of Ortiz Cofer's own. As the young girl watches a chameleon run through its palate of colors, she suddenly senses that the chameleon is also watching, and it expects her to change color as well. She cannot compete at that level, however. Unable to change skin color, ethnicity, or mingled accents, she will always show against any background.

Throughout *Silent Dancing* and *The Latin Deli*, Ortiz Cofer investigates this frustration of growing up Latina in fact and in religion. Although as an adult she no longer tries to wash away her heritage the way she once tried to wash the color from her skin, she still protests the restrictions placed upon Latinas/os from within and without their increasingly mixed culture. Her writing voice is often that of a confused and angry young woman buffeted by the process of physical, emotional, and cultural maturation. While the tone remains more plaintive than self-realized, it does indicate a desire for understanding, acceptance, and forgiveness. One believes that the speaker desires a dialogue that is more fruitful than her one-sided protest.

8

A Loss of Presence

Yet another young character who takes on her contradictory times and cultures is Margarita Forté (Maggie), one of the main characters of Edna Escamill's *Daughter of the Mountain* (1991). Maggie is an adolescent whose heritage and situation differ considerably from those of Ortiz Cofer, the Mirabals, or Huitzitzilin. She carries Spanish, French, and Yaqui Indian blood, and she lives among the poor in the southern Arizona village of La Milpa, which is undergoing economic colonization by U.S. developers during the Korean War era. The new copper smelters bring pollution, the ranches bring fences, and the economic philosophy brings a certainty that the land can be owned. The invading workers and vacationers find the pastel shanties of dusty La Milpa an eyesore too close to their own substantial homes, lawns, and pools, and with government backing they will replace the shacks with low-income apartments that will be neither private, nor personalized, nor owned by the people put into them. No one asks the villagers if they want the war, the industry, the fences, the apartments, or the government assistance.

Trying to find themselves in this tense and changing community are Maggie and a boy named Balestine (Bale), who have been friends since childhood. Both children find themselves at odds with the village because of their racial mix. Maggie's light skin, lanky body, blonde hair, and slanted black eyes set her apart from the shorter, darker population of La Milpa and from her family. Her Anglo features infuriate her stepfather. Bale also feels misplaced because his Spanish-Yaqui heritage includes blood from a distant mountain tribe, and he is shorter and more solid than the slender young men of desert La Milpa. The children's uncommon physical features seem to trigger ancient prejudices that are accepted without question, even by the children themselves. The villagers, particularly the males, behave as if the children's *mestizo* looks evoke the shame *of La Malinche* and revive old resentments about women who have loved, married, or been enslaved by an invader and produced *mestizo* children. Maggie and Bale are unwilling reminders of conquest and humiliation for a people so damaged that they don't recognize and cannot reject the legacy of self-hatred.

Through their physical nonconformity, Maggie and Bale suffer borderland tensions not experienced by the Mirabal sisters, Huitzitzilin, or Ortiz Cofer. These two young people lack the pure bloodlines that initially protected the Mirabals and that identified Huitzitzilin as the last true Mexica. Politically, they possess less power and mobility than the Mirabals or the Ortiz Cofer family. Instead, they resemble the poor Puerto Ricans described by Ortiz Cofer: they are born U.S. citizens, but they are treated like foreigners or immigrants until the U.S. needs men for its armed services. The Korean War disrupts La Milpa just as the Cold War and Vietnam fracture the families of Puerto Rico.

Spiritually, Maggie and Bale find themselves in a wasteland of contradictions and futility. They know little of bygone wars that displaced their indigenous ancestors, named their national citizenship, created their physical features, and dictated their current existence. The Catholic leadership they have trusted to guide them remains silent against the mainstream economic, social, and physical intrusions of their own era. The local padre and the three female religious workers called the Tres Hermanas prescribe only humility and penance in response to events old and new: humility because Christ was humble and because the poor have no other treasure to share, and penance because mankind as a whole must continuously atone for its long history of sin. In this absence of spiritual nurture, more than in any other area of their experience, Maggie and Bale resemble the Mirabals, Ortiz Cofer, and Huitzitzilin. Their inherited religion no longer helps them address the challenges of a changing life. Maggie will forge a broader spirituality and will survive. Bale will not.

The difference between them is that Maggie benefits from the spiritual guidance of her paternal grandmother, Adela Sewa, a pureblood Yaqui who teaches Maggie that everything one is and knows can be used to sustain life. Rejecting the path of humility and penance, Maggie learns to value her mixed religious and cultural heritage as a source of multiple abilities and solutions. At Adela's shack, she not only escapes her stepfather's verbal and physical blows, she also finds acceptance for her curiosity, her independence, and her love for the desert. Although she does not completely shed her distress over her blonde similarity to the invading whites, she does begin to recognize the hidden blessing of *mestiza*: she has within her a multiplicity of unexplored options. She must not cling to just one but must glean the wisdom and reject the destructive content from each element of her heritage. Through examining her alternatives, she finds a way to forgive and protect her unstable mother, accept the loss of her birth father, and deny the impulse to destroy her abusive stepfather. Spiritually, she renounces the joyless and mercenary behaviors of the white population and the submissive posture of her Church.

Bale has no male model to parallel Adela Sewa. His sole guide into male adulthood is his poverty-stricken mother, who is hampered first by her low status as a widowed mother of *mestizo* children and second by her unquestioning acceptance of the padre's joyless and futile spiritual pathway. She cannot initiate Bale into the cultural code of *machismo*, so he adopts the interpretation offered by the men of La Milpa. For him, being male means that he must defend and support his fatherless family, recognize and protect all good women, and be the voice of judgment against bad women. He cannot accept advice from those who love him best because they are women. On his own, he must become a bold provider who can flirt with death and ignore pain, and he must do so despite a dominant culture that tears down his home, limits his opportunities, and denies him the right to date its daughters. To that culture, he is useful only as a negative example or as an expendable body to send to Korea. To them, Bale's people and their homes are an embarrassment that needs to be disguised or eliminated. Amid these pressures, Bale cannot find a way. He spirals into self-hatred, despising himself first for belonging to his poverty-stricken culture and then for betraying that culture by his hatred. The desert that has been his solace loses its healing power as the invaders violate its powerful spaces and creatures. When the rattlesnakes and hawks become trophy sport for visitors, Bale finally crumbles. From that point on, he will prefer death to assimilation and continued powerlessness.

Bale's Church might be expected to offer him a sense of personal worth, but it does not. The padre, a victim of Euro-centered values to the same degree as the villagers, appears to believe that Euro-Americans deserve superior status, that a people's place in the official hierarchy accurately defines their worth, and that divine complicity in this plan must not be questioned. He counsels himself and the villagers to endure their poverty and low status with humble patience, and he reinforces the message by asking Bale to carry a heavy wooden cross in a Christian reinterpretation of the ancient Day of the Dead customs of the Southwest and Mexico.

For Maggie and Bale, this padre fails as a model of manhood. He may be powerful in the village, but he wears a long black dress and lacy white cassocks sewn by poor women like Bale's mother, women who wear clothing not nearly so fine. To the padre, the hot reaches of the desert are a metaphor for eternal damnation, not an ancestral home breathing with familiar spirits. Such a man cannot guide Maggie, Bale, and the rest of the villagers back to a sense of cultural and personal integrity. Like the developers, he can scarcely appreciate their love of place when he doesn't even admit they have a place or a functioning culture. In return, Bale and Maggie cannot accept a priest who offers only disapproval and penance.

The failure of culture and Church to comprehend a people's love of homeland is not a fiction invented by Escamill. Certainly, this failure is strong in fictional La Milpa, but Latina writers of nonfiction and memoir record it as a part of daily experience. Notable among these writers is Gloria Anzaldúa, whose comments in *Borderlands* (1987) specifically accuse Christian religions of damaging the peoples of the Americas. Like Escamill, Alvarez, Ortiz Cofer, and Limón, she accuses these Churches of misusing their power and defaulting on their duty to use their symbols and rituals to increase the people's sense of personal and communal importance and belonging. In the Spanish Americas, she says, the Catholic Church declared the previous earth spirits, shamans, patterns of worship, and festivals to be pagan, and therefore sinful, and they likewise condemned later imports such as *Santería* and *espiritismo*. Furthermore, missionaries convinced the people that the road to salvation lay in humility and self-mortification.

Other critics of colonizing Churches and cultures agree that the clash of ideas is destructive, perhaps even mutually so. Understanding the religion of another culture is more difficult than simple observation, imitation, or even ethnographic study. Louis Owens (1995), commenting on misconceptions about Native American religious beliefs, points out that real understanding is very difficult to achieve because an outsider cannot automatically draw upon a cultural referent or grasp a precise shade of meaning. Long immersion is required before even the most sincere outsider can recognize the subtle difference between an object of cultural importance, which can be incorporated into body or home decoration, and an object of sacred religious importance, which may only be used ceremonially. Casual intercultural contact often results in the dominant culture using the sacred ceremonial symbols of the other culture in inappropriate places, such as on T-shirts, key chains, and other tourist trinkets.

An illustration of a parallel abuse against a Euro-American religious symbol would be a disregard for the Catholic communion bread or "host." This flat, white disc of unleavened bread is a symbol so central to Catholic experience that it permeates Western and Latin literature in both physical and metaphoric form, but its complexities are rarely explained and are not generally known outside the religion. This host, before it is "consecrated" or blessed by a priest, is important in a symbolic sense because it is grain, a substance many religions honor as a symbol of sustenance and community. Unblessed, the host would be respected by Catholics, but it would not be revered. That is, if it were treated casually, eaten, or even scattered by nonbelievers, the action would be highly offensive, but it would not be an unforgivable desecration. Once the bread has been blessed, however, it is sacred. For this reason, when Trujillo seizes the consecrated hosts and distributes them in the novel *In the Time of the Butterflies*, he is seen as crossing all lines of religious propriety. At that time in Church history, only a priest was allowed to touch a consecrated host. The devout could receive it only by mouth. Therefore, the reluctance of the Church leadership to punish Trujillo for his sacrilege was a meaningful failure.

The host becomes an even more complicated symbol when viewed in the context of Church history. Practices change, and since the 1960s, Catholic parishioners in much of the world have been allowed to participate in distributing the communion bread, giving and receiving it among themselves with their hands. Touching the host is no longer a sacrilege, but the consecrated host is still sacred and the unconsecrated is not. What has changed is the people's relationship with the symbol.

In *Daughter of the Mountain*, the old religious symbols retain their sacred power for some of the people, particularly Adela Sewa, Maggie, and Bale. The creatures of the desert, as well as the desert and the mountains themselves, demand a reverence they do not receive from hunters, developers, mining companies, or even the village priest. As with the host in Catholicism, the spiritual satisfaction or awe or fear associated with these entities would have to become established through experience, not through logic. In the Americas, both the Spanish colonizers and the indigenous peoples lacked this experience, so neither group could fully understand the religio-cultural system of the other. The Spanish solution was to try to eliminate the indigenous system, and later Churches and governments have continued that program of destruction through military and social means.

In the era depicted in *Daughter of the Mountain*, the Spanish Catholic practices have nearly obliterated the Amerindian ones. The villagers of La Milpa are a long way from describing, justifying, and praising themselves as a viable culture. Realistically, the town will never throw off its original colonizers, whose bloodlines will be forever in evidence; nor can it undo the secondary colonization by the U.S.; nor can it resist the present colonization by developers. The cultural memory of the people continues to erode as a result of actions such as the padre's reinterpretation of the Mexican festival for remembering the dead, or the government's decision to raze the homes that represent independence to the poor. The resulting spiritual crises underlie the actions and outcomes of *Daughter of the Mountain*.

Maggie and Bale are not allowed to respect the bits of their ancient culture that remain. In the Day of the Dead ceremony, for example, the remnants of older and more consoling practices are barely visible. In the old times, the people honored the dead by thinking about them, talking about them (or even to them), and enticing them back by decorating the graves and clearing a pathway to the family homes. In spirit, the dead could be brought close to the community one more time. The foods, flowers, and practices fostered continuity and belonging, not grief, fear, or punishment.

However, as the padre at La Milpa interprets it, the Day of the Dead is a time to focus on the sorrow of past losses, the likelihood that the dead are suffering, and the duty of the living to share this suffering so the dead may escape to heaven. His mournful procession is a carryover from the Spanish Catholicism of the Conquest era, which included long, penitential pilgrimages to religious shrines. A means of atonement and self-mortification, these journeys proceeded on foot and involved other forms of self-denial. Adapting this pilgrimage model to La Milpa, the padre requires the people to don black clothing and undertake an hours-long, silent walk beneath the midday sun. The people know the impracticality of such a walk, but they have accepted that their sinful nature necessitates their earthly suffering. Even the children, though uncharacteristically quiet during the preliminaries, do not resist the ordeal. They have been taught that suffering benefits them and their dead, so they join the adults in praying for the relief of those who require purification in purgatory before they may enter heaven. They offer up their suffering to earn forgiveness for their own sins or to make themselves worthy of divine favors in the future.

These acts of suffering and praying for someone already at rest make no sense to the children. Neither do the Latin prayers that drift back from a priest who is himself visibly wobbling under the weight of his large gold cross. When the procession stops for lunch, the children fight their natural impulse to share smiles with their friends because they know joy is somehow inappropriate on the walk. Much later, nearly at dusk, they reach the shrine, an iron-gated cave beneath a hillside dominated by a tall white cross. In its gloom, they light candles and offer prayers before a statue of the tear-stained Blessed Mother receiving the ravaged body of her crucified son.

Disturbed at the pathos of this mother and the evidence of violence done to her son, Maggie urges her mother away from the shrine. All the children leave this shrine eagerly, but not just because they are confused or scared. With the padre's imposed celebration finished, they will be released into a much more comfortable sharing of food, laughter, and companionship under the stars. The children are unaware of the age or importance of this private fiesta relegated to the free time of the villagers, but they know it comforts them more than any ritual they have encountered at church. The graves their families decorate do not frighten them, nor does the dark.

This contradiction between the tortuous pilgrimage and the soft evening among the graves emphasizes an often-overlooked element of literature about the Latino experience. The scenery, the action, and the characters themselves serve to oppose the pre-Conquest metaphors of darkness and light with the metaphors brought by the conquering culture. The imported Catholicism has always associated whiteness with purity, goodness, and peace, while it has linked darkness with sin, evil, and destruction. However, Amerindian traditions connected whiteness with distress. Many details of the padre's Day of the Dead procession reveal whiteness or brightness to be disturbing to the villagers: the harsh midday light shatters on the glaring white cassocks and shiny gold cross; the cross above the cave glows white-hot and inaccessible on its steep, distant hill; and the candle flames fail to warm the cave where the pale Mother of God receives her dead son with large, colorless tears on her white face. The procession itself contradicts logic, for it gathers the community not for fun or solace, but to lead them in sorrow to an iron gate they must force open. The shrine behind it honors death rather than resurrection, and it lies far removed from the family graves marked by crosses painted the same pastel colors as the village houses. Only in the darkness after the blinding, exhausting day may the people move undisturbed among their extended families, living and dead. There, under desert stars that comfort the night, the people find food, drink, conversation, belonging, cooler air, and rest.

The Church's imposition of suffering, guilt, and hopelessness shows more than once in *Daughter of the Mountain*. Maggie avoids succumbing to it because, unlike Bale, she has a rebellious elder to follow. Grandmother Adela recognizes the inconsistencies between the padre's ideals and the realities of La Milpa life. Although her return to ancient ways has caused both Church and community to reject her, she functions without bitterness. Through her isolation, she is able to provide her granddaughter a safe haven from the certain physical abuse and the potential sexual abuse by her stepfather. Equally important to Adela, she can protect Maggie from the emotional abuse of a system that labels her inadequate, ugly, sinful, and destined to humble service. Adela teaches her granddaughter to forage for healing herbs and takes her to ancient and unsanctified shrines like that of El Tidadito, a traveler who was long ago robbed and killed on the road. He performs miracles for the poor because the poor women who discovered his body gave him proper cleansing and burial. He and his miracles are not recognized by the Church, and this papal rejection makes El Tidadito's shrine a place of innocence to Adela. Spiritually, she herself embraces the wisdom and holiness of outcasts, including those who have been condemned outright by Christians. In her shack is an altar to the ancient mother goddess she calls the Dark One, a renegade deity attuned to woman and therefore not welcome in the Church.

Grandmother Adela's spiritual breadth enables her to guide Maggie through the contradictions of cultures, religions, and colors. By preserving alternative deities, altars, rituals, and medicines, she gives Maggie options that her mother and the female religious resources of the village—the Tres Hermanas—cannot. These Tres Hermanas, three Catholic lay women devoted to the spiritual and physical wellbeing of La Milpa, themselves need salvation from their austere, demanding lifestyle. Two of them, Josepha and Emma, can only encourage Maggie to follow the unfruitful path of submission. Rule-bound and joyless, they fail at hope and charity. Josepha, who is always in a hurry to get to church, doesn't recognize the personal failures in her own past. Not only did she sanctimoniously refuse to help Adela Sewa out of her self-destructive bout of alcoholism, but she also turned away from Maggie's struggling mother and the infant Maggie. Her failure to forgive and assist survives in her present rejection of the sober Adela, whom she continues to call a savage even though Adela has saved herself, Maggie, and Maggie's mother. Resentful of Maggie and Adela's mutual affection, she blames Adela for Maggie's adolescent mistakes.

The second sister, Maggie's godmother Emma, also appears to be emotionally crippled. She expresses her love of desert birds by trapping and caging them. Focused on the control if not the elimination of jubilance, she obsesses over the household consumption of food and lamp oil. She incessantly scolds at the third sister, Consuela, a disorganized and perpetually cheerful dreamer. Consuela is a bad fit for the religious role she has chosen, but she endures with humble patience. Of the three sisters, only she offers Maggie any love or tenderness, and her presence makes the home of the three sisters a haven for Maggie during her early school years.

The presence of Consuela in this trio provides an essential balance in Escamill's implied evaluation of Catholic care of the poor and disadvantaged. Without her, the image of the Church is bleak indeed, and to be that bleak would contradict the common Latina viewpoint that the Church is seriously flawed but not worthless. To dismiss it entirely would be to condemn an essential element of the culture. Furthermore, Consuelas do exist. Even though Escamill's Consuela represents only one-third of the female Catholic leadership of La Milpa, her generosity and connection with the land and its people speak louder than Josepha and Emma's righteous disregard. As a model of the openness required to inspire real hope among those in physical and spiritual need, she mirrors Adela's tolerance for syncretism and her willingness to accept unusual and even contradictory viewpoints as reflective of daily, lived life.

The real-life presence of characters like Consuela is verified by Díaz-Stevens (1994), who has studied the organization called *Las Hermanas*, a group of Catholic lay women and nuns who joined forces in 1971 to advance their role in the hierarchy of the Church. They chose to work in small communities rather than in urban convents, schools, or churches, and in doing so, according to Díaz-Stevens, they entered a new reality. The demanding lifestyle taught them new skills, but more than that, they encountered the strength and intelligence of commoners and a more flexible interpretation of Catholicism. When they gave respect, they received it in return. As described by Díaz-Stevens, their experience appears to confirm that in hundreds of years, the moral of the story of the Indian, the priest, and the cows has not changed: one needs to listen and observe as well as to instruct, for the faithful have wisdom to share.

In the story offered by Escamill, however, the cheerful Consuela sickens and dies, and in her absence, Maggie can't face life with Josepha and Emma. She turns to desert life with Adela for its focus on the respect and preservation of life. There, the line between life as it asks to be lived and life as the local Church defines it sharpens again at the deaths of Adela and Bale. Grandmother Adela, who long ago was reborn to sobriety and health by a return to the life-affirming old ways, peacefully returns to the mountain called *La Madre*. She prepares for a respectful but joyous journey, selecting her best clothing and favorite red shawl because she does not consider her transition a somber event. In an open convertible, with Maggie driving and *La Muerte* waving a crepe paper banner in the back seat, she goes as promised to her beloved mountain, where she symbolically reunites with the earth mother by sealing herself into a cave. As a result, when Maggie needs her grandmother's advice, she can consult her through healing dreams and prophetic visions on *La Madre*.

Bale's spiral toward death lacks this sense of peace and completion. He remains overwhelmed with doubt and confusion, quite certain that good is not rewarded because his good father was taken despite all the family's devotions. Bale pities his mother for her constant efforts to pray her husband out of purgatory and petition her sons into good fortune. His remaining hopes fail through his attraction to Doreen, a girl of higher social class whose family will not allow him to date her. Bale's bitterness turns to self-hatred. He cannot tolerate even his own short, broad-chested body, for he doesn't know that it would be an enviable body among the mountain-dwelling ancestors he has never seen. He grows strangely silent, and Maggie, herself still too immature and distracted by her own dilemma, doesn't recognize his signals of distress. When he says he'd rather die than accept the encroaching white ways, she fails to take him literally.

The story doesn't clarify whether Bale's death is intentional or accidental, but his words and actions indicate that he is morose and possibly suicidal. Perhaps his fatal car accident results from a flirtation with death rather than a deliberate act, just as his brother Eddie's death seems likely to result from his fascination with riding rodeo bulls. Ultimately, this question of suicide is moot; Bale's inability to confront change has already left him spiritually dead. As he parties for the final time with Maggie and Eddie, he is watched by a more mature and perceptive woman who warns Maggie that Bale has too little regard for life. Maggie understands her meaning too late.

Though devastated by Bale's death, Maggie will not follow him into despair and self-destruction. Unable to find consolation at his funeral, she leaves the church and seizes the gun her stepfather taught her to shoot, but she spends her rage at a nearby firing range, as if she can deny annihilation by aiming it away from herself. In the coming years, she will do as her grandmother taught her, forcing death behind her and using every aspect of her heritage to sustain her own life and the life of her people.

Maggie does finally achieve a tenuous cultural balance. She honors the Catholic forms for the comfort they give the community, but she chooses to practice the Yaqui spirit religion as well. She accepts the U.S. education system because it will eventually enable her to help her people on their own terms. In these choices, she resembles some of the other characters offered by U.S. Latina writers. Looking for guidance in the face of the destruction of her culture, she places Catholic and Indian ways side by side and reveals the need for continued searching, just as Huitzitzilin does. She sets the realities of U.S. Latina life next to reality as described by the Church, and she finds discrepancies, just as Ortiz Cofer does. She embraces the rebel code in order to create a more useful and satisfying theology, just as the Mirabals do.

As different as their situations are, these characters come to a similar conclusion: no single code meets all the needs of all the people, but each code contributes experience and information to the people as a whole. Hatred and separation are unproductive. If answers exist, they can only be found through ongoing search and negotiation. The quest is worthwhile, for the answers that emerge will help create a balance in the joy and suffering of *la lucha*, the struggle that is Latino life.

9

A MALLEABLE RELIGION

Despite complaints about the failure of Catholicism to properly nurture and lead its poor and dark-skinned members, U.S. Latinas continue to label themselves Catholic or at least catholic in their memoirs, *testimonios*, poetry, and fiction. Whether they criticize the religion sharply, as Anzaldúa, Castillo, and Cisneros do, or simply let it lapse, as Ortiz Cofer and Mora say they have, they admit that their religious heritage continues to influence their perception of the world.

The paradox of simultaneously embracing and rejecting Catholicism may be understood more easily in terms of *mestizaje*. The authors, like the characters they create, may be partly Catholic, partly Spanish, partly Jewish, partly Amerindian, partly Anglo, partly African, and so on. More important, they believe that being mixed doesn't mean being reduced or limited; rather, it means having a multitude of options at hand. As *mestizaje* applies spiritually, it allows the Latina to draw upon several belief systems to use what is helpful and sideline what is not. She may fill in the gaps with non-Catholic or non-Christian customs, she may test secular philosophies, she may combine all these sources, or she may reject them all. Flexibility, not rigidity, is the key. She is free but for one rule: she must respect her complex origins. Failure to do so is *el olvido*, the sin of forgetting roots and thereby sacrificing wisdom.

Individual efforts to negotiate this hybrid religious zone show clearly in both fiction and nonfiction. Some writers seek a balance within Catholicism itself by discarding just those elements that may lead to unwarranted guilt, self-hatred, or despair. Others integrate Catholic practices with Protestantism, Amerindian religions, spiritism from Africa or Europe, Judaism, evangelism, Islam, or Buddhism. They may retain a Catholic identity through movements such as *mujerista* theology, or they may redefine themselves completely. The mix, no matter what it is, is always visible in the literature; spirituality is text or subtext in nearly all the writing produced.

Of all the challenges involved in settling the question of personal spirituality, the most difficult appears to be the intentional separation from their ingrained Catholic responses. Their deeply embedded Catholic rhythms, word patterns, and moral codes bleed through and demand attention. Julia Alvarez, in her semi-autobiographical novel *How the García Girls Lost Their Accents* (1992), offers a particularly interesting example of such intrusions as she records the years before and after the García family fled to New York City to escape the dangerous politics of the Dominican Republic. The outspoken García girl Yolanda (Yoyo), who was already wavering among the spiritual alternatives present on her home island, lets many Catholic practices lapse during her early adult years in the U.S. However, her conscious rejection is interrupted by ineradicable Catholic longings, such as her occasional desire to dig out her old crucifix and return it to its once comforting place under her pillow. The figure of Jesus, separated from the cross through years of use, has been reconnected with a rubber band. The unglued Jesus is an apt metaphor for Yoyo's fractured spirituality: the parts of her old religion have separated, but she can rejoin them whenever and however she finds practical. Although she may no longer view Jesus as a personal savior, she can continue to seek the sympathy of this courageous fellow sufferer.

Another author who reveals the surprising tenacity of her spiritual upbringing is Cherríe Moraga (1993), who does not call herself a Catholic but who occasionally still invokes traditional religious phrases. To tell her mother about her own profound response to an eclipse, for example, she automatically chooses the appropriate phrase:

"Ahora conozco a Dios, Mamá" [Now I know God, Mama]. And I knew she understood my reverence in the face of a power utterly beyond my control. She is a deeply religious woman, who calls her faith "catholic." I use another name or no name, but she understood that humility, that surrender, before a sudden glimpsed god. Little did she know god was a woman. [p. 70]

For Moraga, as for many others, the name of the religion—or the gender of the god, or the particular manifestation of the great one—is not the point. The point is the ability to talk about those intense spiritual moments experienced by the living.

Surprising variations on Catholicism are not unusual among Chicanas/os, according to Gloria Anzaldúa, who writes in *Borderlands* (1987) that she was raised in a folk Catholicism that borrowed from both Christian and pagan religions. She herself, like Moraga, recognizes the Virgin of Guadalupe as a powerful female deity. The official Catholic Church, on the contrary, accepts this Virgin only as a variant of the Blessed Virgin Mary of European tradition. It doesn't sanction her in the militant and sensuous form preferred by Anzaldúa and many other Latinas who conflate Guadalupe with Coatlalopeuh, a potent earth goddess central to the ancient Mexica beliefs. Similarly conflated goddesses appear elsewhere, as well, as in Cristina García's (1992) stories about Cuba. There, La Señora de la Caridad del Cobre and Our Lady of Regla are associated with Yemaya, an African goddess transplanted to Cuba along with the Lucumi slaves. According to the *mujerista* thought of Isasi-Díaz and Tarango (1988), Yemaya, the Goddess of the Sea, is too strong, passionate, and sensual to permit official association with the chaste, mild Mary; yet that strength and commitment to ongoing life is precisely what the people of Cuba need. Like other Latin Americans, Cubans encompass a complex religious ancestry and deserve access to all of it:

. . . the Amerindian, the African, and the Spanish. Not all of these cultures are equally present in the different Hispanic Women's groups. Hispanic Women with ethnic roots in the

Mexican culture are mostly influenced by Amerindian and Spanish culture. Hispanic Women with ethnic roots in the Caribbean, both Puerto Ricans and Cubans, are mostly influenced by African and Spanish culture. However, some small strands of all three cultures appear in all three groups. [p. 5]

Some of these influences are visible in rituals described by authors such as Ortiz Cofer and Alvarez, who respectively note that European and African spiritism are commonplace and acceptable in Puerto Rico and the Dominican Republic. Furthermore, these beliefs have traveled to the mainland U.S. along with the islanders who have moved there in pursuit of better lives. Isasi-Díaz and Tarango (1988) believe that U.S. Catholicism has greeted spiritism with official efforts to "either denounce it and work actively against it or look for ways of purifying it, of 'baptizing' it into Christianity, accepting only those elements that can be Christianized" (p. 67). That its practitioners nonetheless have continued to support this fusion of beliefs is borne out in Latina literature. Fictional and nonfictional characters alike maintain home altars populated with seemingly incompatible sources of hope, consolation, or intercession: Jesus, Mary, and the saints; Yoruban deities and saints; photos of family members or sympathetic world figures such as John F. Kennedy or Mother Teresa; bird bones or rocks given by the earth spirits; medicinal herbs; and personal mementos. Official Church law would declare this syncretic collection to be chaotic or even sacrilegious, but secular writers and *mujeristas* find it acceptable because for them, the daily, lived experience takes precedence over Church law. Díaz-Stevens (1994), a sociologist not associated with the *mujeristas*, expresses a similar confidence in the Latina flexibility that allows women to discard patterns and values that are destructive to female social progress, but to hold on to healthy elements that constitute their identity. Many Latina writers go further than the *mujeristas* and Díaz-Stevens by scoffing at the whole concept of religious law. To them, the term "Catholic" means heritage, not dogma or rules; they are "Catholic" because their families have traditionally been baptized into that Church and have followed some of its practices.

Orlando Espín (1994) elaborates upon the centuries-old tendency of Latin congregations to take license with Catholic rules once they realize that the local clergy is relatively powerless in the overall Church hierarchy. In his opinion, the local clergy itself has promoted such freedoms in the interests of maintaining control and keeping church attendance high enough to justify funding by the official Church. Without the alliance between official and popular interpretations, the Church effort would have lost ground, and the people would have lost the social, educational, medical, and personal benefits the Church could offer. In this way, a symbiotic need has continued to preserve and control, relax and expand the definition and practices of Catholicism.

U.S. Latina literature reveals this relaxation and expansion in a variety of ways. Some writers, such as Pat Mora, celebrate the comfort they find in the multifaceted heritage of the Mexico–U.S. borderland. Mora's memoir *House of Houses* (1997b) sings the unity of family and honors the syncretic spirituality that has helped sustain it. For Mora, the Catholicism of her family's history and practice is more about intuitive adjustment than about rules. It is an awareness drawn from the habits, symbols, and vocabulary of daily family life, and as such, it reflects twentieth-century U.S. secular philosophies as well as Amerindian and Catholic beliefs and traditions. Mora and her family have absorbed this spirituality as they have absorbed the borderland culture, and they could shrug it off no more easily than a first language. *House of Houses* proclaims that she does not wish to reject this rich, precious heritage, regardless of its contradictions.

Mora's other works also suggest that religion and spirituality are not the same thing, and that a personalized spirituality is the better choice. In her *Borders* poem "To Big Mary from an Ex-Catholic" (1986), the speaker wonders whether the Blessed Virgin Mary will reject her because she has abandoned religious devotions. She reasons that as a truly caring, heavenly mother, Mary will continue to sympathize with a daughter lost in a maze of options. In other stories and poems, Mora stresses similar personal relationships between individuals and their spiritual guides.

Her extended family knows their saints in a way not derived solely from printed biographies. Their saints have specialties, preferences, weaknesses, obsessions, a tendency toward humor, and differing degrees of accessibility. Mora's own intimate knowledge of them shows throughout her work, particularly in the poems of *Aunt Carmen's Book of Practical Saints* (1997a), a collection of highly personal meditations on the meaning and value of the family's favorite saints. Echoes of these meditations resound in *House of Houses* (1997b) as heavenly beings wander through the action. Even Grandfather, who finds the Catholic Church unsupportive, stays in touch with St. Joseph, the patron saint of many Mexican men, for he can believe that Joseph will pity and understand the difficulties of a displaced man with a family to support.

Just as they choose to honor or reject a saint, Mora and her family choose to honor, reject, or modify individual elements of Catholicism and other borderland religions. Although Catholicism has molded the people who have lived under its influence for centuries, she asserts, the people have shaped it in return. Mora herself no longer practices the religion, but she admits its attractions. In *House of Houses* she mentions her gentle longing for "the old church, the Latin church, the invisible choir, the priest's back rather than his face, the intoxication of incense and flickering candles" (p. 18). That "old church" is the Catholic Church of her growing up, the traditional Church before the changes of Vatican II and the 1968 Medellín conference, the Church of the *muy católica*, and the Church dedicated to weaning its people from folk Catholicism. The vocabulary and rhythms of that Church are called forth as she defines her heritage in the memoir. Just as the title itself plays upon the biblical definition of "house" as lineage, the story abounds in religious references. Prominent in it are Aunt Lobo's prayerbook, the family's patron saints, the communion host, the rosary, the sign of the cross, and the liturgical seasons with their accompanying prayers and music. These are the context in which her family has always functioned and within which she remembers them. To ignore their influence would be *el olvido*.

Central to *House of Houses* are the shared Catholic experience and its effect upon the telling and comprehension of favorite family stories. Indeed, Mora worries that she has robbed her own children of their heritage by not raising them in the ways of the Catholic Church. A very small incident pierces her cultural conscience: her children cannot grasp a family story about genuflection, that quintessentially Catholic practice of demonstrating humility by touching the right knee to the floor during worship, before entering a church pew, or after leaving the pew. Mora's sister recalls her own ingrained impulse to genuflect: one day she forgot where she was and touched her knee to the floor before entering a row at the movie theater. To the adults who grew up with the practice, the story is evocative, an inside joke, but for Mora's children, it requires explanation, and even then it seems quaint and a bit ridiculous. This gap in her children's background troubles Mora because she understands the importance of children retelling family stories. A story they do not value will be lost to their children, subtracted into the great silence of the forgotten.

As if to stave off that loss, Mora textures every page of her memoir with details of Chicano Catholic life, whether she is speaking of family celebrations, petitions to the saints, escape from Pancho Villa's forces, or survival during the Great Depression. Although she complains about shortcomings in leadership and humanity among the priests and the largely non-Latino congregations her family encounters, she consciously seeks a peaceful acceptance of the religion's ongoing good influences on her family. She respects the consolation her elders have derived from their private devotions to the Christ Child, the Virgin of Guadalupe, or their patron saints. Clearly, Mora wishes to preserve these and other Catholic contexts as she seeks the meaning of the interwoven Mora and Delgado houses.

Catholicism is not the only spiritual influence she must reveal, however, for interwoven into family practices are seemingly contradictory, non-Christian traditions. To resolve the paradoxes and sustain her theme of harmony, Mora creates a device that reflects two ways of knowing. The first is the recursive habit that sends the mind over and over the chronological facts, looking for patterns, links, causes and effects. Mora caters to this approach when she reports the family's literal history in the appropriate Western time frame, for these facts derive from officially dated family records. Likewise, she provides a family tree in which generations are discernible even when specific dates are unavailable.

The second way of knowing is the intuitive awareness that comes from internalizing natural and social rhythms. Human sensitivity to light patterns, for example, might inform a family of the approaching solstice, or a glance at public decorations may reveal the coming or passing of a holiday. When Mora tells family stories, she invokes this kind of time, a flexible time more concerned with the accumulation of family wisdom than with factual accuracy. She further stretches the standard chronology of calendar months through references to the nonsynchronous Christian and Mesoamerindian liturgical calendars, the moon-measured months as counted before Western contact, and the task-identified year of the gardener.

This flexible approach to understanding complex personal histories is not unique to Mora. The antichronological, recursive, multivocal style of many Latina writers encourages this tolerance and advocates for the constant reinterpretation of events. Cordelia Chávez Candelaria (1997) maintains that this writing style imitates the way Chicanas communicate within their own cultural group. Feminist critic Julia Kristeva (1991) devotes considerable thought to the idea that women's writing may reveal a different perception of time, one based upon cyclic repetitions and significant events. It is not linear or precisely measurable. Kristeva finds that females view time as fluid or as existing in large, amorphous chunks such as the unpredictable length of a pregnancy, the span of one's childbearing years, the years in a generation, or the duration of the journey from childhood to maturity. Kristeva insists that economic and psychological systems need to recognize the benefits of this flexible model of time.

Mora seems to follow a similar philosophy in the structure of *House of Houses*, which stresses re-examination as it organizes the

events of many years into recurrent cycles. She jumbles themati-
cally related memories into each representative month of her
memoir, and she rounds out the memories through contributions
by numerous speakers. In a sense, the recursive nature of *House
of Houses* allows her to revalue her family's space in Mexican and
U.S. history, culture, and religion. The family story is one of years,
moons, seasons, and births-deaths-rebirths. Information flows
through generations of linked females just as the Río Grande flows
through their history. Like the river, they are always the same
and always different. The Río Grande both protected her family
from Pancho Villa and severed them from Mexican nationality.
The river provided the very substance of the family's adobe house,
a central metaphor that merges the place, the house, the body, and
the spirituality of her Mora and Delgado roots.

By invoking this flow of history, Mora (1997b) emphasizes the
layers of generations, places lived, memories, and religious beliefs
that surround the members of a family "nesting like bodies inside one another" (p. 3). Viewing her family as a "house" in her
imagination, she describes a home built on a concentric design.
Orchards surround this home, which itself presents a smooth
adobe wall to the outside but allows guests to enter increasingly
more intimate zones until they reach the very heart of the family.
In this house, the rooms face inward to a covered porch, which
in turn encloses a garden, which in turn surrounds the life source,
a central fountain. The internal sphere is a separate world of flow-
ing water, living greenery, shifting shade, and timeless intimacy:
a personal space, the womb of the family. Of it, Mora asks, "What
does the house, the body, know?" (p. 4).

The house knows what is important about religion, history,
and family, but it can only share the knowledge through Mora
and Delgado voices, the prophets and scribes she trusts. One voice
belongs to Aunt Lobo, a celibate but motherly woman, a handsome, educated priestess as powerful as the author's father. Others belong to her Aunt Chole, her grandmother Mamande, and her
great-grandmother Mamá Cleta. These and other family members,
mostly women, spin out the family history and pass on the beliefs

and values of the nearly forgotten ancestors. Much of the advice they offer has to do with adaptation, a skill which Aunt Lobo calls "the generational pattern for women and the dark-skinned and the poor" (p. 22). Moreover, the spirits teach Mora that adaptation is a matter of addition rather than reduction. It requires acknowledging and tolerating the existence of other means to an end, but it doesn't require embracing them or rejecting previous ones. Mora extends this concept of addition to her language, her culture, and her religion. She records that *adobe*, the familiar Mexican name for the very material of her house, came from the Spanish colonizers, who in turn had mimicked the Arabic word for *brick*. Likewise, the ubiquitous rosary of Catholicism originated in twelfth-century Europe and has similarities to Muslim prayer beads. Even some nonreligious folk customs originated far away, as did the art of cutting decorative patterns in tissue paper, a skill adopted from the Chinese. Ultimately, Mora declares, "cultural purity is a myth" (p. 96).

Another myth she dispels is the ability to eradicate one's heritage. Although she herself has abandoned the formal practice of her religion, at Christmas she gravitates toward the planning, cutting, baking, and storytelling that precede the holiday. Almost unconsciously, she continues to fill at least part of the role Díaz-Stevens attributes to the Latin American Catholic woman: helping the community prepare for liturgical and agricultural festivals. When she insists that her children help arrange the traditional manger scene, she is actually protecting the history of family treasures, for handling the pieces will teach the children their many shapes and origins as well as the years of communal effort required to collect them. By involving her children in the family ritual, Mora gives them over to the older women of the family, who relate prayers and religious stories and thus supply the background she herself has neglected.

Through her calendar-based memoir, Mora discovers how deeply the religious events embedded in her culture have continued to influence her perceptions. Starting with the poetic prelude "House of Houses" rather than the traditional first month of

January, she mimics the Catholic liturgical year, which starts with Advent, a period covering the four Sundays before Christmas Day. During Advent, the faithful hear again the promises of the Old Testament and anticipate the stories of Christ's life and teaching that will fill the coming year. The repetition offers an opportunity to understand the message a little better in the coming year, and better yet in the years after that. On a personal and family level, Mora follows similar logic as she prepares herself to review family habits and teachings in the coming chapters. Condensing the stories and admonitions of many years into the representative seasons of the year, she hopes to understand her heritage more fully.

In this prelude, Mora subtly invokes the symbols of Advent. Just as the Bible story recalls the House of David that engendered Christ, she recalls the houses of Mora and Delgado that joined to create her. In this past-yet-present house, "time loses its power and past ∞ present braid as they do within each of us, in *our* interior. The clock ticks, the present becoming past, a current that like the wind resists control . . ." (p. 4).

Anticipating the coming year, she refers to a Mexican folk practice of guessing the year's weather by analyzing the first twenty-four days of January. She thereby reinforces the overall structure of the book in two ways. First of all, she shows that calendrical time is only one way of predicting change. Second, she reaffirms that the best information comes from juxtaposed systems. By examining numerous cycles and conflicting beliefs, she may come to understand the complex Catholicism she has inherited.

In this title chapter for the memoir, the women plait the braid that binds many seasons into one representative season. One strand is the gardening year, a good example of what Kristeva (1991) calls cyclical time, for the day to plant and the day to harvest will come, though no one knows exactly when. The speed and success of plant growth will depend upon uncontrollable natural elements. The filling and waning moon will exert its magic pull, but not on the same dates as in the year past or the year to come. The seasons will create an average by never being average. Knowing these things, the family women anticipate their spring garden, confident that plants "nourish, inspire, intoxicate. . . . [They are] like our subconscious, fertile and full of promise" (Mora 1997b, p. 8). Always, the emphasis is on nurture and continuity, on the usefulness of the past and the certainty of a future.

As the memoir progresses, Mora follows the interwoven strands of time, nature, growth, family, and religion. One significant strand is Aunt Lobo's missal, her copy of the biblical readings as they appear in order during the Catholic year of Masses. Holy cards and family pictures alike tumble from its pages, for Lobo believes that family and its special moments are just as important as Catholic saints and scripture. The family women, most of whom are present as spirits, examine this missal in the liturgical ambiance of a scented candle as they drink tea brewed in a "sacramental" (p. 11) act. They begin reconstructing their past on the orderly plan of a twelve-month Western calendar, but they soon superimpose the flexible time of family generations as well as the rotating, astronomically influenced calendars of the Catholic Church and the pre-Conquest Mesoamericans. Catholic liturgical seasons do not always begin on the same calendar date, and even fixed dates such as Christmas land on different days of the week each year. All celebrations follow the lead of Easter, which falls upon the first Sunday after the first full moon after the vernal equinox. When Mora recites the Church seasons from Advent to Ordinary Time, she notes they are "rhythmic as the seasons" (p. 12).

Significantly, Mora also refers to the *Popol Vuh*, the oldest recorded origin stories of the Quiché Maya, and she consistently invokes the moon seasons as named by other indigenous groups: Snow, Awakening, Sprouting Grass, Full Flower, Full Rose, Full Thunder, Big Harvest, Full Long Nights. Her layering of time imitates the complex cyclical calendars of the Aztec and Maya civilizations, calendars that allowed the priests to predict how a single day might be influenced by its simultaneous representation on differing but superimposed cycles. Mora and her family have absorbed this layered perception of time along with their Catholic and secular calendars. These time wheels provide the context in which the family has always functioned.

In *House of Houses*, the first interval after Advent runs roughly from January through April. During these months, Mora refers to the events of the Church calendar from the arrival of the Three Kings to the death and resurrection of Christ. She condenses family history, as well, presenting an overview of the Mora and Delgado lives from the great-great-grandparents down to her own children. Continuing the garden parallel, she makes herself receptive to the seeds of stories and the strenuous period of gestation: "We probably dig some of ourselves into all that we pursue, but there's something eerie or maybe appealing—all the Catholic dust-to-dust stuff—about digging ourselves into earth, loosening the soil and burying some of our essence . . . even while we're alive becoming part of the compost" (p. 67).

This "dust-to-dust" period of self-examination gains impact around March, a month that always finds the Catholic Church in its penitential season of Lent. Accenting the Lenten practice of self-denial, Mora calls this penitential season the "'I Won't' season" (p. 69) because of all the pleasures she won't enjoy for the duration. Outside, the garden shivers. The vernal equinox approaches, but too slowly. During this dark time of year, the period of the Snow Moon and March wind, the family stories are sorrowful. Aunt Lobo tells of Pancho Villa's attacks and the hardships of being displaced from Mexico to Texas, a history consistent with the liturgical year and its devastating stories of Christ's passion and death. They invoke the bitterness that must be endured while awaiting resurrection, the Awakening Moon, and renewed life in the garden and the family.

March must become April, however, and the Awakening Moon must follow the Snow Moon. Mora contemplates the spiritual rain of Easter and the physical rain of spring, both of which renew life. Fittingly, she tells of her father Raúl, who holds death-bed conversations with the Virgin and his dead ancestors. Such visits gratify rather than disturb the family because their personal

Catholicism embraces a pre-Christian conviction that the dead remain accessible to the living. As Mora says later, her father believed that the family dead "have no use for cemeteries, staying underground. They drift through the rooms like incense, like a prayer, a melody, a breath" (p. 268). Comforted by this belief, Raúl and his family trust more in his spirits than they do in the final sacramental rites performed by the priest. Whereas the spirit visitors promise Raúl joyful relief after his years of mental and physical pain, the Church rites remind him of a lifetime of error and threaten him with more punishment. In April, with its parallels of Easter, an Awakening Moon, young animals, and green shoots, the family chooses hope over despair. Four days after Raúl dies, Mora finds him at her side in memory as she strolls their favorite market.

The other miracle in this miraculous month is the improving eyesight of Aunt Chole, who physically has been almost blind for years. Always capable of "seeing" by means of her unerring intuition, Aunt Chole has communicated equally well with birds, children, and spirits. She has forced people to read to her or describe to her what she can't see, and in return, she has told them what they don't see, don't notice, or don't remember. With other family elders, mostly women, she has spun out the family history, adding the detail, nuance, and depth of long memory. Still, she and the family rejoice in her enhanced sight. Her physical improvement, like Raúl's sudden spiritual presence, expresses rebirth and offers the gift of seeing once more and in a new way.

May to September provides a long season of garden growth that must be supported by dedicated watering, a duty echoed in the baptism and ministry of Christ as it is told during Catholic Ordinary Time. Mora examines the family stories of culture clashes and racial biases—those directed toward the Moras as well as those they directed toward others. Such stories lead Mora to wonder if her own children have sometimes been made to hate the heritage she wishes them to love. Suddenly she realizes how deeply European her family is, in both its religion and its names. She realizes she knows neither the songs nor the names of her Amerindian ancestors. They are lost because the garden of memory withers without care.

In early autumn, the family lingers for gentler stories. The liturgical year dallies, too, delaying the contemplation of death and darkness until early November. During this golden interlude, Mora tells of Mamá Cleta's charming spirit party for Saint Rafael, Our Lady of Guadalupe, and all the rest of her favorite spirits. All of them attend, of course; such camaraderie persists between the house and its heavenly darlings. The Virgin even searches her pockets for seeds for the parrot. When Jesus shows up in the form of the Holy Child of Atocha, the Virgin gathers him onto her lap and fusses over his manners and his little shoes, which he wears thin as he dispenses mercy around the world. Mora wistfully recounts these friendly modifications of the austere Mary and Jesus of Catholicism. Such adaptations have long sustained her family.

In November, the parties for the departed have a more somber tone, but they avoid the penitential demands of the Day of the Dead celebration described by Escamill in *Daughter of the Mountain*. In their echo of pre-Conquest practices, the women entice the spirits back for a visit, even if they will come for only one night. Their sensual invitation includes the tang of crushed marigolds, the taste of sugar skulls and *pan de muerto*, the touch of familiar sand and tile, the noise of the gathered living, and the quiet flicker of dozens of candles. Pathways glow with golden petals that lead through the open door and up to the family altar. And the family spirits do gather. Mora and her children give their spirit relatives appropriate spirit gifts, a practice reminiscent of Amerindian traditions, and later, they escort the departed back to their invisible realm by floating lighted candles on the Río Grande, one light for each of the deceased, even for the children who died so young no one remembers their names. Then, her year finished and her stories told, she prepares to start the cycle again, wiser than before, and wise enough to know that she will learn still more in the new year.

Having gone full cycle, *House of Houses* culminates with December and Advent. Again, Mora emphasizes gathering the family, sharing stories, expanding the traditions, and anticipating future generations. During these rituals, Grandma Lito reminds them to taste and enjoy every season, and she salutes the joy and hope that permeate the weeks of Advent in the liturgical year. Mora agrees. The memory year has renewed her belief in the importance of family solidarity. Furthermore, it has proven her earlier impression that, like the Holy Family of Catholic tradition, her family "is a holy body too, crazy, but holy" (p. 43).

Mora's redefinition of the Holy Family, like her redefinition of time, isn't unusual among Latinas, who often note the difficulty of equating the Church family model with any human family they know. Norma Alarcón (1996) mentions the impracticality of the Jesus-Mary-Joseph model as she comments upon Helena María Viramontes's story "Snapshots" and Cherríe Moraga's play *Giving Up the Ghost*, both of which reveal the hopeless bind in religio-cultural definitions of woman and her role in creating and maintaining the family. In reality, Alarcón points out, children are not Christlike, and most families have multiple children to raise rather than just one. Mothers grow impatient, and fathers, particularly stepfathers, do not always preserve and protect their spouse and offspring. Poverty and abuse are rampant. However, women still must quietly and humbly hold the family as close as possible to the model of Joseph and Mary, the perfect human parents to a divine only child.

This questioning and redefinition of the Holy Family has centuries of precedent. As Espín (1994) explains in his essay on folk Catholicism, the reconfigurations of both the Holy Trinity and the Holy Family began as soon as the Spanish missionaries introduced these units. Both trinities were unacceptable to the Mexica and Antillean peoples because neither one conformed to indigenous perceptions of the proper relationships among deities. A Holy Trinity composed of Father, Son, and Holy Spirit ran counter to the belief that a god must mate with a goddess to generate divine offspring. The idea of Jesus the Son of God being part of an all-male Trinity had to give way to a family structure: God the Father had to have a female counterpart, and the reasonable choice was the Blessed Mother. Together, they could produce Jesus, the son of gods. Mary's lack of divinity in Catholic doctrine didn't deter them; they simply elevated her anyway, with the Mexica further associating her with Guadalupe and lending her the qualities of the powerful earth goddess Coatlalopeuh.

In the same way, the people had to adjust the Holy Family, for Joseph and Mary were not gods and couldn't produce a god. Over the years, the partially converted Mexica and Antilleans came to think of the Holy Family and the Holy Trinity as the same unit. According to Espín, they decided that the Roman Church had mistakenly given Christ's stepfather Joseph too much value, while it had not valued his mother Mary nearly enough. Again, the people solved the dilemma by deifying the Blessed Mother, making her an appropriate partner for God the Father and providing the proper religious logic for the creation of the Son of God. They continued to honor Saint Joseph as an ideal model for earthly fathers and stepfathers.

The writers who continue the folk Catholic traditions don't specifically challenge the Church on the structure of its official Holy Trinity or Holy Family. They identify the Trinity as God the Father, God the Son, and God the Holy Spirit, but they express little devotion to the unit or its individual deities. Likewise, they speak respectfully of Joseph as a patron and role model for men, but they seldom find him essential to their stories. Instead, they celebrate Mary in her Guadalupan form, a caring and powerful mother goddess revered *and obeyed* by her son. Perhaps these adjustments originally were cosmetic, merely an attempt to preserve a measure of the old religion without bringing down the wrath of the conquerors, but they have persisted. The spirit of the militant Mary pervades Latina stories.

For Mora specifically, Mary and the saints exert a more gentle influence. As much as she follows a broader spirituality than that offered by her former Church, she tells Norma Alarcón (1986) that she prefers subtlety and a tempered stance on potentially divisive issues. Mora's *House of Houses* embodies this approach and leaves a good feeling behind it. In her poetic effort to re-member a family strongly influenced by its Catholicism, she respects differences and seeks common ground. Though less outspoken against the Catholic Church than Anzaldúa, she is willing to temper her beliefs with traditional wisdom from both sides of the great oceans and both sides of the Conquest. Like Moraga, she can experience the power associated with God without giving that power the same name her relatives do. Like Alvarez, she is drawn back to those elements of the family religion that have unified and comforted the generations. Together with many other Latinas, she asserts that the point is not to forget her Catholic heritage but to recover the larger heritage, a *mestizaje* both physical and spiritual.

10

A FLEXIBLE STORY

Although Latina writers often criticize Catholic or Christian religious policies, they consistently express a belief in the possibility of change. Perhaps because they write literature rather than history or sociology, the authors tend to search for meaning more than fact and to explore what is and could be more than what has been. While they may agree that the present is a flawed result of a colonial past, they also recognize it as a starting place, and the challenge of beginning anew in a *mestiza* consciousness powers the stories they tell. In this general search for a better future, small moments may trigger great revelations, as if a better way has existed for some time, waiting for someone to follow it.

These small moments manifest themselves differently, sometimes suddenly, and always personally, as when Patria recognizes the complicity of Church and state in *In the Time of the Butterflies*, or when Mora understands that in her house of houses, a loving family can absorb large differences. Such stories end with a beginning, a new awareness that will inform the future. Patria discovers a larger spirituality and Mora reconnects her old beliefs with her new, and a country and a family benefit.

Another story in which a character suddenly turns the past into a bridge to a better future is Edna Escamill's *Daughter of the Mountain* (1991). At the outset, the *mestiza* girl Maggie, who is burdened by her overwhelmingly Anglo appearance, faces a future with no discernible role in her own village or in Anglo society. Her grandmother leads her toward an appreciation for her own strengths and abilities, but Maggie must achieve this recognition on her own. Midway in this journey of discovery, in one of the many breakthroughs she must make, Maggie takes an unexpected step forward: at a community gathering, she spontaneously changes the ending of a popular folk story. Her new ending defies the social, economic, gender, and class structures under which she lives, and for her, at least, it opens a new way to operate in her cultural borderland.

The story she alters is a Chicano quasi-religious tale commonly called "Dancing with the Devil" or "Devil at the Dance." According to ethnographer José Limón (1991), this story gained popularity among the Mexican Americans of South Texas during the middle of the twentieth century. Other ethnographers have reported its presence across the U.S. Southwest as well as in northern areas that employ migrant workers. Often mentioned in books about Chicano or Latino culture, it enjoys multiple versions that can be reduced to the following common plotline:

> A young, unmarried Latina attends a village or community dance. There, she trades glances with a very attractive outsider, often an Anglo, and eventually she not only accepts his invitation to dance, but continues to dance with him for the rest of the evening.
>
> Her behavior is scandalous for a variety of reasons. She may have been forbidden to attend the dance in the first place. She may have been told not to dance with anyone more than once, or with anyone unknown to the family, or with anyone not properly introduced to her and her chaperone. She may have been warned against this very stranger. The stranger's inappropriateness as her dance partner is recognized by everyone at the party, even those who would trade places with her if they dared. He is too suave, too tall, too handsome, and too attentive. That is, he is too good to be good for her.
>
> At the climax of the story, the foolish young woman notices with horror that her elegant partner has the feet of a chicken (or some other animal). He can be none other than the devil. Knowing she is ruined, she faints or even dies in shock and

dismay, and the stranger escapes, often disappearing in a burst of smoke. Even if the woman lives, she will suffer a social death. She is forever tainted, forever unmarriageable, forever prevented from having legitimate children.

The story unmistakably reinforces the religio-cultural view of woman as corrupt or at least easily corruptible, for the devil finds success with her, not with a man. She disobeys and takes chances, like Eve; she consorts with the intruder, like *La Malinche*. She pays the price her predecessors paid: removal from society, if not from life.

In Limón's opinion, this tale functions both as class resistance and as social control. In terms of class, it reinforces the image of Anglos as rich, immoral infiltrators who are best avoided. In terms of the social structure, it justifies the strict moral restraint imposed upon village women, particularly the young and unmarried. Indeed, Limón finds the tale accepted wholeheartedly by all age and gender groups in the villages *except* the young, unmarried women. The village men, whether married or single, believe the woman in the story exhibits all the worst faults of women: she is vain, loose, greedy, and unappreciative of village men. They believe she gets just what she deserves. The married women consider the woman a threat because she is just the type of girl who would enjoy seducing the married men of the village. The village elders, male and female, think the woman's behavior is just one more example of the continuing breakdown of traditional moral values. In their minds, the people have carelessly invited the devil into their midst, and the woman wants to make him permanent by being his partner.

The young, unmarried women, however, find the situation more ambiguous. They agree that the woman behaves badly, but they sympathize with her for wanting to do so, for she shares their own yearnings for a clean, handsome, economically secure man who will cherish his woman and be true to her forever.

Limón interprets the story from a Marxist point of view, saying that its frequent telling helps the community resist the social, political, and economic influences of capitalism. The Anglo represents the rich man who lures the women away from the very men upon whose backs he has built his attractive lifestyle. The men believe that if their culture is to survive, the Anglo and his system must be driven off, and if that fails, then the young women must be kept away from him. The young women, on the other hand, wonder if some of the Anglo's secrets might be useful to their own people. Therefore, for Limón, the young women offer the possibility of toppling the system and insisting on a share of Anglo wealth.

Interested in this potential economic revolution, Limón doesn't consider the possibility that the story itself may have to change before the people can. Escamill, retelling the story through Maggie, explores that possibility. The girl stuns herself and her village when she deals with the devil at the dance in a new way. Although her action doesn't break the power of the elders, the married men and women, or the bachelors of her village, it does mark the beginning of a *personal* revolution. The reader is left to speculate whether the people around Maggie will think new thoughts.

Maggie breaks the story pattern at a moment of great impact: a fireside storytelling session that follows a day of communal food-gathering in the mountains. This community celebration has a special purity because it occurs away from the Anglo-tainted village and it involves only the people who still follow the traditional ways. Old stories shared in such a setting do triple duty: they reestablish the rightful balance of the social structure, they entertain the people, and they impart the culture to the young. Any tale told here will perpetuate itself. An aberrant tale will receive such strong notice that it will be difficult to silence. Even if the elders disapprove of it, they will retell it in the act of expressing their disapproval. Even if they forbid its repetition, the ending-that-cannot-be-told will remain in the memory of everyone present. The young, in their curiosity over the resulting furor, will wonder why the ending caused such an uproar, and they will whisper it in sweet and secret disobedience.

When she begins her tale, Maggie doesn't know she is about to destroy a convention. She simply intends to relate a familiar story as dramatically as possible. Assuming that she has heard her version of the story somewhere else, probably from her grandmother Adela, she doesn't even recognize it as her own creation. But she is wrong. The story has formed in her subconscious during her conscious battles against the triple burden of color, class, and gender that she bears daily.

In Maggie's version, the dancing woman is as beautiful as the story requires her to be, but she is also strong and self-possessed. She dances with the stranger again and again, ignoring her parents' command to return home. In fact, she behaves so disgracefully that the chatting villagers who have been ignoring the familiar old tale suddenly find themselves drawn into it once more.

Maggie pauses dramatically when the dancer notices that her partner has goat feet. The audience waits breathlessly for the silly woman to suffer complete and delectable destruction. A child breaks the tension by asking to hear the woman's fate, and Maggie delivers the new ending: no fainting, no smoke, no ruin. Instead, the woman turns into a black jaguar and bites off the man's head.

The children are thrilled, and the same child asks which creature seemed more terrible to the people at the dance. Maggie assures everyone that the jaguar outdid the devil, for only she could recognize him, and she made his defeat so fearful that all the watchers ran away.

Maggie's revision and the responses of her listeners are particularly interesting in light of José Limón's comments. The elders, who already disapprove of Maggie because of her Anglo features, her troubled family, and her unconventional grandmother, probably hear the story as further evidence of the depravity of the younger generation. The women of the village know that the men, single or married, are likely to be outraged. In hundreds of years, the men have not been able to exorcise the Anglo devil. They have barely been able to control their women. Now, a woman not only has defied their rules, but also has defeated the devil and cast out the newcomer in a spectacular fashion they cannot equal.

Aware that the males will feel threatened by the new story, the women immediately hush their children and hide whatever response they themselves may have had to the change. They know the anger of the men too well, and they know their duty to initiate their children, particularly their daughters, into the mysteries of avoiding it. They will have to decide later, among themselves, whether they admire this jaguar-woman and whether they will keep the new story alive.

It is the children, a group not addressed in Limón's study, who appear to be the promising element in Escamill's story. A child— and notably, one not assigned a gender—asks the question that triggers Maggie's invention. The child's action would be culturally proper and even expected, since one of the purposes of communal storytelling is to make children want to know the results of forbidden behavior. This child doesn't know the "correct" ending for the story. No doubt the watching adults wear indulgent expressions as they anticipate the child's reaction to the dancing woman's terrifying punishment. And no doubt their expressions change when the woman becomes a jaguar, bites off the stranger's head, and inspires the children to cheer.

Escamill has chosen particularly meaningful details for Maggie's brief but long-reaching rendition of "Dancing with the Devil." A jaguar is a powerful, rare, and stunning beast by any measure, but more significantly, it is known to have been a sacred symbol in the pre-Columbian religions of Mexico. Maggie can't invoke its presence without also invoking the village's powerful ancestors, and she can't attach the jaguar's power to Woman without also summoning the awesome authority of the ancient Mexica earth goddesses. Furthermore, this jaguar-woman increases her power when she bites off the head of the Anglo and thereby adds his knowledge to hers.

Maggie's jaguar-woman achieves omnipotence and omniscience because she alone recognizes the true nature of her dance partner. He is the devil, all right, but his temptations include the sins ingrained in her own culture: unfair gender roles, self-hatred, loss of cultural pride, and economic submission. She is the jaguar of action and self-definition, and her violent act rejects centuries of destructive thinking. Her summons to new ways of perceiving Woman and *mestizaje* is indeed powerful. No wonder the rest of the revelers ran away.

In religious and metaphoric terms, Maggie has also told a revolutionary tale. In its original form, the story is ambivalent about the identity of evil, and it confounds the cultural and religious metaphors of light and dark. The foolish woman is dark-skinned, but it is the devil, not the woman, who is the epitome of evil in the story. To be consistent with Spanish Catholic definitions of good and evil, he should bear Indio-dark, not Anglo-white, features. Even before Maggie's alterations, therefore, the story already resists white domination through its combination of the pre-Columbian perception of dazzling white things (threatening, empty, and rigid) and the postcolonial perception of the Anglo (dangerous and destructive). Once Maggie turns the easily manipulated young woman into a sleek, powerful, agile black jaguar, the Christian partiality toward Anglo whiteness is not only overcome, but obliterated, eaten.

In the aftermath of telling her story, Maggie becomes the revolutionary woman she has conjured. She faces down her abusive stepfather, cares for her emotionally ravaged mother, accepts the death of her grandmother, and copes with the suicide of her best friend. She bites off the knowledge of the Anglo by pursuing an education that will enable her to help her people. Eventually, she will identify her own inner devils and be the jaguar that dispatches them. She will make her mixed heritage her medicine rather than her burden, and in the life she plans for herself, she will teach her people that the old, old story of race and class discrimination can have a better ending.

The "Dancing with the Devil" story appears elsewhere in Latina literature, though seldom with the impact it carries in *Daughter of the Mountain*. Another novel that uses it to advantage, however, is *Face of an Angel* (1994) by Denise Chávez. In this novel about men, women, men and women, the eternal triangle, love, women's solidarity, and the need for self-acceptance, the folktale provides a position from which to question religious and cultural expectations. The validity of the tale crumbles as the main character, Soveida Dosamantes, studies the personal suffering in her small Chicano town and then redefines herself, the devil, angelic behavior, woman, man, and the nature of service.

In *Face of an Angel*, a version of "Dancing with the Devil" is repeated during the last hours before Soveida is married. While she is out of the room, her grandmother, Lupita, tells her mother about dancing with the devil, invoking the traditional ending. The disastrous fall of the woman is familiar to the women of the Dosamantes family, who for generations have suffered the infidelities of handsome but wandering men. Mamá Lupita insists that Soveida's groom, like the man in her story, is a mooching nobody with chicken feet and a lingering smell of sulfur. She believes Soveida should never have encouraged him in the first place, but should have kept to her childhood plan to become a nun. Soveida's mother, Dolores, unwilling to invite evil by speaking of it, prevents Mamá Lupita from repeating the story to Soveida, and the wedding proceeds.

As Chávez structures the novel, the groom, Ivan Eloy Torres, emerges as a potential devil at the dance long before this wedding is even planned. When Soveida first meets him, she connects him with all the glitter and polish of city society. As she gets to know him, she discovers he not only is dark and handsome but has a penetrating gaze, a sense of worldly wisdom, an air of self-ease, a strong sexual allure, and a great talent for dancing. As he awakens her to the plight of farm laborers, the work of César Chávez, and the pride of being Chicano, she comes to see him as an angel, but her mother cautions her that men who dance may not be angelic. Her boss's mother tells her Ivan is too pretty to be good, and her family's old servant and friend, Oralia, warns her to listen to the advice women give her. Regardless, though somewhat less joyfully, Soveida marries Ivan. She would undoubtedly do so even if Mamá Lupita did tell her about the devil at the dance.

In the events that follow, the devil tale appears to have been an accurate prediction. Ivan Eloy's selfishness and infidelity destroy the marriage and disappoint the elder Dosamantes women, who had hoped that at last one of them would marry well. Contrary to the traditional outcome of the story, however, Soveida is not destroyed physically, emotionally, or socially by the divorce. She keeps the peace with family and friends, works her job, and continues to write her *Book of Service*, which is a handbook about real life—about *lo cotidiano*—even though it masquerades as a manual for waitresses. She doesn't give in to hatred or despair, though her handbook does include a warning about dark, handsome, unfaithful men who limit their love. Unfortunately, she does remarry, this time to an emotionally damaged Anglo named Veryl, who cannot love her physically or emotionally and who devastates her by committing suicide. Later, she has an affair with J.V., a creative writing professor who puts his career ahead of their developing relationship, and then she becomes pregnant through an affair with J.V.'s married brother, Tirzio.

At first glance, these multiple failed relationships do seem to validate the cultural logic of "Dancing with the Devil." However, the tale cannot be laid over the story without leaving gaps and overlaps. From the outset, the identity of the devil-man is blurred. He should be an outsider, preferably an Anglo, and he should sweep her off her feet with his polish. None of Soveida's men fit this model. Veryl is Anglo, but he is hardly impressive, even to Soveida, who is not surprised when he turns out to be selfish, stingy, impotent, insensitive, and unsupportive. Ivan Eloy is Spanish, dark, and elegant. J.V. and Tirzio are handsome and impressive, but they are Chicanos whom she meets under acceptable circumstances, not outsiders she accepts without knowing anything at all about them. That they are her half-cousins because of a common unfaithful ancestor is a secret learned late in the story.

Even the men's similarities to the devil don't create a convincing parallel between tale and novel. True, Soveida's lovers are all male and all distrusted by the female elders. Likewise, all of them disappear. However, Soveida enters all four relationships with her eyes open. Furthermore, neither the courtships nor the men's departures are noteworthy in terms of social impact. Ivan Eloy leaves through a divorce that draws little attention and leaves no stigma. Veryl's pathetic suicide may be empty and cold enough to reinforce the anti-Anglo model, but the act results from Veryl's own demon, and it affects Soveida alone and leaves no apparent social stigma. J.V.'s career move to Germany is greeted philosophically all around, and Tirzio's existence and paternity are never shared with the family. Even Tirzio's inability to leave his first family is a foregone conclusion to Soveida. Not one of the men leaves with the fire, smoke, and devastation of the devil's departure from the dance.

Because of this ill fit, the folk tale cannot reinforce the validity of folk belief in this situation. It can, however, strengthen a countering theme in the novel. Both *Face of an Angel* and Soveida's *Book of Service* begin with observations about gender roles. They reveal a religious society that has been structured so God and the male are expected to take, not to give, and women are expected to serve both. If women find the arrangement demeaning, according to this novel they can and must redefine it.

In *Face of an Angel*, the women who perpetuate the original ending of "Dancing with the Devil" cannot change their own stories. Almost to the end, they blame marriage failures on themselves and offer convent life as the only viable alternative. Soveida, observing the daily realities of life, finally is able to offer them a different conclusion. She discovers that the devil may be male or female and may come from anywhere. She decides that the devil's presence is not the sinful fault of woman. Rather, women are often the victim, and their suffering places upon them the face of an angel, the wise and loving face of the spirit of understanding and improvement. As Sister Lizzie tells Soveida, even God needs to be improved, and the nuns are working on it. Soveida determines that men and women can also be improved, if the basic religious and cultural stories are reinterpreted. The devil's power was created by men and sustained by men and women, but women can refuse to sustain it any longer. First, women must learn that their service, even when it is hard and dirty, does not sully them but gives them grace. Second, people are not to blame for their attractions, and the causes of unhappiness are many and complex. Third, the magnitude of need and pain in all aspects of life creates in every person the duty to understand, to serve, and to forgive. Fourth, everyone who tries to help others through the struggle of daily life wears the face of an angel regardless of his or her righteousness in the eyes of the Church. And last, service, love, and improvement may be possible only when the old ending of the story gives way to a new beginning.

11

A SPIRITIST ELEMENT

In Latina literature, the spirit world manifests itself in various ways, depending on the part of the Americas portrayed. Writers such as Mora, Castillo, and Limón refuse to relegate their family dead to some distant and inaccessible heaven or hell. For them, the dead remain invisibly among the living, present in a parallel universe and sometimes able to comfort and advise their loved ones. These dead aren't fearsome, and the living do not require an intermediary to communicate with them. Thus, Mora can have tea with her ancestors and a saint or two, and Huitzitzilin can speak the old language with her courtyard spirits. In other situations, such as the Day of the Dead celebrations described by Mora and Escamill, the invited spirits may visit the family home but may not be visible or approachable.

A different familiarity with the dead pervades works by Latinas who live or have roots in the Caribbean islands. Included among these authors are Judith Ortiz Cofer, who writes about Puerto Rico; Margarita Engle and Cristina García, who write about Cuba; and Julia Alvarez, who writes about the Dominican Republic. While these authors differ in the number and importance of religious references in their works, they all reveal a population practicing Catholicism alongside *Espiritismo*, *Santería*, or Voodoo. The spirits surrounding their characters are less likely to be deceased family members who come willingly with consolation or advice. They are powers from the beyond who must be ritually summoned by a priest-like intermediary,

167

usually in a particular setting and sometimes with blood sacrifice. Some of them bring harm.

One type of spiritist practice came to the Caribbean with Yoruban slaves from Africa, and another came from the "scientific" spiritism of nineteenth-century Europeans such as the French Hippolyte Revail (aka Allan Kardec) and the Spanish Amalia Soler (Brandon 1993). In these practices, communication with the dead requires the assistance of a medium who has been born to the position, spiritually chosen for it, or trained into it. The types of spiritism differ in their rituals and in the types of favors that the intermediary may request. Properly summoned, a spirit may offer a solution for a victim of physical or emotional pain, provide information privately to a spiritist in a trance, speak to everyone present through a medium at a séance, or be persuaded to block the activities of some other spirit. In Voodoo, evil spirits may be invoked and directed.

In the communities described by Caribbean-American authors, Catholic and spiritist beliefs themselves are complex, and their interwoven practices vary among and within nations across Latin America. As a whole, these are not blends but syncretic composites in which varying deities, beliefs, and rituals exist alongside each other. They create a mix or aggregate like gravel: the individual components retain their identity. No two samples of the mixture are likely to be identical, but the result can be recognized and named.

Spiritism's deities, who likewise are syncretic, may combine the physical traits and the mystical powers of Yoruban deities and orishas (saints) with those of Christ, the Blessed Virgin Mary, and the Catholic saints. They vary from depiction to depiction, and any icon may draw from the repertoire of symbols related to either of the originals. The result is composite deities such as Shango (of various spellings), who may appear as a combination of the Catholic Saint Barbara and the Yoruban deity Shango. In Catholic legend, Saint Barbara was tortured for converting to Catholicism and refusing to marry, and she is linked with thunder and lightning; in Yoruban practice, Shango is the god of passion, thunder, lightning, and fire. Caribbean spiritist iconography of Shango and other saints/orishas undeniably favor Roman Catholic depictions of the saints and Mary with the child Jesus. The most noticeable differences are in skin color and the addition or substitution of accompanying symbols. For example, one statue of Ochún, a river goddess and the wife of Shango, presents her as *la Señora de la Caridad del Cobre*, the virgin patroness of Cuba, but this virgin wears the white cloth sacred to Ochún and shows boat imagery in her crown and at her feet (Lindsay 1996).

Of the spiritist influences in folk Catholicism, the most difficult for the official Church to accept is *Santería*. Although broad definitions often present *Santería* as a combination of Catholicism and African Yoruba, more detailed discussions reveal disagreement about whether this spiritism is a variant of Catholicism, a variant of an African religion, or a separate religion altogether. Catholic theologian Espín (1994) declares *Santería* a separate religion and refuses to recognize it as a form of popular Catholicism. He points out that the differences between the *Santería* practiced in the Caribbean and the Yoruba religion practiced on mainland Africa are as great as those between popular Catholicism and Roman Catholicism. He agrees that Yoruba practitioners may have superimposed some Catholic elements on their religion as camouflage to protect it from religious or political persecution, but he insists that Latino Catholicism itself has not absorbed elements of African Yoruba. He resists spiritism as fervently as he does Protestantism, Pentecostalism, and other behaviors that many U.S. Latinas/os have adopted while continuing to call themselves Catholic. He's uncomfortable with it even though he is not uncomfortable with Amerindian spirit influences in the popular Catholicism of the U.S./Mexico border.

An opposing view of the origins of *Santería* is offered by George Brandon, who devotes most of his study to Cuban *Santería* but also addresses other types of spiritism. While he agrees that Caribbean slaves were forced to learn Catholic prayers, he contends that Catholic beliefs were not absorbed into African religions. Rather, African practices joined Catholic ones to create a new kind of Catholicism. Some of the changes may have occurred in individual homes as African house slaves shared their rituals, particularly those related to healing, in the process of helping their Spanish mistresses raise children and maintain plantation houses. Other far-reaching changes may have occurred in sixteenth-century Cuban cities, where the Church sought to indoctrinate the Africans through *cabildos* or religious brotherhoods. In order to attract and hold the African members, the Church may have allowed them to worship in their own style. Because the *cabildos* were also recreational clubs, Brandon maintains, African music and dance were permitted, and these forms of expression could not help but pass into the Catholic celebrations. Although the Catholic Church and the government eventually suppressed the *cabildos*, the practices continued in private, and the groups re-emerged on their own in the nineteenth century. Thus, Brandon credits the Catholic Church with both creating the syncretic form of *Santería* and slowing its development.

Both *Santería* and a more Spanish form of Catholicism have encountered additional obstacles in communist Cuba, particularly between 1959 and 1965. Perhaps, as Brandon maintains, the Castro government was more opposed to Catholicism and Protestantism than it was to Afro-Cuban religions, in part because it associated Catholicism with Western values and powers, but linked *Santería* with the cultural heritage of the people. Indeed, religious practice, especially Catholic practice, became more dangerous under communism. A ban on processions affected all religious groups, and any sect could be investigated as potentially political or even subversive in nature. In the face of such suspicion and repression, even the followers of *Santería* would be watched, and the similarities between their religion and Catholicism would be noted. In addition, any ritual expressions tolerated by the regime could also be subject to the regime's dictates about place, time, type, and audience. Eventually, *santeros* withdrew to private or even secret worship.

Recent novels by Margarita Engle and Cristina García call attention to this suppression of religion in Cuba, and they also affirm that both *Santería* and Catholicism are practiced carefully in order to avoid the suggestion of political or social activism. Engle's novel *Singing to Cuba* (1993), the title of which honors the pastors who were sent to labor camps for their refusal to give up liturgical song, carries a stronger tone of political exposé than García's. To Engle, all types of song, poetry, and rejoicing have been crushed in Cuba and can be heard only from the underground or from outside the island. Although religion is not her main focus and the religion she mentions most often is Catholicism, she does refer to the persistence of *Santería*, which she associates with the African Cuban population. Her main characters view it as a separate and frightening practice.

The two religions coexist more comfortably in García's novels *The Agüero Sisters* (1997) and *Dreaming in Cuban* (1992). García's characters, even characters in the same family, tend to favor Catholicism, spiritism, or no religion at all, but in most cases, they don't allow religion to separate them permanently any more than they allow politics or exile to do so. In *The Agüero Sisters*, the passionate Reina Agüero identifies with her beloved island itself, devoting little attention to any religion. Symbolically, however, she can be linked with the goddess Oyá, the fire-ruling wife of Shango, particularly after she is struck by lightning and reconstructed through skin grafts from friends and family. Dedicated to Cuba and the loveliness still remaining in the island, Reina seeks to re-create it as she herself has been re-created, gleaning assistance from whatever quarter seems promising: the *santero* and the Virgin; the wisdom of ancient Cuba and the politics of the new Cuban communities in the U.S.; the hard science pursued by her deceased father; and the magical cosmetics brewed by her sister, Constancia, in her U.S. kitchen. For Reina and for her sister, a disregard for formal Catholicism translates not into a lack of spirituality but into an openness to alternatives, religious or secular. What they oppose is anything that offers violence and deception, whether to their families or to their beloved island. At the end of the novel, Reina and Constancia embark on a quest recommended by a *santero* but conducted as much with Catholic prayer as with spiritist potions and dress. Their much-needed but much-resisted reconciliation results.

The characters in García's *Dreaming in Cuban* also become dissatisfied with one-sided solutions. Mother Celia tries to be a good communist, daughter Felicia chooses *Santería*, and daughter Lourdes holds her Catholicism in exile with her in New York City. Lourdes's observant daughter, Pilar, looks beyond them all and concludes, "I get the feeling that it's the simplest rituals, the ones that are integrated with the earth and its seasons, that are the most profound. It makes more sense to me than the more abstract forms of worship" (p. 199). The new generation represented by Pilar reels from its experience with the contradictory political and religious ideologies of its two "home" countries. Pilar herself, raised Catholic and anti-Castro in New York City, cannot find the balance point between mother and grandmother, new country and old, or capitalism and communism. Nor can she completely accept or reject either the saints and miracles of her mother's Catholicism, the saints and magic of her aunt Felicia's *Santería*, or her own agnostic leanings. Only by fleeing New York to sample her grandmother's life in Cuba can she begin to make her choices and learn to understand anyone else's. Like the islanders themselves, she ends up preserving as many options as possible so that life and family unity may continue.

Literary portrayals such as these by Engle and García cannot settle Espín and Brandon's argument about whether Catholicism absorbed some parts of Yoruba, Yoruba adopted some Catholic ways, or *Santería* is a third, separate religion altogether. However, the stories do reveal Catholicism and spiritism existing alongside each other in the same community, the same family, and possibly even in the same household. Ultimately, Latina writers do not seem troubled by the problem of religious genealogy that preoccupies Espín and Brandon. They know that Catholicism and spiritism coexist because they have witnessed it daily. Some authors, such as Achy Obejas, include *Santería* as another aspect of their *mestizaje*. In her stories in *We Came All the Way from Cuba So You Could Dress Like This?* (1994), Obejas mentions it alongside Catholic and

Amerindian practices, even allowing one character to gauge the depth of a friendship by her own willingness to describe her mixed practices. She and others, regardless of their own affiliations, appear to recognize that religious rituals of all types help the people to honor the joys and cope with the trials of living. Ignoring the presence of these rituals would not only separate the writers from their heritage but diminish the honesty of their writing. They present spiritists as real people rather than monsters, saints, or caricatures. They depict *Santería* and *Espiritismo* not as either/ or alternatives to Catholicism but as elements of their total spirituality, their total set of options in times of need.

The daily trials for which a person might consult a spiritist include physical and emotional suffering. One author who repeatedly defends *Espiritismo* as a healing practice is Judith Ortiz Cofer. In her mixed-genre book *Silent Dancing* (1990), her novel *The Line of the Sun* (1989), and the short story "Bad Influence" in *An Island Like You* (1996), she includes a benign spiritist in the form of a grandfather with a mystical conduit to hidden knowledge. The grandfather's insights are a gift he humbly accepts and freely offers to those who need guidance. In the *Silent Dancing* essay "Talking to the Dead," Ortiz Cofer praises her own grandfather for his *mesa blanca* spiritism. She writes that Grandfather accepts his clairvoyance and insights with a humble, respectful sense of gratitude and honor. Patiently enduring the daily trial of his wife's skepticism about his gift, he maintains his altar and his mahogany wand and continues to worry over the problems of his supplicants. Grandfather eventually proves himself to Grandmother by divining the location of their son Hernán, who has dropped out of contact with them after seeking work in the United States. Grandfather's spirits reveal that Hernán has fallen victim to a labor recruitment scam through which New York farmers import cheap labor on the promise of good wages. Treated more like prisoners than workers, the men are unable to escape their captors because they have no idea where they are geographically, they are not allowed outside contacts such as personal mail, and they are penniless after the growers deduct living expenses from their pay. Only through Grandfather's spirit messages can his family locate Hernán and begin legal procedures to free the enslaved workers.

In the story "Bad Influence," Ortiz Cofer offers a more skeptical view of the supernatural aspects of *Espiritismo*. Here, the narrator's spiritist grandfather is asked to heal an adolescent girl who has quit eating. The narrator, an adolescent herself, asks her grandmother why the girl's mother doesn't hire a psychiatrist instead. The grandmother explains that mental illness requires a psychiatrist, but soul sickness requires someone who will ask the girl's sympathetic spirits for guidance. In this story, the grandfather determines that the *mala influencia* affecting the girl comes from a man living with the girl's mother, and he convinces the mother to throw the man out. Later, the girl insinuates that she planned the whole interlude. Unable to think of any other way to get the abusive boyfriend out of their home, she says, she refused to eat so her mother would be told the truth about her boyfriend by the spiritist, an adult she would believe. This claim and the narrator's acceptance of it suggest that spiritist healing results from psychological manipulation rather than miraculous intervention. Ortiz Cofer herself seems to entertain this explanation. When her grandfather talked about his interventions and his supplicants, she reports, he discussed them in terms closer to psychology than religion. Echoing a nineteenth-century European view of spiritism, she insists that the *Espiritismo* she includes in her own creative works never exceeds what can be explained logically (Ocasio 1994).

Such a view of spiritism as psychology or natural law, if it is widely accepted among island and mainland Puerto Ricans, may help clarify the easy mix of Catholicism and spiritism in Puerto Rican life. If the people see spiritism as folk psychology rather than worship, as Ortiz Cofer says she does, then spiritism is not a matter of religion at all. However, such a facile division of science and religion raises several concerns. First of all, since the Catholic Church opposes spiritism in a way it does not oppose the science of psychology, the Church must define it as an infringement on its religious hegemony. Also, the symbols and iconography of *Espiritismo*—the *mesa blanca*, as well as the representation of the Catholic deity and saints on that altar—suggest a spiritual connection not typical of psychology. Indeed, Ortiz Cofer does not explicitly deny that Catholicism and spiritism have joined forces. She mentions both beliefs when she describes the rituals she avoids even though she accepts that they comfort many Puerto Ricans. In her interviews as well as in her creative works, she indicates that the practices proceed side-by-side, both on the island and on the mainland. Among the people she describes, a spiritist is thought to be blessed in a more spontaneous and valuable manner than a priest. More important, the spiritist has the advantage of being trusted as one of the people.

While the Ortiz Cofer stories don't resolve the paradoxical relationship between Catholicism and spiritism, they do reveal the friction between *Espiritismo* and *Santería*. In *Silent Dancing* Ortiz Cofer writes that the powerful matrons of the village are willing to consult her grandfather, but they avoid *santeros* as devil worshipers. In *An Island Like You*, her story "Bad Influence" reveals a similar rejection of *Santería* when the grandmother insists that her *espiritista* husband works only through the powers of heaven. To some extent, Ortiz Cofer discloses, their antipathy follows class and color lines: "*Santería*, like voodoo, has its roots in African blood rites. . . . *Espiritismo*, on the other hand, entered the island via the middle classes who had discovered it flourishing in Europe" (p. 30). Brandon mentions this same division, pointing out that *Espiritismo* came from Europe, and like Catholicism, it tends to follow Spanish genealogy; but *Santería* is from Africa, and in recent decades some African Americans have embraced it as part of their ethnic heritage. According to Brandon, these racial issues complicate the effort to join or completely separate *Espiritismo* and *Santería*. He addresses the dilemma by putting them at opposite ends of a continuum and then locating individual populations and locales somewhere on the line connecting them. Furthermore, Brandon maintains that Catholic and spiritist influences also fluctuate by population and locale, but not congruently with the varieties of spiritism. He agrees that the Roman Catholic opposition to both *Espiritismo* and *Santería* has not eradicated the presence of either one in the folk Catholicism that originates in the Caribbean. He represents the relative components of this folk Catholicism by superimposing a second continuum over the first, this time using Catholicism and spiritism as the end points.

The interrelationships among Catholicism, *Santería*, Voodoo, and *Espiritismo* include the importance of healing ceremonies and the assumption that spirits are able to cause suffering and ill fortune. The ancient Catholic Church accepted the presence of evil spirits and instituted a ritual for their exorcism. Today, the rite still exists, both in its simple form during the sacrament of Baptism and in a solemn form, which requires the officiating priest to have permission from a bishop. Before approving such a serious invocation of Christ's power to free the victim from evil influence, the leadership must ascertain that the illness is spiritual, not psychological (United States Catholic Conference 1997).

The spiritist approach to controlling evil spirits is likewise ritualized and entrusted to specialists. According to Brandon, both the *santero* and the *espiritista* are considered healers, but the *espiritista* is relegated to a trainee position and limited to expertise in *causas*, those less potent but still bothersome spirits who can bring about disease. The more powerful *santero*, on the other hand, commands the right to conduct worship of the orisha and to persuade them to act. In general, the *espiritistas* and the *santeros* maintain separate meeting times, meeting places, and symbols, and only the *santeros* insist upon being paid for their services. These generalities, of course, are drawn from a pool of widely varying individual cases. Brandon asserts that a clear distinction doesn't exist in reality.

The separation of these practices isn't clear in most Latina creative writing, either. In the works of Ortiz Cofer, the practices identified as European spiritism are sometimes closer to *Espiritismo* and other times closer to *Santería*, and all are practiced by "Catholics." In *Silent Dancing* and "Bad Influence," the behaviors are much closer to *Espiritismo*, and they are treated in a positive tone as European-based, benevolent, and successful. In *The Line of the*

Sun, however, only the Puerto Rican islander, Papá Pepe, is defined as following an innocent, European-based *mesa blanca* spiritism, and he is ineffectual against his grandson, Guzmán's, problems. The *espiritista*, Rosa, also an islander, receives less respect than Papá Pepe, partly because she is a single woman living alone outside of town and partly because she has been influenced by a New York City *santero*. This tainted woman not only cannot help Guzmán, but she casts the boy and herself into a hopeless, obsessive love relationship when she tries to cleanse him. In later but unrelated events after the characters have relocated to Paterson, New Jersey, a Puerto Rican *espiritista* and an African *santera* join forces against labor union problems, and they unintentionally set fire to their apartment building and kill many of their neighbors. Stories such as these preserve a prejudice against *Santería*, but at the same time they blur the distinction between *Espiritismo* and *Santería* rituals and capabilities. The narrator of *The Line of the Sun* admits, "the rites and philosophy of spiritism were much more complicated than I cared to know" (p. 238).

In *The Line of the Sun*, political turmoil provides the context in which spiritism operates. Similar turmoil backgrounds the Julia Alvarez novel *How the García Girls Lost Their Accents* (1992), and it receives further mention in her later collection of personal essays, *Something to Declare* (1998). In both books, Alvarez refers to Haitian Voodoo, a practice closer to *Santería* than to *Espiritismo*. The spiritists themselves are Haitian servants who practice on their own with powders and spells, but who are not priestesses. Although the fictional García family and the real Alvarez family are Catholics who rarely seek Voodoo help, neither one objects to a visit to a *santero* if it is made discreetly. The children seem to be particularly aware of Voodoo, perhaps because they spend more time with the family servants. In this respect, the children may be a twentieth-century urban echo of the colonial plantation mistresses described by Brandon. Because they often face problems that their own religion doesn't solve, they remain open to approaches suggested by the Haitian maids, particularly those with a noticeable aura of power and mystery.

In *How the García Girls Lost Their Accents*, Alvarez describes the concerted effort of the Haitian maid, Chucha, to enjoin her spirits against the Trujillo forces that threaten the García family. When two agents of the secret police show up at the house while the mother is absent and the father is in hiding, Chucha delays and misleads the men until the mother returns. Then, with the attention no longer on her, she covertly sprinkles a powder and grumbles as she leaves the room. The García girl, Yoyo, recognizes these actions and knows Chucha has cast a spell to neutralize the power of the agents. It does.

Chucha's spiritual practices include a strong Christian element, as well. Fifi, the youngest García girl, compares the taciturn woman to a nun because she remains single, keeps quiet, rarely leaves the grounds, and offers Catholic prayers to ease the García family into Catholic heaven. Chucha's own contributions to this multivocal novel reveal the loyalty, compassion, and benevolence she has felt toward her employers since they gave her refuge during Trujillo's 1937 massacre of Haitians living in the Dominican Republic. Nonetheless, Chucha's pious behavior takes place in the private room she has to be given because the other maids fear her Voodoo and her habit of sleeping in a coffin. She is a memorable individual with a demeanor and style of her own, not a stereotyped representative of a counterculture. She differs greatly from other practitioners in the novel, most notably from the Haitian-Dominicana Pila, whose Voodoo includes convincing everyone that she consorts with demons in the coal shed. As unfaithful to the family as she is hostile to her fellow servants, Pila eventually disappears with many García family treasures.

Alvarez's personal memories of Voodoo also emerge in her essays in *Something to Declare* (1998). In "My Second Opera," she details the result of her grandmother's request that the Haitian maid, Misiá, seek Voodoo intervention so the government will allow the Alvarez family to visit the United States. Young Julia is allowed to attend the ceremony with Misiá for a reason that helps define the range of petitions taken to *santeros* as well as the casual attitude with which they were consulted: she goes because "a minor petition, along with the big one that we all escape the country, was that I learn to be a fine young lady instead of the loud-mouthed tomboy I was bent on becoming" (p. 33). The ceremony involves chanting, drumming, and dancing; its symbols include candles, images, nuts, spices, fragrant water, and a goat garlanded with flowers. Miraculously, a week later, the entire family receives permission for an indefinite stay in New York City.

This escape, however, is not the only outcome of the incident for Alvarez. The spectacle of the Voodoo rite remains in her mind, not just because it is unique for her but because she has noticed its similarities to the Catholic high masses she attends with her family. Years later in New York, upon seeing the opera Aïda, she recognizes the parallel between its Egyptian pageantry and the two kinds of religious celebrations she has witnessed. In her mind, the three link up as "similar in spirit" (p. 34). Each has been able to inspire awe and wonder in her. As Alvarez writes in the essay "Writing Matters," "the function of ritual is not to control this baffling universe but to render homage to it, to bow to the mystery" (p. 280).

A similarity of spirit may well be the element that invited spiritism into popular Catholicism and keeps it there today. Perhaps this similarity of spirit allows many people to view the systems as complementary sources of expression, help, and healing. Certainly, spiritism and Catholicism coexist in Latina stories about the Caribbean and those areas of the U.S. and Mexico influenced by contact with or migration from the Caribbean. To varying degrees, Cristina García, Judith Ortiz Cofer, Julia Alvarez, and others accept or even appreciate this multifaceted spirituality that has helped sustain the people they love.

12
A Goddess

One indication of the religious debate that underlies much Latina writing is the frequent use of religious motifs. When studied closely, these patterns present not only a persistent, underlying habit of thought but also an ongoing redefinition of Catholicism. Significantly, the redefinition extends to the most basic level of belief, that of deity. Through it, the Virgin of Guadalupe or another Dark Virgin becomes a goddess.

The ubiquitous appearance of this Virgin/goddess deserves considerable analysis. That the metaphor itself would be manipulated is not hard to accept. As Díaz-Stevens (1994) points out, the transmission of religion and culture has been largely the duty of a matriarchal core that keeps the family together, remembers its stories, and furthers its faith life. The existence and power of this core is also recognized by Latina writers, who re-create it in their stories and refer to it frequently in interviews and articles. They affirm that the female elders of the family—mother, aunts, grandmothers—transmit the culture and insist upon religious observances. Furthermore, this core confirms their confidence in womanhood itself for its rebellious power, its adaptability, its sense of community, its long memory, and its dedication to a future.

The strength of this female unit is reinforced by the presence of its deity, the Virgin of Guadalupe, who always stands ready to help her people. Since her appearance in sixteenth-century Mexico, she has been a major religious and cultural symbol for Latin Americans as a whole, regardless of their religion, nationality, status, or gender. Guadalupe is a spiritual guide who inspires her people to resist political, social, economic, and religious domination from outside or inside the country. She stands on her own as a vestige of the Mesoamerican ancient past, and as such, she sanctifies the land, the old religions, and the non-Spanish blood of its people. Although Guadalupe has been admitted to official Catholic iconography as one form of the Blessed Virgin Mary, she differs significantly from the official Mary.

One characteristic of the Virgin of Guadalupe that bases her solidly on the soil of the Americas is the tradition of her appearance on Mount Tepeyac, the sacred mountain of the Mexica earth goddess Tonantzin. This tradition allows her an intermediate position between a ruler of the fertile earthy dominion and the demure, virginal Mother of God brought by the Spanish. Another characteristic is her reputation as a rebel who has interceded for the poor and the dark-skinned ever since her sixteenth-century appearance before Juan Diego, a Christianized Mexica man. At that time, her miraculous image on Juan Diego's cloak forced the Spanish bishops of Mexico to listen to him despite his color and his poverty; and indeed, the power of her intercession appears to have continued into the twenty-first century with the canonization of Juan Diego as a Catholic saint. Robert Ellsberg, author of the 1997 book *All Saints*, comments that Juan Diego has become a symbol of the poor and marginalized who are dear to God (Pattison 2002), and Father Eduardo Fernández (1997) writes of the people's feeling of visibility and equality when a church in Las Cruces honored their *Morenita* (Guadalupe, the "Little Dark One") by moving her statue from the church entry to the church proper.

A third significant aspect of the Virgin of Guadalupe, and one that increases her importance for many Latin American women, is her fertility, an element emphasized by the black sash that gathers her gown above her waistline and announces, in the way of her people, that she is pregnant. Latin American women inside and outside of the United States interpret this openness about pregnancy as a blessing on woman's role as a sexual being. Through her sexuality, their "Lupe" participates fully in the lives of the common people. She is poor and *mestiza*. She is pregnant, perhaps not entirely by choice. She must give herself and her child into the care of a stepfather. Eventually, she sees her child die when the government does not protect him. In spite of all that, however, she remains powerful. In heaven, she commands Christ's filial respect and influences his actions. On earth, as a cultural icon, she wields power over the males who control Church and government.

These are tremendous feats that cannot be completely explained by Guadalupe's link to Tonantzin. Even before the Conquest and the arrival of the weaker Mary of the Catholic Church, the power of Tonantzin and the other female earth powers was already being overshadowed by the emerging war god of the ruling Aztecs. These former protectors of crops and regeneration took on frightening features and became deadly deities, and the Catholic missionaries naturally reinforced this degradation, for they opposed devotions to any pagan goddess, particularly one wearing a skirt of snakes and a necklace of human hearts (Castillo 1995a). Still, the Virgin of Guadalupe somehow overcame her implied association with demons and the snake of Eden. Recovering Tonantzin's former power but adopting the gentle appearance of Mary, she has attracted men and women alike. By avoiding assimilation into the meek Mary, she has defeated male domination in a way that Tonantzin and the Spanish Blessed Virgin Mary could not. As a result, *la Virgen* can be trusted to provide understanding, comfort, joy, and identity, particularly for Latin American women.

The earth goddess/Guadalupe conflation permeates Latina literature. Edna Escamill invokes her blessing to open her novel *Daughter of the Mountain* (1991), and Escamill's character Maggie learns to relate this constant female power to the mountain called *La Madre* by her curandera grandmother. Maggie survives the confusing and dangerous pathways of *mestizaje* by remaining centered on La Madre regardless of her own physical distance from the mountain. The place and its nurturing female deity replace the distant, constantly suffering and dying Christ and saints petitioned by the village priest.

An equally loving but more militant goddess emerges in the Denise Chávez novel *Face of an Angel* (1994). Soveida, who finds no positive models among the priests, fathers, and husbands of her acquaintance, also rejects God the Father as a source of spiritual healing. She prays to God the Mother, a figure far different from the loving but powerless Blessed Virgin Mary of the Catholic Church. God the Mother may be an ephemeral sister, but she is one who agitates, who makes herself known and feared. She laughs at gender roles.

This changeability of the goddess/Virgin is an apt example of the reciprocity between art and life. Artist Felipe Ehrenberg (1996), discussing the varied depictions of Guadalupe, finds her darning socks, sporting about in tennis shoes, table dancing, or protesting the treatment of migrant workers. Theologian Orlando O. Espín (1994) also notes her appearance on posters, on publications of every sort, and even on walls as graffiti as she appears to sponsor numerous Latin American social and political movements. Indeed, political activist Margaret Randall (1996) reports that many Latinas associate their Lupe with guerrilla rebellion. Randall cites 1969 statistics revealing that almost 50 percent of the Latino people in the U.S./Mexico borderland proclaimed Guadalupe their favorite over God himself.

The practical relationship noted by Ehrenberg, Espín, and Randall is important to any discussion of the popularity of Guadalupe in U.S. Latina literature. Among fluctuating ideas, beliefs, and practices, the Virgin occupies the shifting middle ground. Guadalupe doesn't emerge as the *only* alternative but as *another* alternative, as a model useful in conjunction with others. She has held her place for nearly five centuries, but she has not aggressively displaced other religious powers the way that the Aztec war god, Huitzilopochtli, once pushed aside the goddesses of earlier cultures, or the way that the Spanish God the Father superseded the Aztec gods. To consider Guadalupe the ultimate answer would be to deny her the very adaptability and balance that have preserved her.

Neither is Guadalupe a symbol for lost matriarchal superiority. The Aztec political structure was matrilineal, not matriarchal: it traced kinship through the mother's line, but it left decision-making to the males, and thus is better described as patriarchal. Furthermore, neither the Aztecs nor their predecessors granted superiority to goddesses. Rudolfo Anaya (1996) reiterates Gloria Anzaldúa's 1987 opinion about the de-emphasis of goddesses by the Aztecs, who favored male power and the violence of the war god. Anaya maintains that the Aztec god Quetzalcóatl, a winged and feathered serpent, shared power and space with the earth goddesses at first, but later he chose the sky over the earth by mating with a heavenly sister instead of an Earth goddess. In Anaya's opinion, Quetzalcóatl thereby abandoned the earth, while Tonantzin remained there; and when the Spanish came, she joined forces with the Virgin of Guadalupe.

Anzaldúa, who links Guadalupe and former earth powers, has noted the similarities in pronunciation between Guadalupe and the goddess Coatlalopeuh, who herself is linked to the goddess Coatlicue, who bore the war god Huitzilopochtli, and the goddess Tonantzin, who preferred animal or bird sacrifices to human ones. During colonization, she insists, the Spanish Church discouraged this link by associating Guadalupe with the chaste Blessed Virgin Mary and shifting the ancient goddess's earth powers onto images of whores, devils, or fearsome icons from the Aztec past. Thus, the human and sexual traits of Guadalupe/Coatlalopeuh became sinful and forbidden. The popular Guadalupe recovers some of her humanity and sexual identity.

Theologian Espín says the Church rejects the reassociation of Guadalupe with pre-Contact figures. Although he recognizes that the orthodox Blessed Virgin Mary and the Virgin of Guadalupe are not duplicates, he doesn't accept even a long-past equivalency between Guadalupe and Tonantzin. Rather, he attributes the modern-day differences between Guadalupe and the Blessed Virgin to a misunderstanding that began during the conversion of the Aztecs. In his view, the conversion effort was severely hampered by poorly educated missionary priests who did not know how to relate God the Father to the male god of the Aztecs. The God the Father they presented did not offer the gender duality typical of Aztec gods such as Ometeotl, who was masculine and warlike but had a feminine, nurturing dimension. Even though God the Father purportedly included the nurturing attributes of God the Son and the Holy Spirit, the early Catholic priests were unable to convince the people that an all-male Trinity could both rule its people and care for them.

Missing the female balance, these Aztecs looked to the Spanish Blessed Virgin Mary, but they found her inadequate in her Church-designated role as "handmaiden," or obedient servant to the Trinity and its goals. Therefore, they deified Guadalupe and assigned her the power and duty to nurture and protect. She became an equal, a balance for the god. This solution also helped the early converts make folk sense of the all-male Trinity, for if Mary/Guadalupe became an equal with God the Father, then the two deities together could produce Jesus, the son of god(s). The Trinity thus would be linked to the Holy Family, and it could be accepted as sovereign. Espín says that the missionaries of ensuing centuries tried but were unable to correct such aberrant doctrines, so even today, the Virgin of Guadalupe is conflated with the Aztec Mary-as-aspect-of-god, rather than with the Catholic Mary-as-chosen-servant-of-God.

Evidence of the difference between these two Marys emerges in an old tale of the Southwest Indian tribes, "La comadre Sebastiana," or nosy neighbor Sebastiana, a representation of death. In this story, a starving man takes a chicken from his wife's flock and sneaks off to the woods to enjoy a private meal. Three separate strangers approach to ask him to share his chicken. The first is the Lord, whom the man refuses on the grounds that the Lord doesn't treat the poor as well as he does the rich. The second is the Virgin Mary, whom he refuses on the grounds that she doesn't use her mother power to force her son to treat the poor equally with the rich. The third is the gaunt Doña Sebastiana. The man shares his chicken with her because he knows she takes equally from the rich, the poor, the beautiful, the ugly, the old, and the young. Doña Sebastiana rewards the man with the power to cure the sick, but she warns him that this power will not be absolute: he must allow her to take the people who are marked to die. Eventually, he oversteps his limits and is gathered among the dead (Griego y Maestas and Anaya 1980).

Two elements of this story reinforce the separation between the Virgin Mary and Guadalupe. The Mary of this story is the Mary-as-chosen-servant-of-God. She does not merit reverence because she will not stand up to Jesus in defense of her people. Even worse, her weakness has allowed the divine power of the universe to tip out of balance. The Lord acts in error because Mary is only his servant, not his mother and equal, and Death can assume control because the life power, the mother power, has not asserted itself.

Modern-day Latin American women inside and outside the United States continue to recognize this distinction between their *mestiza* Virgin and the Blessed Virgin Mary. Sandra Cisneros (1996) admits that she "bolted the door against" the Church version of the Virgin of Guadalupe, who was "nothing but a goody two shoes meant to doom me to a life of unhappiness" (p. 156). The all-or-nothing choice offered by this virgin—that is, to be saintly or to be corrupt—didn't accommodate Cisneros or the women she knew, all of whom wanted to love unashamedly with body and soul. Once Cisneros associated *la Lupe* with the ancient goddesses, however, she no longer felt guilty about her own sexual power and desires. She came to honor the conflated Guadalupe as a goddess dedicated to helping Chicanas redefine themselves. This Lupe would inspire and *forgive* the poetry Cisneros (1995) elsewhere admits she writes to "anguish the Pope and make fathers cry" (p. 114). This is the Lupe a reader might recognize in the scene offered by another Latina writer, Liliana Valenzuela (1989), whose character Camila asks the Virgin if she really was a virgin. Valenzuela's Guadalupe remembers sexual desire and enjoys her own body. Furthermore, she blesses the human yearnings of Camila's heart.

U.S. Latinas who question Latin American religio-cultural attitudes toward sexuality often turn to Guadalupe for understanding. As girls, many of them questioned the traditional belief that Mary bore a child without having lain with a man. They later rebelled at the guilt imposed by the attitudes that only an immoral woman enjoys sex and that there is something inherently degrading about marriage and pregnancy. The Church message, according to the autobiographical writing of Rosario Ferré, has been that marriage means a regrettable loss of virginity, but marital sex will not be sinful as long as the wife suppresses her pleasure during intercourse. Sociological information about Mexican-American women verifies widespread resentment against this double standard that condones male sexual activity but labels the behavior sinful for women. These women are further incensed that the double standard has even been used against the victims of rape (Moore 1994).

Cisneros, who agrees that the Church maintains a double standard in sexual matters, prefers to believe that sexual passion, regardless of orientation, is understood and condoned. In her story "Little Miracles, Kept Promises," she seeks a goddess who resembles Coatlicue: "bare-breasted, snakes in your hands . . . swallowing raw hearts and rattling volcanic ash" (1991, p. 127). Cisneros's goddess is similar to the "Dark One" recognized by Escamill's character Adela Sewa, who accepts exclusion from the Catholic community in order to devote herself to a deity who has sharp, powerful teeth and who loves the desert and woman. This is also the goddess Ana Castillo (1996) describes as powerful in the realms of both the living and the dead, as opposed to the heavenly Mary of the Church.

For Pat Mora, too, the great female god contains multiple forms. She's a family friend in *House of Houses* (1997b), and in the 1997a *Aunt Carmen's* poem "La Buena Pastora (the Good Shepherdess)," she watches over a field of sheep in a manner usually associated with Jesus. In the *Agua Santa* (1995) poem "Cuarteto Mexicano," Mora joins the power and wisdom of Coatlicue, *La Malinche*, Guadalupe, and *La Llorona* to create a divine presence who urges women to test their inner voices, resist religio-cultural stereotypes, recognize their ability to inspire, and share their wisdom.

The Virgin of Guadalupe typically models action and fosters an awareness of alternatives. In *Daughter of the Mountain*, her shrine is a candlelit hiding place of linked spaces, open windows, and adobe walls. Built from desert materials and decorated with folk art, it is the kind of safe, integrated place that is often unavailable to Chicanas, who have neither the room of their own mandated by Virginia Woolf, nor the comforting "here" Gaston Bachelard praises in his discussion of the poetics of space. To Maggie, the chapel provides the safe zone that is unavailable in her abusive home, in the stern residence of the Tres Hermanas, or in her local church.

The Virgin is steadfastly present for the desperate characters in Estela Portillo Trambley's (1983a) play *Puente Negro*, as well. Here, Guadalupe presides over a hiding place for Mexicans illegally crossing from Juárez, Mexico, to El Paso, Texas. These people lack a safe zone in Mexico, in transit, or in the United States. They also are deluded by the American Dream, which promises an escape from poverty but actually may deliver them into virtual slavery under employers who threaten to expose them to *la Migra*. Their *coyote* Chaparro knows these dangers. Squat and tough as her dwarf oak namesake, she tries to avoid emotional connection with her clients, but she carefully protects them from *la Migra* and abusive employers. Chaparro has established an overnight refuge where she once unearthed a Virgin statue at the mouth of a hidden arroyo near Puente Negro, a border landmark on her trail. She maintains the Virgin's altar in the shelter and uses the place with some confidence until one night she arrives to find an aged Chicano sleeping there. Against her advice, Chaparro's softhearted clients insist that the man share their shelter and food, and in the morning, he reports them to *la Migra* to collect the bounty on *mojados*. The group escapes, and the Virgin stays behind in the now-useless shelter. Her sympathy with the rebels is clear, but so is the message that the people must stand with her against the political tyranny of borders and the economic temptations of the American Dream. The people and their leaders must remain alert and mobile in the dangerous zone between nations, religions, and cultures. The Virgin's protection of the hiding place fails because the people are betrayed from within.

A dark-skinned Virgin similar to Guadalupe signifies understanding and concern for the people of the Caribbean, as well. There, she is the Black Virgin thought to be associated with the black Guadalupe of Cárceres, Spain, a miraculous black statue first revered in the twelfth century in the Extremadura region of that country (Ehrenberg 1996). She is believed to have appeared frequently among the poor people of the islands. In Puerto Rico, the original "Black Virgin" was a black statue that the Spanish soldiers brought to Ponce in the eighteenth century. Rosario Ferré (1996) writes that her nursemaid once told her to stay in league with this powerful Virgin, for she was a fighter who expected her petitioners to fight alongside her.

The Black Virgin is said to have appeared many times in Puerto Rico. Ortiz Cofer, herself not a practicing Catholic, nonetheless respects this Virgin for the comfort her patronage gives the women of Hormigueros. In *Silent Dancing* (1990), she affirms that "being a woman and black made Our Lady the perfect depository for the hopes and prayers of the sick, the weak, and the powerless" (p. 44). Esmeralda Santiago verifies this role of the Black Virgin in family matters. In *When I Was Puerto Rican* (1993), she reports that although her mother professes no religion and her immediate family's religious observances are casual, the traditions surrounding the Virgin still influence her life. When Santiago's extended family suffers the death of an infant, their *curandera* prescribes the proper devotion: a pure young woman among them must close the baby's eyes to invoke the Virgin's protection for the rest of the children. Regardless of Esmeralda's terror, her mother insists that she comply because she is the available virgin, and the proper thing must be done.

Only when Esmeralda is much older does she appreciate the Virgin as powerful, aggressive, and able to protect her people. In

Almost a Woman (1998), she describes dancing the part of Our Lady of Lourdes under the guidance of her free-spirited coach. As Our Lady she leapt onto the stage, then stalked the kneeling Bernadette "like a hungry tigress, my long robes hissing, . . . a terrible vision . . . a warrior Virgin, mourning my Son" (p. 143). This "terrible vision" confounds the sweet apparition of Lourdes with the elemental presence of Tonantzin. This Lady wears a woman's gown, but the gown accentuates rather than conceals her sensuous movements, and it hisses like Coatlicue's skirt of snakes. This Lady leaps and paces, mourns with the drama of *La Llorona*, knows the wild power of her tiger gaze. She will demand action, not prayer; righteous anger, not humility.

A dynamic Black Virgin also reigns as Our Lady of Regla or as La Caridad del Cobre in Cuba, undaunted by government efforts to suppress Catholicism. Her miraculous representation is a wooden statue, little more than a foot tall, that was found floating in the sea near the copper mining area of El Cobre. Isasi-Díaz and Tarango (1988) link this Virgin to the highest-ranking Lucumi goddess Yemaya, a sea deity who came to Cuba long ago with the African slaves, and they credit her with strength, passion, and sensuality. In their opinion, Our Lady of Regla would be the preferable symbol in matters of morality and sexuality, for in nature and demeanor, she resembles Guadalupe more than she does the Blessed Virgin Mary. As she appears in the works of Cuban-American writers, Our Lady of Regla displays sensuality and a guerrilla instinct for leading the disadvantaged in unified action. Just as the Virgin of Guadalupe protects the illegal aliens of Trambley's *Puente Negro* only as long as they support one another, the Virgin of the Caribbean demands that her followers stand together.

In Cristina García's *Dreaming in Cuban* (1992), a beleaguered Virgin emerges through the creative instinct of Pilar, a teenage artist whose mother has coerced her into painting a Statue of Liberty for the Yankee Doodle Bakery. Pilar's portrait of Liberty combines the traditional Church iconography for Mary and the Cuban flair for colorful representation. In the finished painting, Liberty stands against a background that looks "irradiated, nuked out," her torch hovers out of reach, she wears a safety pin in her nose, she has "black stick figures pulsing in the air" around her, and the base of her statue reads, "I'M A MESS" (p. 141). The painting reiterates everything *Dreaming in Cuban* says about U.S. politics, Cuban-American attitudes, Latino religious beliefs, divided families, lost freedoms, and tarnished ideals in the wake of Castro's revolution and the Cuban exodus to the U.S. Family members on U.S. soil are no more tranquil than those still in Cuba, and devotions are ineffectual whether directed toward God, the Blessed Virgin, the Virgin of Cuba, the Statue of Liberty, or the portrait of Castro. The Virgin's loss of power in Pilar's eyes is symptomatic of a shattered culture. While Pilar depicts a Virgin under siege, however, she doesn't depict a defeated one. The hope for the Virgin in her story, and in many other Latina stories, lies in earthly cooperation with her, a cooperation specifically requiring the solidarity of female generations.

Certainly, most Latina writers place some form of the Virgin in the midst of Latina life and consciousness. However, they do not let her represent the entire Latin American culture or even its entire religious component. As Debra Castillo points out in *Talking Back* (1992), women's writing is not served by literary criticism that reduces their works to simplistic images of a mother goddess. The ancient earth goddesses and Guadalupe are individual elements among the many that authors explore as they relate the Latina experience. Likewise, their presence is but one element in the impact that the literature has on Latino culture and religion. Such forces are reciprocal. Guadalupe is in the literature because she is in the religious culture, and the more ways she is depicted in the literature, the more multifaceted she becomes in the culture and the religion. Ultimately, culture, religion, and literature influence and reflect each other, and to speak of any one of them is to have to consider the other two. Thus, the Virgin is not the whole, but neither can she be subtracted from it. Like their cultural and religious heritage, she is in the people and with them forever.

13

A Priestess

For all their power, adaptability, and appeal, the Black Virgin and the Virgin of Guadalupe still belong to the abstract, each existing as a symbolic or felt presence rather than a physical one. For all their solidarity with humans, they dwell in the spiritual realm. Thus, in the crises of daily existence, someone else, someone earthly—a priestess of sorts—must be accessible. In much Latina literature, this intermediary takes the form of a grandmother or a *curandera*, a flesh-and-blood fellow sufferer.

Priestess is an apt term for these women. They are holy, not in the sense of devotion to a particular Church, but in their dedication to the continued existence of their people and culture. They are trained not through convents but through their participation in the mingled sorrow and blessings of *lo cotidiano*. They are ordained through the confidence and respect given them by the ones who ask their counsel and healing.

Many of these characters seek peace and enlightenment by wandering alone in the desert or the mountains, as did Christ, John the Baptist, and countless others, or they go on pilgrimage and come back with an altered spiritual understanding. They learn to confess and to hear confession, to forgive and to accept forgiveness, and to move forward with hope. They keep their needs simple and their doors open. Their altars may well honor Christ, the Virgin, and the saints, but they may also welcome orisha, tarot cards, bird bones, flowers, stones, herbs, and pictures of loved ones and heroes. Accepting their human limits and mortality, they share their wisdom so later generations may build upon it.

The Grandmother or *curandera* need not be a literal grandmother. She might be an elderly aunt or friend, an aged midwife, a medicine woman, or any other female who is old, experienced, and devoted to the survival of the people. She nurtures the troubled family, especially the women, by her presence, her labor, her *cuentos*, and her command of family and community history. She monitors the younger generations and is accepted by them in a way their parents are not, so sometimes she can bridge over the mother–daughter and father–son rifts typical of adolescent years. She decides when the parents as well as the children are ready to receive and understand her guidance. The family who loses their Grandmother loses their compass, and the female members lose themselves, for the official priests and other males in their lives generally provide them with impractical counsel and unattainable goals.

According to Ana María Díaz-Stevens (1994), the Grandmother tradition is not a figment of literary imagination. Díaz-Stevens found it healthy and active in a Latino population she surveyed in New York City in 1980. When asked to name the individual they respected the most, not counting their own parents, two-thirds of the respondents named a person who fit the Grandmother model. The women they trusted were elderly, well known within the community, and experienced in leading the prayers and rituals that come from folk rather than Church traditions. Fully half of the young people said they had confided in such a woman, and another quarter thought they might do so if the need arose. Half of the respondents also agreed that they preferred the older woman to the local priest because she lived the same life they did, and she could understand the problems they brought to her.

U.S. Latina writers regularly include such Grandmother figures in their works. Many times, this elder is a self-sufficient single woman who can survive without male support and thus can operate outside of patriarchal rules and demands. Their model of passive resistance may have been developing since colonial times, when the indigenous woman lost even the small power she had held in her original culture. As Díaz-Stevens suggests, one function they retained was the direction of folk celebrations that surrounded official Church services and festivals. Through the hard work disdained by the priests—the cooking, the decorating, the gathering of family, and the other enhancements they devised for the required worship—they gradually imprinted folk custom on Church practice and became vital to the people's accommodation of the new religion. In a way, the devout female elder became a folk priestess simply *because* the patriarchal Church would not let her be a priest or nun. The haven and model their independence provided may well have inspired others to follow them, and thus their role became established.

During and after colonial times, the women most likely to possess the legal and economic freedom necessary to carry out this role would be widows, spinsters, and nuns, all of whom are abundant in Latina literature. With few exceptions, the nuns in the literature provide the weakest guidance, perhaps because their role in Latino culture has been too narrowly defined. In most stories, the nuns are a past memory from the middle-to-late twentieth century, a group of not-quite-women who may be sympathetic but who are paralyzed by their vows and hampered by their subservient position within the male-dominated Church. As recently as 1978, Enrique Dussel argues that in theory, a nun's unmarried status frees her for activism because men and children are not draining her energy or creating a vulnerable zone through which an enemy could strike. Dussel complains that Latin American nuns haven't capitalized on this opportunity to become activists, a failing he blames on their psychological servitude to outdated role models of humility and drudgery. To these religious women, he offers the model of Sor Juana, a nun who seized a share in the intellectual life of the sixteenth-century Spanish colony of Mexico.

Dussel himself may suffer psychological servitude to stereotypes. His choice of model is inappropriate, considering that the Church ultimately silenced Sor Juana. Furthermore, he insists that women who are not nuns cannot be politically involved because of their duty to husband, family, and home. He misses the point that people operating in isolation from the daily life of the people are doomed to fail. He would better admonish all women, secular as well as religious, to dedicate their minds and voices in a united effort. Such solidarity has apparently existed among the secular female population for centuries.

Disheartening and outdated as it is, Dussel's evaluation of the mindset of nuns seems to describe the role they play in much U.S. Latina literature. Although the writers don't treat Church women with the same tone of criticism and disrespect they attach to priests, they nonetheless portray nuns as puppets and victims. In Limón's *Song of the Hummingbird* (1996), the nuns surrounding Huitzitzilin behave hatefully, treating the old Mexica woman as if she were evil, demented, and contagious. They do what they must for her, speak doubtfully of her humanity, and disappear into the privacy of their convent lives as soon as they can. The nuns drawn by Ortiz Cofer and Alvarez show more personality and more engagement than this, but they still limit themselves to unobtrusive and ultimately ineffective acts of resistance. In Escamill's *Daughter of the Mountain* (1991), the three lay sisters take shape as individuals, but they still live prudish, pedantic lives that offer no useful model to Maggie. If these religious women hold any attraction for the young women they influence, it is the chance to trade an active, involved life for a peaceful, safe engagement with abstractions.

Only rarely does a nun stride onto the page the way Sister Margaret Elizabeth does in Denise Chávez's *Face of an Angel* (1994). Sister Lizzie seems to have launched a crusade to improve God. A self-proclaimed lesbian and feminist, she believes nuns deserve respect for the work they do. If they are to sew or cook for the priests, they need a better reason than Church tradition. Sister Lizzie reserves her own right to go out for pizza and beer with her Newman Center students, just as a priest might. She asserts that the choice to serve others does not eliminate one's own right to be active and to be loved. Rather, she is going to change God and tell the Church that people cannot face life alone and still be well, happy, and devout. She rejects all types of isolation, whether that of a homosexual, a lesbian, an unwillingly celibate person, a married person abandoned by a spouse, or anyone else cut off through role or custom. Sister Lizzie is undeniably a force, but she's unique among nun characters.

The women who consistently do surface as leaders are grandmothers and *curanderas*. These women have survived the trials that the common folk endure daily, be they ordinary burdens such as marriage and parenthood, or grievous ones such as rape, alcoholism, or domestic abuse. One such woman is the Yaqui Indian Adela Sewa, the grandmother in *Daughter of the Mountain*. Broken by a life of poverty and military disruption, ostracized by her Mexican village for having married a Spanish soldier, and almost defeated by alcoholism and despair, Adela returns to the more life-affirming practices of her ancient ancestors. In actions that suggest a turn toward the matriarchal core of spiritual leadership, Adela goes on pilgrimage to the sacred peak called *La Madre*. There she endures a symbolic death of her degraded self and a rising in the spirit of family and community. She becomes the conduit for this wisdom, passing it to young Maggie via casual advice, *cuentos*, straightforward talk, folk remedies, and a combination of Native American and Catholic rituals. To remind Maggie of the need to speak one's own presence amid a complex population, Adela tells her the story of the mystic ceremony performed long ago to free Maggie's tongue. To teach her to look everywhere for answers, she shares ancient Yaqui symbols and rites that the village priest won't condone. Through Adela's guidance, Maggie discards attitudes and behaviors that nurture neither interpersonal nor interracial peace. She learns to look for power within herself. She accepts that life is uncontrollable and that death must come. She accepts that her own journey into adulthood, like her pilgrimage with Grandmother to the shrine of El Tidadito, is a long walk to light a candle and return home, never looking back. When she has to leave La Milpa for the education that will allow her to smooth the path for other Native Americans in the Anglo world, she will still be able to find her way back to *La Madre*.

As a model of female spiritual leadership, Adela Sewa has much in common with the *curanderas* threaded through numerous other stories. Like them, she lives by herself, gathering plants for food, medicine, and barter. She is a controversial figure among the Anglos and the Anglicized natives, suspected of being a *bruja* because of her questionable past and her earth-centered practices. Never, however, does she pursue the negative or destructive ends associated with the evil sorcerers of Anglo tradition. A medicine woman is not a witch.

Pat Mora details the difference between the *curandera* and the witch in one of her *Nepantla* (1993) essays. *Curanderas*, she says, are a force for good. The folk medicine and folk psychology they practice are comforting traditions based on familiar and accessible natural elements, as well as seasonal and verbal rhythms. If they are able to cast a spell, they do so through the spiritual and cultural power that the people grant to *abuelitas*: the soothing, generous-spirited power of love and familiarity with the family. Through that power, an old woman like the one in Mora's poem "Abuelita Magic" (*Chants*, 1985) might know how to calm both her frantic daughter and her daughter's wailing infant by rattling a dried chili pod in the rhythm of a ceremonial chant. Through it, the *abuelitas* of countless other stories know how to brew teas, concoct poultices, recite folk wisdom, and tell the appropriate cautionary tale at the proper moment. And because of it, the younger generations, men and women alike, know to listen.

As a rule, grandmothers are also lovingly connected with the earth, as are the grandmothers in Mora's *House of Houses* (1997b) or Adela in *Daughter of the Mountain*. Even in big cities they will be linked to some type of garden, window box, or bit of yard. Aurora Levins Morales (Morales and Morales 1986), descended from a New York City family of Puerto Rican, U.S., and Jewish backgrounds, still finds references to the earth in the advice she receives from her great-grandmother, who insists that all one needs to have a home and family is the dedication to plant and care for them like a garden. In a more literal reference to cultivation, an elderly friend tells Aurora the earth cannot be fertile unless someone first loves it. Both statements bring to mind Pat Mora's fondness for gardens and the magic of sinking her essence into the mud that came from the Río Grande to feed her family and give them material for adobe. It is this reverence for life and common origins that marks the grandmother, female elder, or *curandera* as a priestess of the great Mother.

Curandera power may also be described as an attention to natural law. Ana Castillo, in *Massacre of the Dreamers* (1995a), insists that medicine women are neither *espiritistas* nor *brujas*. If they appear to be supernatural, it is because they are so completely attuned to the natural. Their depth of understanding, not magic, hones their powers of massage, herbal medicine, midwifery, and counsel. A belief that nature abhors separation and inequality fuels their efforts to maintain connections and value all elements of life.

Castillo's own character Doña Felicia in *So Far from God* (1993) demonstrates this sensitivity to a need for balance. Felicia is alone but not isolated, poor but not dependent. Castillo writes few details about the trials that taught Felicia her skills, but whatever they were, they prepared her to accept that all the bizarre happenings in Sofia's family have meaning and purpose. What she can do for the destroyed, resurrected, and re-destroyed girls, she does, even if sharing her knowledge involves putting up with the horse, Corazón, and the tenants from hell, and even if it means allowing Caridad to return to the earth first at Chimayo, then at the mountain cave, and finally at the bottom of the cliff. One of Felicia's great wisdoms is that her cures "in and of themselves are worthless without unwavering faith" (p. 59). Another is that one person or even one group alone doesn't have all the possible answers, and a third is that she cannot change the future, only prepare for it, for "knowing and preventing are two very different things" (p. 54).

Felicia, though unique in herself, belongs to a type familiar in Latina literature and life. According to Díaz-Stevens, the *curandera* role might also be filled by a *partera* who has inherited her role from her ancestors and who may herself have attended the births of several generations of the local families. The *partera* cares for the expectant mother and unborn child, and she claims the right to baptize the newborn immediately after birth. The community trusts her as a member who understands hard realities like poverty, dirt, pain, or loss, as well as the great joys of camaraderie, laughter, birth, marriage, and the many aspects of love. Moreover, she is dedicated to life and to whatever adaptation will preserve it. Escamill's Adela Sewa belongs to this wise but human company. She recovers the control of her own life partly so she will be able to bring Maggie into the world and then keep both Maggie and her mother alive. She also "births" Maggie into adulthood by teaching her to respect her *mestizaje* for the extra alternatives it will give her for functioning in an Anglo world.

Not restricted to the cultures of the Mexico/U.S. border, the midwife *curandera* has also accompanied the Caribbean migration to urban centers in the U.S. Northeast. Ortiz Cofer relates the well-known family story of her birth in Puerto Rico at the hands of the same midwife who had delivered her grandmother's twelve children. Although this old woman needed assistance because she had become forgetful, the family did not consider leaving her out of the event. In her later years in Paterson, Ortiz Cofer recognizes midwifery in the actions of neighbors who foster continuity for displaced Puertoriqueña/os. In "The Latin Deli: an Ars Poetica" (1993), she describes the barrio grocer who imports foods from the island. This deli owner, "a woman of no-age who was never pretty," attracts customers who just need to "gaze upon the family portrait/of her plain wide face" (p. 3). She satisfies spiritual as well as physical needs by "conjuring up products/from places that now exist only in their hearts—/closed ports she must trade with" (p. 4). The urge to draw forth and welcome, the ability to comfort and sustain—these mark the grocer as *partera* and *curandera*.

Among rural folks and in small villages, medicine women like these answer a very real need. Doctors and hospitals may not be available, and even if they are, the poor people may not be welcome there or may not wish to place their trust in the strangers there. Such a community appears in the Sandra Benítez novel *A Place Where the Sea Remembers* (1994), which is set in a Mexican coastal village that has only occasional service from an itinerant doctor. Even when the doctor visits, many of the people there prefer to rely upon the *curandera* Remedios and the *partera* Esperanza to support their spiritual and physical well-being. Some of them also resort to the *brujo* don Picho Lara, who charges to work his black magic. Remedios's actions underscore the difference between the benevolent power of a *curandera* and the negative power of a male witch doctor, for she labors for years to reconcile the sisters Marta and Chayo after Marta pays a *brujo* to curse Chayo's pregnancy. Remedios gains power through her accord with the elements and creatures of earth, fire, water, and air, all of whom are honored beside the Catholic symbols on her white altar. Like doña Felicia of *So Far from God*, she ministers by meditation and counsel over time, and like Felicia, she accepts that people must prepare to accommodate what cannot be changed. Because the curse was called down by Marta's malevolence toward the village and her own family, Remedios can only foster forgiveness and reconciliation between the sisters. One day the balance will have to be paid, for Marta continues yearning to move to El Paso. The story of discontent is one the elderly Remedios knows well because she has listened to all the stories of all the generations of all the families of the community. In the end, she cannot prevent Marta's flight to probable destruction in El Paso.

This lack of certainty, this human ability to occasionally fail, as Remedios and Felicia do, may be central to the cultural appeal of the *curandera*, *partera*, or grandmother. These women eat with the people, laugh and hurt with the people, die with the people. They live free from the officialdom and intellectualism that burden clerics and nuns. They don't have to prove anything because like all priestesses, they love their people, remember their stories, and intercede for them in any way they can.

14

A TRINITY

With the notable exception of *Song of the Hummingbird* (1996), which begins with Huitzitzilin stranded as the last survivor of her people, a significant number of Latina stories emphasize the need for united action among linked generations of women. Over and over, this core of women responds to a multitude of practical and spiritual challenges.

The literary insistence on female interconnectedness is too widespread to be ignored. It is not merely a stylistic device, or worse, a stock motif. It is not just the result of women preferring to tell stories about women. Rather, it reflects the realities of Latina experience. As revealed by Church and secular studies, Latino cultures foster a strong sense of family. Furthermore, it assigns the women of the family the duty to perpetuate cultural and religious practices. In populations threatened by discrimination, deportation, inner-city violence, and poverty, problem solving may well belong to the family, also, since they cannot always trust government agencies or afford professional help.

In families headed by women, solving problems *within the family* means solving them *among the women*. Even in male-headed families, women's problems have traditionally required women's solutions, for such problems are considered unworthy of male attention. Perhaps the women even prefer to be left alone in these matters, having discovered over time that they have more freedom to speak when they are among women than they do when they are in a mixed group. The literature produced by U.S. Latinas during

the last decades highlights the freedom and effectiveness of female solidarity. Family women and female communities share their
wisdom and energy to cope with economics, education, religion,
health, counseling, childrearing, and all the other demands of daily
life. They respect themselves and are respected for their efforts
to perpetuate life, culture, religion, and stories. Their unit, a self-
perpetuating triad of grandmother, mother, and daughter figures,
belongs to the here and now, not the abstract. As individuals, they
make mistakes and pay for them. They laugh, swear, cry, have
babies in or out of wedlock, love their men and despair over them,
understand sexual passion, know the satisfactions and trials of parenthood, and maintain a paradoxical relationship with their religion. They know *cuentos*, folk remedies, and family secrets as well
as the proper time to share them. They provide immediate, tan-
gible, audible assistance when they are physically present, and
when they are not, their remembered words furnish it.

In García's *Dreaming in Cuban* (1992), a typical triad in an
atypical situation survives their post-revolution separation despite
serious differences in politics and religion. Although they live in
two separate countries, they remain devoted to their common
Cuban history, and they continue to preserve each generation's
right to enter the discussion from its own standpoint. Sandra
Benítez, in *Bitter Grounds* (1997), similarly describes a pair of families that survive the divisions caused by sixty years of political
violence in El Salvador. Though the families vary greatly in status, with one belonging to the peasant poor and the other to the
plantation rich, each relies on its triad of grandmother, mother,
and daughter to negotiate similar issues: the loss of their men
through desertion, war, death, or disappearance; the family es-
trangement over political controversies; the religious confusion
due to Catholic disregard for the indigenous religion of one member and the Islam of another; and the distrust of a Church that
appears to side with the oppressive government and the abusive
property owners. In each family, in each generation, the flexibility and peacemaking efforts by the women provide the only hope
of preserving a sense of kinship and a possibility of reunion.

The pattern is the same among the generations of women affected by political unrest in the Dominican Republic, as shown by *In the Time of the Butterflies* (Alvarez 1995a). It repeats itself among the women who keep the displaced Mora family together in *House of Houses* (1997b). Even in stories set in the peacetime United States, and even when families do not face daily threats of deportation, barrio violence, domestic violence, or rape, the female core opposes other obstacles to family unity. They fight abandonment, poverty, single parenthood, low-paying jobs, narrow opportunities, and biases against their language or color. In Denise Chávez's *Face of an Angel* (1994), Soveida recognizes her position as the family woman most recently left by a faithless man, and while the family pattern does not comfort her, she does find relief in the knowledge that her mother and grandmother understand her situation. When she becomes pregnant through an affair with a married man, she finds the courage to release the man and raise the child on her own because her mother and grandmother bless her pregnancy and offer their help. Observing her family, all of whom have suffered, she realizes that the "face of an angel" is neither the genderless, remote image favored by the Christians nor the humiliated, suffering countenance demanded by a culture that wants its wives to be faithful, asexual homemakers. Instead, the angelic face belongs to a loving, connected, community-conscious, sensual, decision-making woman. The face mirrors everything that women are, not just what men have wished them to be. Welcoming this new angel in the form of her unborn child, Soveida calls the baby Milagro, for the girl will be stronger for being a woman among women, a part of the core.

Chávez reiterates her confidence in family women in her 1987 play *Novena Narrativas y Ofrendas Nuevoamericanas*. The character Isabel says, "When I feel alone, I remember behind me stand my grandmother, my mother, all the women who have come before me" (p. 156). Recalling the day she thought she heard her grandmother's voice but turned to see a complete stranger, she recognizes the "thread that connects me to all women, everywhere. Wherever I go, I *know* the women. I know their deepest joys and pains" (p. 156). The main character of Edit Villarreal's 1989 play *My Visits with MGM* (*My Grandmother Marta*) likewise connects with her deceased Chicana grandmother. Young Marta Feliz is the mother of four children: one each from three failed marriages, and a fourth by Father Ernesto, the priest who is sent to save her. She presents a free and delightfully practical figure as she talks through her moral dilemmas in imaginary conversations with MGM. MGM's Catholic spirituality may be highly unorthodox, but it is more active and life affirming than the strict morality available from Marta's joyless, aging housemate Florinda or from the crusading priest. Following MGM's advice that suffering is *not* the only road to virtue, Marta Feliz recovers her home and asserts her right to love. Along the way, she convinces Father Ernesto to preach the better sermons of joy and community.

Both Isabel, who hears her grandmother in other women's voices, and Marta Feliz, who communes with MGM in memory, summon their loved ones in a manner that resembles Pat Mora's invitation to her family saints in *House of Houses*. Like Mora, who lights a candle and joins the departed at tea, Isabel and Marta refuse to relegate the deceased to a place unapproachable by the living. Rather, they hold the spirits close to them on earth, certain that linked generations guard the composite strength of past, present, and future: the knowledge of family and community history, the body of old information to balance the new, and the potential for new ideas. Each individual will be powerful as long as they all support one another.

In a very real way, this earthly female trio meets needs that are not met by their men, by the Catholic Church, or even by the Church Godhead, the Holy Trinity. The members focus not on power and punishment but on communication, forgiveness, peace, and rebirth. They plead for a better understanding of women's lives, both on earth and in the heavens, in real life and in literature. The Ortiz Cofer story "Nada" (1993) offers examples of this difference, revealing the inadequacies of the male-dominated society and the male-dominated Church. It also clarifies the importance of the female unit and the damage that results when it fails to transfer intact into a new culture. In this story, the woman Doña Ernestina, transplanted from Puerto Rico to Paterson and then widowed, suffers another blow when her son dies. The narrator of the story ponders the inability of the men to understand Doña Ernestina's excessive mourning. The men of the apartment building leave the matter to the women, the priest offers platitudes, and the government treats her son's body as a commodity and seeks to satisfy her with a medal, a flag, and a military funeral on some unspecified date.

Other writers also reveal women's anger over what Ortiz Cofer calls "a man's world, and a man's heaven" (1990, p. 44). They have difficulty relating to God, particularly in his aspect of God the Father. In Castillo's *So Far from God* (1993), La Loca criticizes God for condemning *La Llorona* to wander simultaneously in hell and on earth, when he has forced no other sinner to do so. In several other stories, women call the Lord unjust and unwise in his decision to let children die. Where men and God fail so completely, they agree, women must devise their own approach to keeping people whole, alive, connected, and hopeful. Their methods include raising their children and their gardens, feeding the extended family, and communicating with their saints and spirits.

Procreating, feeding, consoling, and unifying—these are the duties of a god. Still, U.S. Latinas as a rule do not deify their female triad as a Trinity or even revere it as superhuman; they keep it firmly based on earth. They speak of grandmothers, aunts, sisters, daughters, *curanderas*, and female friends. Every woman is automatically a member of the unit, but she isn't a good member until she discovers and lives her role. The link between triad and Trinity is metaphoric, the same as the link between the Communion of Saints and the community, between the Grandmother/*curandera* and the priestess, or between the Virgin of Guadalupe and the Earth Goddess. Metaphorically, the female trinity exists to provide the leadership and care that the Catholic Church promises from the male Trinity, but that the male Trinity has not been able to deliver.

Among the Latina works written in the U.S. during the last few decades, Ana Castillo's satirical *So Far from God* comes the closest to deifying the female trinity. On the surface, *So Far from God* resembles other Latina stories of mothers and daughters: it tells of Sofi, a Catholic Chicana butcher living in New Mexico, who raises her four daughters alone after driving out their gambling father. She and her girls are assisted by an ancient *curandera* who combines Catholic and earth-centered practices. A series of disasters leaves Sofi parentless and childless, but she continues to work against the forces she believes are destroying not only her community but also the entire planet.

Though familiar in its outline, *So Far from God* offers additional insights through its design as an allegory. Its lengthy chapter headings, facetious as they are, call to mind the didacticism of John Bunyan's *Pilgrim's Progress* and the satire of Cervantes's *Don Quixote*. The women's names represent human virtues: Sofi (Wisdom), Fe (Faith), Esperanza (Hope), Caridad (Charity), Felicia (Gladness), and La Loca (a God-touched Madness that fosters foresight). The men's names indicate behaviors idealized in Church philosophy: Father Jerome (Asceticism), Francisco el Penitente (Self-Denial), and Domingo (Dedication to God). Caridad's affectionate but unwise horse is Corazón (Heart), and her beloved is Esmeralda (Emerald). Besides the significant names, certain actions recall the symbolic devotions of the *muy catolica*: Sofi and Caridad make pilgrimage to the blessed soil of Chimayo, Sofi and La Loca follow the Way of the Cross, and La Loca and Caridad return purified from encounters with death. La Loca, Caridad, and Doña Felicia stand separate from the general community in their style of life and ministry, and all three offer spiritual healing to family and community. Numerous characters honor the earth spirits as well as the Virgin and the Catholic deities. In an oblique imitation of Jesus, Sofi encourages the people to become shepherds. Francisco el Penitente tries to rid himself of temptation, and the gambling Domingo reforms and returns to his family. In spite of this adherence to proper Christian duties, however, the characters regularly suffer violence and barrenness.

Additional culprits are present but unnamed in the story. No one is called Greed or Social Class, but money and social aspirations certainly kill Fe. Theft and Patrimony hide in Domingo's gambling loss of Sofi's property, an action that imitates the Spanish colonization, the later seizure of Mexican lands by the United States, and the ongoing displacement of indigenous peoples by Anglos. Social Apathy allows faith, hope, and charity to die before anyone begins to question traditional Church values of humility and suffering. Surely Environmental Irresponsibility is at large. The most eloquent statement against human self-destruction is not Sofi's organization called M.O.M.A.S. (Mothers of Martyrs and Saints), but the sorrows of the Way of the Cross Procession, an extraordinary event that protests ruinous human practices by placing them parallel with the traditional fourteen events of Christ's journey to crucifixion. It is a global death walk involving man and woman, Church and people. One participant, whose baby's birth defects were caused by the uranium dumps on the reservation, protests that her people have become endangered along with whales and rain forests even though they themselves "have always known about the interconnectedness of things; and the responsibility we have to 'Our Mother,' and to seven generations after our own" (p. 242). Her plight reinforces the representative nature of Sofi's suffering. Not just Sofi but the entire community must make itself heard if anyone is to survive.

As part of its social and religious allegory, *So Far from God* quite openly compares the three generations of females to the traditional Catholic Trinity. The Holy Trinity joins three "persons" or manifestations of God into an inseparable godhead. God the Father is the powerful creator of heaven, earth, and humans. God the Son is a half-divine/half-human teacher who has forgiven sins, endured temptations, performed miracles, loved the poor and the outcast, fed his followers, and instituted the unifying sacrament of communion. He has endured a terrible death, visited hell, come back to life, and returned to heaven. For the comfort of the humans left behind, the Holy Spirit replaces Christ as an unseen presence that continues to inspire goodness on earth. This male Trinity is intangible, eternal, and unchanging. It represents love, unity, and power.

Parallel in form and actions, Castillo's female trinity also creates, forgives, feeds the family, suffers terrible deaths, visits hell, rises again, and maintains an inspirational presence on earth. However, these actions are not delegated to specific women but are shared by the continuously renewing generations of women. The generations themselves trust the Virgin of Guadalupe/ Tonantzin more than any male god.

In the novel, as family troubles mount, the literal and symbolic references to Trinity and the Virgin begin to build. Mother Sofi, like the Mother of God, breaks into sobs at the sight of her beaten, pierced, and sacrificed girls: "a permanently traumatized daughter, another who was more ghost than of this world, and a third who was the most beautiful child she had given birth to and who had been cruelly mutilated" (p. 34). Fe, the one "permanently traumatized" by social realities, eventually dies from toxins in the workplace; she is the only one of the girls to remain in her grave. The ghostly La Loca, who has intuitive powers, comes back from the dead two times. At the age of three, she revives during her funeral, much to the consternation of Father Jerome, who has more difficulty accepting this miracle than does the community as a whole. The priest is particularly displeased that La Loca claims to have visited hell, purgatory, and heaven during her Christlike two nights of death. Worse than that, she tells him that God has sent her back to pray for him and the villagers. She links them all with the doubting apostle Thomas of the New Testament, warning them that they can't enter heaven until they believe. La Loca, as innocent as the apolitical Christ, dies again as a young woman, inexplicably killed by AIDS even though she has had no infectious contact with anyone or anything. Shortly before her death she accompanies Sofi in the Way of the Cross Procession. Like Christ and Fe, La Loca suffers terrible physical pain and dies from a condition that the government fails to address. In dying twice, she also imitates Christ, who is said to have remained on earth for a time after his crucifixion and resurrection, and then left once more through an ascension to heaven. La Loca physically returns to her family after her first death, but after her death from AIDS she rises in spirit only.

The third sister, Esperanza, seeking truth as a war correspondent, dies in the Persian Gulf War. Her body is never returned to Sofi, but she apparently has risen, for her spirit converses with La Loca. The final daughter, Caridad, wastes herself as a playgirl until she is viciously mutilated by a strange evil force. She miraculously regains her health and beauty, but by then she desires only the company of her horse, Corazón, her lover, Esmeralda, and the unbelievably ancient *curandera*, Doña Felicia. Accepting her own healing powers after a Christlike period of solitude in the wilderness, Caridad understudies Doña Felicia, but she doesn't live long enough to succeed her. Relentlessly stalked by the religious fanatic Francisco el Penitente, she and her lover Esmeralda leap from a cliff to merge cleanly with her soft, safe Mother Earth. Like the Holy Spirit, the spirits of Caridad, La Loca, and Esperanza remain with the living. Rather than being invisible and inaccessible, however, they assume their human forms when they converse with their loved ones.

Through these parallels in community service, sacrificial suffering, resurrection, and spiritual presence, Sofi and her family imitate the supernatural attributes of the male Holy Trinity. At the same time, however, they reject the austere separation from the people practiced by that Trinity. Rather than usurp the status of God or interfere with community reverence for the distant deities, they live as real humans among real humans. Their community neither worships them for the goodness of its life nor blames them for its harshness. As representatives of three generations, Doña Felicia, Sofi, and her girls remind the community of its duty to its own future, to *"las siguientes siete generaciones"* (p. 7). The community learns to help itself. Nonetheless, its very need for action from its own members suggests that the official Church and its Trinity have failed to be accessible and active. This community truly remains "so far from God," and its salvation may lie with a deity so very different from him.

Overall, Sofi and her girls imitate many of the actions of God the Son in his human form, and in this respect they typify numerous groups of women in Latina literature. The preparation and sharing of food, a form of nurture frequently modeled by Christ, appears in most stories as a way to celebrate, to give comfort, or to unite the family one last time when a separation is imminent. Sofi identifies the giving of food as the most basic and reliable act of nurture, "the beginning and end of what a mother knows to do for her offspring, even when she doesn't know what to say" (p. 48). A similar emphasis on sharing meals runs through Mora's *House of Houses* as her family spirits take food and drink in the sacramental atmosphere of candlelight and peace. In this work and others, parallels between shared food and the communion host abound. Recipes and litanies of food likewise dot the writing of Ortiz Cofer, Alvarez, and others. Escamill presents Adela Sewa, Maggie, and their village in the act of gathering traditional foods such as acorns, the sap of mesquite trees, or medicinal herbs.

An important feature of all these sets of nurturing generations is that they must cooperate to be effective. In this respect, they both imitate the heavenly Trinity and differ significantly from it. Whereas the Holy Trinity is infinite, unchanging, unified, and all powerful, the female trinity is finite, shifting, fallible, and occasionally inharmonious. Even in its broadest sense as a self-perpetuating worldwide phenomenon, this totally human trinity remains subject to separation, dissent, and death. It doesn't pretend to have divine power even though the tasks it undertakes are the tasks of a deity.

One of the most powerful elements of the Grandmother-Mother-Daughter configuration is its flexibility in the face of human challenges, and this element alone would differentiate it from the Holy Trinity. The Holy Trinity is a single, all-encompassing essence whose wisdom is infinite. Paradoxically, each member of it encompasses the other two but also remains separate from them. If it were diagrammed, its members might occupy set positions at the points of an equilateral triangle, a rigid unit with three distinct, unchanging angles. Theoretically, a midpoint or center for the figure could be determined.

The trinity of family women resists any such geometric representation. Because it reflects the changeability of earthly life, the lines and angles must shift constantly. As in the male Trinity, roles overlap because grandmothers have been both children and mothers, mothers have been daughters, and daughters carry the potential to become both. However, the actual women are unique and mortal, so they must constantly learn their roles, and no single one of them remains present forever. The terms Grandmother, Mother, and Daughter are themselves generic rather than specific, so a great-grandmother, another female elder, or a *curandera* might supplement or fill in for Grandmother; an aunt or friend might do the same for Mother; and any number of young women, relatives or not, might be Daughter. The configuration reshapes itself as roles are added or lost. The arrangement suggests a changing polygon or rough sphere that rotates and shifts its shape, unsettled but cohesive, a shape that implies a center but can't provide its coordinates. It is the very depiction of rejected borders and hierarchies. Each position presents another swirl of questions and answers. Information flows in all directions. Change is perpetual because each generation is constantly in the process of becoming the next one. Knowledge is fluid rather than set; it constantly is accumulated, re-evaluated, adapted, passed on, misplaced, and rediscovered.

The dynamic of this female trinity may be the new paradigm that Isasi-Díaz and Tarango (1988) have found Latin American women to be seeking—a paradigm that might be recognized as the ancient but newly appreciated model called the matriarchal core by Díaz-Stevens. It also is consistent with theoretical constructs by postcolonialists and feminists who challenge the marginalization of nonmale and non-Western groups in Western male-dominated cultures. Its shifting nature creates a free space amid contending generations, the type of space where identities may stretch and shift in the constant struggle between the desire for separation and the desire for unity.

U.S. Latina works suggest that a woman's personal balance derives from recognizing her relative place in this shifting trinity. Neither automatic nor permanent, this balance comes through her keen observation of patterns and her ability to adapt. Denise Chávez (1994) reveals a young woman recognizing this stability within change when she has Dolores tell Soveida that women do not just grow to look like their ancestors, they actually *become* them. Dolores finds comfort in this permanent presence of mothers and grandmothers who have passed on. In her memoir *Almost a Woman* (1998), Esmeralda Santiago views the combined history and prediction in family faces from another angle. As an adolescent applying makeup to age her face for a school play, Esmeralda frightens herself with a glimpse of her future: "I faced the mirror again and saw my grandmother, Abuela. . . . But if I turned to the left, there was Tata, the grandmother I lived with" (p. 83). Even more startling to her than the evidence of her heritage is the realization that even though her Puerto Rican heritage remains permanently visible, the non-Puerto Ricans who see her will never truly understand what that identity means. She will have to establish self-knowledge without the help of peers. Her models must be drawn from family women, so she watches them and listens to their cautionary tales, which she calls a roadmap revealing the dangers ahead, a guidebook by which she might choose a better way. Tempted to flee with a lover, she chooses to stay near her mother and grandmothers, for she knows the family women have always found men to love, but none of them could ever find a replacement for each other. She refuses to break that link.

Over and over this sense of familial and cultural continuity surfaces for Latina characters. For Celia, the grandmother in *Dreaming in Cuban* (García 1992), the birth of a granddaughter enables her to stop adding to the pile of unsent love letters she has been writing for years. Celia knows her granddaughter Pilar will become her living record of family lore. As a teen, Pilar accepts the role: "Women who outlive their daughters are orphans, Abuela tells me. Only their granddaughters can save them, guard their knowledge like the first fire" (p. 222). A similar reference to keeping the flame alive appears in Escamill's *Daughter of the Mountain* (1991) when Maggie kindles a new fire on La Madre mountain to signify the understanding gained through her three-day consultation with grandmother Adela's spirit there. The fire marks her own symbolic death in the male order and her rising in the female.

This solidarity among Grandmother, Mother, and Daughter results largely from the persistent nurture that flows around the trinity. The Mirabal sisters of *In the Time of the Butterflies* (Alvarez 1995a) foster the family even as they resist the complacency of their mother, but they never abandon her or are abandoned by her. Mothers themselves, they assume the Grandmother role as well, sharing the care of their children and finally entrusting them to Dedé, the only sister to survive, the one who can keep the deceased mothers present through storytelling. By the end of the story, Dedé is on the cusp of being Grandmother, and the girls are old enough to soon replace her as Mother. This Mirabal trinity is simultaneously held together and torn apart by its members, who wish to preserve the family even as they must alter its social and religious orientation. The women negotiate in a shifting alignment that preserves knowledge and offers the possibility of new solutions.

The importance of trinitarian continuity to the social and spiritual welfare of the community itself becomes markedly clear when members of the trinity fall away. In Cristina García's novel *The Agüero Sisters* (1997), Grandmother is absent and Mother can't understand Daughter. Each generation accuses the others of abandonment, which is the sin of *el olvido* at its most personal. The action of the novel exposes the details of Grandmother's murder and teaches Reina and Constancia, the two Daughters-become-Mothers, how far nostalgia has led them from the truth about their family and Cuba. In a novel of pervasive death and warring personal philosophies, the deteriorating Mother–Daughter relationship—that is, a withering remnant of trinity—restores itself through shared information and a continuing desire for connection.

García's *Dreaming in Cuban* yields similar insights, with a sharper focus on the ability of religion and politics to unite or divide family women. Pilar's family is beyond the Virgin's help because of its earthly disorder that physically and emotionally separates the younger women of the family from the elder. Grandmother Celia, isolated by geography, religion, and politics, cannot provide wisdom and guidance. Only when Grandmother, Mother, and Daughter reunite do peace and productive action have a chance. In this novel, as in *The Agüero Sisters*, the most information and leadership comes from the elder women, who must find the truth and tell it in a way that enables the others to understand it, accept it, and reconnect with one another in hope.

In other stories, such as *Face of an Angel* or the autobiographical essays of Ortiz Cofer, information originates with Daughter, who has greater skills in the dominant culture's language and possesses better cross-cultural coping skills. In *Face of an Angel*, Daughter Soveida negotiates a balance between service and self-respect, preserving the culturally important goal of improving others' lives while eliminating the destructive need to be the *sufrida*. Her discovery is reinforced by her half-sister, the flamboyant Sister Lizzie, who remains dedicated to the family despite her position outside the reproductive cycle. Soveida and Lizzie's new Daughter wisdom flows upward to Mother and Grandmother, convincing the older women that they can sever their ties with unfaithful men without suffering social or eternal damnation.

In some cases, a woman must learn to be a proper Daughter before she can advance to Mother. In these stories, Daughter learns to nurture and respect others by watching Mother relate to older and younger generations. Difficulties arise if Mother withholds information and if Daughter gives in to her adolescent nature and refuses to seek advice. Both Ana Castillo and Judith Ortiz Cofer have written poems in which Mother and Daughter have not shared an essential conversation. In Ortiz Cofer's (1993) "Orar: To Pray," the daughter first hears her mother beg her philandering husband to remain home, then hears her ensuing prayers: sad, weighty murmurs that give the girl a premonition of the burden she herself will carry as a woman trapped in passivity. Because this mother and daughter are isolated on opposite sides of a wall, however, they cannot comfort each other.

Neither can the mother and daughter in Castillo's "El ser mujer," in which the speaker is a grown woman lying beside her sleeping husband. Full of the questions she hadn't known to ask as a child, she petitions her absent mother:

> Must I be a woman now? I know
> I bear the reflection of your youth.
> Yet I am not ready to echo those
> trying years.
> . . . .
> Mami, I'm afraid! [1995b, p. 138]

Eventually, she follows her mother's advice to pray, but she alters the model: she prays to Mother, not to God.

Sometimes a frightened, confused Daughter like this must gravitate toward Grandmother because Mother hasn't yet discovered her own role. In *Silent Dancing* (1990), Ortiz Cofer admits being such a Daughter. Telling the story of her birth, she reports being cared for by older women "until my mother came out of her adolescent dream to take charge of me" (p. 43). Even in later years, she can't rely upon her mother, who pretends she is in Puerto Rico no matter where she is physically, and thus is unable to help her daughter navigate the Puerto Rico/Paterson zones of cultural and spiritual friction. The young Ortiz Cofer relies upon her grandmother instead. Years later, with her mother sustaining herself with extended family in Puerto Rico, she begins to realize how much her mother's experience with displacement differed from her own, and she approaches a new Mother–Daughter rapport.

The fictional teenager Maggie of *Daughter of the Mountain* has an even more difficult pathway, for she must trade positions with her mother and become the nurturer and protector of the pair. With her Grandmother Adela spiritually but not physically available, Maggie must proceed in the absence of female relatives and medicine women. To some degree, because even her community does not accept her, she is a cultural orphan like Huitzitzilin in *Song of the Hummingbird* (Limón 1996): a fading voice trying to pass the spiritual wisdom of Grandmother, Mother, and Daughter to someone outside the family. Huitzitzilin's situation, of course, is most extreme. The potential recipient of her wisdom belongs to a different color, gender, culture, and religious sensibility. A celibate male, he is a poor substitute for Daughter, but his education, power, and mobility as a male make him her only hope for keeping the ways of her people alive until they can be understood and appreciated. She can't rely upon the convent nuns, for even if they listen to her, the insights they gain will die in the silence of their cloister.

Sofi in *So Far from God* is orphaned in a way different from these two. All four of her girls die childless. Left without heirs, Sofi ponders the same question Father Benito asked Huitzitzilin: "What would we do if all the mothers deprived of their children murdered the men responsible?" (p. 195). Huitzitzilin, having learned the futility of returning violence for violence, would prefer to end the theft of children and thus eliminate the need for an answer. Sofi echoes that hope and labors to make it a reality. Her community aid and awareness efforts succeed because her people still survive and can be returned to their ancient, communal ways. Through M.O.M.A.S. and her co-ops, she seeks to protect the survival of an entire people.

The group called M.O.M.A.S., composed of mothers whose children have been sacrificed, emphasizes the seriousness of lost continuity in a family or a people. The village's Way of the Cross Procession protests a similar devastation on the international level. Through these activities and her programs to revive the village economically, Sofi acts out the commandments of her personal spirituality: Share. Love and honor life. Reject silence and apathy. Remain open to multiple spiritual options, for neither the priests nor the *curanderas* have been able to reverse this terrible progress toward the end of generations.

Sofi's faith does not promote a particular religious code, but rather a connection among peoples and between them and their planet. It requires a belief that solutions may follow when people shift the way they think. One thing is certain for people dwelling so far from God: the existing social, political, and religious practices have led and will continue to lead to sterility, violence, "disappeared" family members, and emptiness.

In *Massacre of the Dreamers* (1995a), Castillo reaffirms this cosmic need for a generous spirituality that undoes the traditional emphasis on the opposition between good and evil. She blames the divisiveness of this concept for bringing the Earth to the brink of its final destruction. Castillo also predicts that women will guide the world toward a better spirituality as they respond to the concerns of their generation: abortion, self-defense, sexual desire, misogyny, racism, and classism. An Earth Mother may be the model for caring leadership, but neither she nor the female trinity nor the male Trinity nor any other system alone will suffice.

In *So Far from God*, single solutions, particularly those that glorify separation, suffering, and death, prove counterproductive. Even Sofi's M.O.M.A.S., which is conceived as a female outcry, eventually overstates itself, creating an extravagant exaltation of mothers and slaughtered children at the same time that it discriminates against bereaved fathers as well as all the concerned parents of living children. Sofi recognizes the error of allowing M.O.M.A.S. to become overly female-centered, and the book ends with her questioning whether women are wise to resort to reverse discrimination to correct previous male excesses. Castillo touches a similar theme in the introduction to *My Father Was a Toltec* (1995b) when she notes that Latinas have reconnected with mothers and grandmothers, but they haven't yet tried hard enough to understand the male elements of their own nature.

Castillo may agree with an observation Díaz-Stevens has made about *madonismo*, a U.S. Southwest peasant tradition that defines motherhood in terms beyond the physical. *Madonismo* deals not with the Virgin Mary or worship, but rather with active service to the family and the community. Thus, the virgins and the barren of a village may gain recognition as nurturers. Perhaps, through the failures of M.O.M.A.S., *So Far from God* suggests that *madonismo* should be extended to male action as well as female.

Such a tradition of surrogate parenthood may very well be a means of ensuring the physical, emotional, and cultural survival of a people. It's a duty, as Castillo says, of each generation to its following seven generations. If Enrique Dussel (1976) is correct in saying prophecy isn't about the future but about the importance of now to that future, then Castillo and other Latinas may well be prophetic. They present the female trinity as a model because it recognizes but is not defeated by the undeniable truths of living: the young and the old die. Daughter resists Mother. Economic and social forces separate families. *Machismo* limits male input. Fathers often go absent. Every individual makes mistakes.

A persistent female network—once oral and now increasingly literary—can't solve these problems, but it can expose them and agitate for change. The leading women in the U.S. Latina literature of recent decades don't insist on a particular course of action; they offer alternatives. They bank their knowledge in the family and they offer it to another culture, not out of an urge to keep things the same, but out of the hope that the accumulated knowledge will save others. Like the Virgin of Guadalupe, they encourage the people to assume whichever shape will sustain them in the endless process of becoming, and like the *curandera*, they believe in bountiful and varied alternatives. Above all, they seek continued dialogue among the generations, the genders, the peoples, and the religions, for in that discussion lies the promise of understanding and the hope of new beginnings.

References

Acosta-Bélen, E. (1993). A *MELUS* interview: Judith Ortiz Cofer. *MELUS* 18(3):83–97.

Alarcón, N. (1986). Interview with Pat Mora. *Third Woman* 3(1–2): 121–126.

———— (1990). The theoretical subject(s) of *This Bridge Called My Back* and Anglo-American feminism. In *Making Face, Making Soul: Haciendo Caras*, ed. G. Andalzúa, pp. 356–369. San Francisco: Aunt Lute Books.

———— (1996). Making familia from scratch: split subjectivities in the work of Helena María Viramontes and Cherríe Moraga. In *Chicana Creativity and Criticism*, 2nd ed., ed. M. Herrera-Sobek and H. M. Viramontes, pp. 220–227. Albuquerque: University of New Mexico Press.

Alvarez, J. (1992). *How the García Girls Lost Their Accents*. New York: Plume.

———— (1995a). *In the Time of the Butterflies*. New York: Plume.

———— (1995b). *The Other Side/El Otro Lado*. New York: Plume.

———— (1997). *¡Yo!* New York: Plume.

———— (1998). *Something to Declare*. New York: Plume.

Anaya, R. (1996). "I'm the king": the macho image. In *Muy macho: Latino Men Confront Their Manhood*, ed. R. Gonzalez, pp. 57–73. New York: Anchor.

Anzaldúa, G. (1987). *Borderlands/La frontera: The New Mestiza*. San Francisco: Aunt Lute Books.

Bakhtin, M. M. (1921). *Toward a Philosophy of the Act*, trans. V. Liapunov, ed. V. Liapunov and M. Holquist. Austin: University of Texas Press, 1993.

Benítez, S. (1994). *A Place Where the Sea Remembers*. New York: Scribner Paperback.

——— (1997). *Bitter Grounds*. New York: Picador USA.

Bhabha, H. (1988). Cultural diversity and cultural differences. In *The Post-Colonial Studies Reader*, ed. B. Ashcroft, G. Griffiths, and H. Tiffin, pp. 206–209. New York: Routledge, 1995.

Brandon, G. (1993). *Santería from Africa to the New World: The Dead Sell Memories*. Indianapolis: Indiana University Press.

Burns. E. B. (1972). *Latin America: A Concise Interpretive History*. Englewood Cliffs, NJ: Prentice-Hall.

Carbonell, A. M. (1999). From Llorona to Gritona: Coatlicue in feminist tales by Viramontes and Cisneros. *MELUS* 24(2):53–74.

Castillo, A. (1993). *So Far from God*. New York: Plume.

——— (1995a). *Massacre of the Dreamers: Essays on Xicanisma*. New York: Plume.

——— (1995b). *My Father Was a Toltec and Selected Poems*. New York: W. W. Norton.

——— (1996a). Extraordinarily woman. In *Goddess of the Americas: Writings on the Virgin of Guadalupe*, ed. A. Castillo, pp. 72–78. New York: Riverhead.

——— (1996b). *Loverboys*. New York: Plume.

——— (1999). *Peel My Love Like an Onion*. New York: Doubleday.

Castillo, D. (1992). *Talking Back: Toward a Latin American Feminist Literary Criticism*. Ithaca, NY: Cornell University Press.

Chávez, D. (1987). Novena narrativas y ofrendas nuevoamericanas. In *Goddess of the Americas: Writings on the Virgin of Guadalupe*, ed. A. Castillo, pp. 153–169. New York: Riverhead, 1996.

——— (1989). Heat and rain: testimonio. In *Breaking Boundaries: Latina Writing and Critical Readings*, ed. A. Horno-Delgado, E. Ortega, N. M. Scott, and N. S. Sternbach, pp. 27–32. Amherst: University of Massachusetts Press.

——— (1994). *Face of an Angel*. New York: Warner.

Chávez Candelaria, C. (1997). The "wild zone" thesis as gloss in Chicana literary study. In *Feminisms: An Anthology of Literary Theory and Criticism*, ed. R. R. Warhol and D. P. Herndl, pp. 248–256. New Brunswick, NJ: Rutgers University Press.

Cisneros, S. (1991). *Woman Hollering Creek*. New York: Vintage Contemporaries.

——— (1995). *Loose Woman*. New York: Vintage Contemporaries.

——— (1996). Guadalupe the sex goddess. In *Goddess of the Americas: Writings on the Virgin of Guadalupe*, ed. A. Castillo, pp. 46–51. New York: Riverhead.

Confraternity of Christian Doctrine. (1970). Psalm 27. *The New American Bible*. Wichita, KS: Catholic Bible Publishers.

Cypess, S. M. (1991). *La Malinche in Mexican Literature: From History to Myth*. Austin: University of Texas Press.

Davis, K. G. (2000a). The Hispanic shift: continuity rather than conversion? In *Bridging Boundaries: The Pastoral Care of U.S. Hispanics*, ed. K. G. Davis and Y. Tarango, pp. 117–127. Scranton, PA: University of Scranton Press.

——— (2000b). Introduction. In *Bridging Boundaries: The Pastoral Care of U.S. Hispanics*, ed. K. G. Davis and Y. Tarango, pp. xiii–xvi. Scranton, PA: University of Scranton Press.

——— (2000c). Still gringo after all these years. In *Bridging Boundaries: The Pastoral Care of U.S. Hispanics*, ed. K. G. Davis and Y. Tarango, pp. 107–115. Scranton, PA: University of Scranton Press.

Díaz-Stevens, A. M. (1994). Latinas and the Church. In *Hispanic Catholic Culture in the U.S.: Issues and Concerns*, ed. J. P. Dolan and A. F. Deck, pp. 240–277. Notre Dame, IN: University of Notre Dame Press.

Dussel, E. (1976). *History and the Theology of Liberation: A Latin American Perspective*, trans. J. Drury. Maryknoll, NY: Orbis.

——— (1978). *Ethics and the Theology of Liberation*, trans. B. F. McWilliams. Maryknoll, NY: Orbis.

Ehrenberg, F. (1996). Framing an icon: Guadalupe and the artist's vision. In *Goddess of the Americas: Writings on the Virgin of Guadalupe*, ed. A. Castillo, pp. 170–177. New York: Riverhead.

Engle, M. (1993). *Singing to Cuba*. Houston, TX: Arte Público Press.

Escamill, E. (1991). *Daughter of the Mountain*. San Francisco: Aunt Lute Books.

Espín, O. O. (1994). Popular Catholicism among Latinos. In *Hispanic Catholic Culture in the U.S.: Issues and Concerns*, ed. J. P. Dolan and A. F. Deck, pp. 308–359. Notre Dame, IN: University of Notre Dame Press.

Fanon, F. (1952). *Black Skin, White Masks*, trans. C. L. Markmann. New York: Grove, 1967.

——— (1961). *The Wretched of the Earth*, trans. C. Farrington. New York: Grove, 1963.

Fernández, E. C. (1997). Seven tips on the pastoral care of United States Catholics of Mexican descent. In *Bridging Boundaries: The Pastoral Care of U.S. Hispanics*, ed. K. G. Davis and Y. Tarango, pp. 81–93. Scranton, PA: University of Scranton Press, 2000.

Ferré, R. (1996). The battle of the virgins. In *Goddess of the Americas: Writings on the Virgin of Guadalupe*, ed. A. Castillo, pp. 79–87. New York: Riverhead.

Fornes, M. I. (1977). *Fefu and Her Friends*. New York: PAJ Publications.

Freire, P. (1997). *Pedagogy of the Oppressed*, rev. ed., trans. M. B. Ramos. New York: Continuum.

García, C. (1992). *Dreaming in Cuban*. New York: Ballantine.

———— (1997). *The Agüero Sisters*. New York: Ballantine.

Gates, H. L., Jr. (1985). Writing, "race," and the difference it makes. In *American Literature, American Culture*, ed. G. Hutner, pp. 463–476. New York: Oxford University Press, 1999.

Goris, A. (2000). Dominican immigrants: social and religious context. In *Bridging Boundaries: The Pastoral Care of U.S. Hispanics*, ed. K. G. Davis and Y. Tarango, pp. 35–50. Scranton, PA: University of Scranton Press.

Griego y Maestas, J., and Anaya, R. A. (1980). *Cuentos: Tales from the Hispanic Southwest*. Sante Fe: The Museum of New Mexico Press.

Gutiérrez, G. (1973). A theology of liberation: history, politics and salvation. In *Americas: An Anthology*, ed. M. B. Rosenberg, A. D. Kincaid, and K. Logan, pp. 229–234. New York: Oxford University Press, 1992.

Harlow, B. (1991). Sites of struggle: immigration, deportation, prison, and exile. In *Criticism in the Borderlands: Studies in Chicano Literature, Culture, and Ideology*, ed. H. Calderón and J. D. Saldívar, pp. 149–163. Durham, NC: Duke University Press.

Ikas, K. R. (2002). *Chicana Ways: Conversations with Ten Chicana Writers*. Reno: University of Nevada Press.

Isasi-Díaz, A. M. (2000). Preface. In *Bridging Boundaries: The Pastoral Care of U.S. Hispanics*, ed. K. G. Davis and Y. Tarango, pp. ix–xi. Scranton, PA: University of Scranton Press.

———— (2001). *Mujerista theology*. Unpublished paper presented at Alaska Pacific University, Anchorage.

Isasi-Díaz, A. M., and Tarango, Y. (1988). *Hispanic Women: Prophetic Voice in the Church*. Minneapolis, MN: Fortress, 1992.

Kristeva, J. (1991). Women's time. In *Feminisms: An Anthology of Lit-*

erary Theory and Criticism, ed. R. R. Warhol and D. P. Herndl, pp. 443–462. New Brunswick, NJ: Rutgers University Press.

Limón, G. (1996). *Song of the Hummingbird.* Houston, TX: Arte Público Press.

Limón, J. (1991). Dancing with the devil: society, gender, and the political unconscious in Mexican-American South Texas. In *Criticism in the Borderlands: Studies in Chicano Literature, Culture, and Ideology*, ed. H. Calderón and J. D. Saldívar, pp. 221–235. Durham, NC: Duke University Press.

Lindsay, A., ed. (1996). *Santería Aesthetics in Contemporary Latin American Art.* Washington, DC: Smithsonian Institution Press.

Lu, M.-Z. (1996). Representing and negotiating differences in the contact zone. In *Reflections on Multiculturalism*, ed. R. Eddy, pp. 117–132. Yarmouth, ME: Intercultural Press.

McClintock, A. (1995). *Imperial Leather: Race, Gender and Sexuality in the Colonial Conquest.* New York: Routledge.

McLaughlin, A. N. (1990). Black women, identity, and the quest for humanhood and wholeness: wild women in the whirlwind. In *Wild Women in the Whirlwind: Afra-American Culture and the Contemporary Literary Renaissance*, ed. J. Braxton and A. N. McLaughlin, pp. 147–180. New Brunswick, NJ: Rutgers University Press.

Menchú, R. (1984). *I, Rigoberta Menchú: An Indian Woman in Guatemala*, trans. A. Wright. New York: Verso.

Moore, J. (1994). The social fabric of the Hispanic community. In *Hispanic Catholic Culture in the U.S.: Issues and Concerns*, ed. J. P. Dolan and A. F. Deck, pp. 6–49. Notre Dame, IN: University of Notre Dame Press.

Mora, P. (1985). *Chants.* Houston, TX: Arte Público Press.

———— (1986). *Borders.* Houston, TX: Arte Público Press.

———— (1993). *Nepantla.* Albuquerque: University of New Mexico Press.

———— (1995). *Agua Santa.* Boston: Beacon.

———— (1997a). *Aunt Carmen's Book of Practical Saints.* Boston: Beacon.

———— (1997b). *House of Houses.* Boston: Beacon.

Moraga, C. (1993). El mito azteca. In *Goddess of the Americas: Writings on the Virgin of Guadalupe*, ed. A. Castillo, pp. 68–71. New York: Riverhead, 1996.

Morales, A. L., and Morales, R. (1986). *Getting Home Alive.* New York: Firebrand.

Morrison, T. (1992). *Playing in the Dark*. Cambridge, MA: Harvard University Press.

Navarro, M. A. (1991). Interview with Ana Castillo. In *Chicana Lesbians: The Girls Our Mothers Warned Us About*, ed. C. Trujillo, pp. 113–132. Berkeley, CA: Third Woman Press.

Norton, J. (2001). Don't restore women diaconate, theologian advises. *Catholic Anchor* 3(16):2.

Obejas, A. (1994). *We Came All the Way from Cuba So You Could Dress Like This?* Pittsburgh, PA: Cleis.

Ocasio, R. (1994). The infinite variety of the Puerto Rican reality: an interview with Judith Ortiz Cofer. *Callaloo* 17:730–742.

——— (1995). An interview with Judith Ortiz Cofer. *The Americas Review* 25(3):84–90.

Ocasio, R., and Ganey, R. (1992). Speaking in Puerto Rican: an interview with Judith Ortiz Cofer. *Bilingual Review* 17(2):143–146.

Ortiz Cofer, J. (1989). *The Line of the Sun*. Athens, GA: University of Georgia Press.

——— (1990). *Silent Dancing: A Partial Remembrance of a Puerto Rican Childhood*. Houston, TX: Arte Público Press.

——— (1993). *The Latin Deli*. New York: W. W. Norton.

——— (1995). *Terms of Survival*. Houston, TX: Arte Público Press.

——— (1996). *An Island Like You*. New York: Puffin.

——— (1997). Where is home? I want to go there. In *Puerto Rican Voices in English*, ed. C. D. Hernández, pp. 95–105. Westport, CT: Praeger.

Owens, L. (1995). *Other Destinies: Understanding the American Indian Novel*. Norman: University of Oklahoma Press.

Paternostro, S. (1999). *In the Land of God and Man: A Latin Woman's Journey*. New York: Plume.

Pattison, M. (2002). Vatican decree on saints draws mixed reactions. *Catholic Anchor* 4(1):3,10.

Randall, M. (1996). Guadalupe, subversive virgin. In *Goddess of the Americas: Writings on the Virgin of Guadalupe*, ed. A. Castillo, pp. 113–123. New York: Riverhead.

Reuman, A. E. (2000). Coming into play: an interview with Gloria Anzaldúa. *MELUS* 25(2):3–62.

Rodríguez, R. E. (2000). Chicana/o fiction from resistance to contestation: the role of creation in Ana Castillo's *So Far from God*. *MELUS* 25(2):63–82.

Said, E. (1978). *Orientalism*. New York: Random House.

Santiago, E. (1993). *When I Was Puerto Rican.* New York: Vintage.
———— (1996). *América's Dream.* New York: HarperCollins.
———— (1998). *Almost a Woman.* New York: Vintage.
Stavans, I. (1995). *The Hispanic Condition: Reflections on Culture and Identity in America.* New York: Harper.
Tabares, F. (2000). Pastoral care of Catholic South Americans living in the United States. In *Bridging Boundaries: The Pastoral Care of U.S. Hispanics,* ed. K. G. Davis and Y. Tarango, pp. 9–33. Scranton, PA: University of Scranton Press.
Trambley, E. P. (1983a). *Puente Negro.* In *Sor Juana and Other Plays,* pp. 1–35. Ypsilanti, MI: Bilingual Press.
———— (1983b). *Sor Juana.* In *Sor Juana and Other Plays,* pp. 143–168. Ypsilanti, MI: Bilingual Press.
Trueblood, A. S. (1988). *A Sor Juana Anthology.* Cambridge, MA: Harvard University Press.
United States Catholic Conference, Inc. (1997). *Catechism of the Catholic Church with Modifications from the Editio Typica.* New York: Doubleday.
Valenzuela, L. (1989). Virgencita, give us a chance. In *Goddess of the Americas: Writings on the Virgin of Guadalupe,* ed. A. Castillo, pp. 92–97. New York: Riverhead, 1996.
Villarreal, E. (1989). My visits with MGM (My grandmother Marta). In *Shattering the Myth: Plays by Hispanic Women,* ed. L. Feyder, pp. 143–208. Houston, TX: Arte Público Press, 1992.
Viramontes, H. M. (1989). "Nopalitos": the making of fiction: testimonio. In *Breaking Boundaries: Latina Writing and Critical Readings,* ed. A. Horno-Delgado, E. Ortega, N. M. Scott, and N. S. Sternbach, pp. 33–38. Amherst: University of Massachusetts Press.
———— (1995). *The Moths and Other Stories.* Houston, TX: Arte Público Press.
———— (1996). *Under the Feet of Jesus.* New York: Plume.
Yarbro-Bejarano, Y. (1991). Chicana literature from a Chicana feminist perspective. In *Feminisms: An Anthology of Literary Theory and Criticism,* ed. R. R. Warhol and D. P. Herndl, pp. 213–219. New Brunswick, NJ: Rutgers University Press.
Zimmerman, B. (1981). What has never been: an overview of lesbian feminist literary criticism. *Feminist Studies* 7(3):451–475.

Recommended Reading

Ashcroft, B., Griffiths, G., and Tiffin, H., eds. (1995). *The Post-Colonial Studies Reader*. New York: Routledge.

Bhabha, H. (1995). Signs taken for wonders. In *The Post-Colonial Studies Reader*, ed. B. Ashcroft, G. Griffiths, and H. Tiffin, pp. 29–35. New York: Routledge.

Bruce-Novoa, J. (1989). Judith Ortiz Cofer's rituals of movement. *The Americas Review* 19(3–4):88–99.

Calderón, H., and Saldívar, J. D., eds. (1991). *Criticism in the Borderlands: Studies in Chicano Literature, Culture, and Ideology*. Durham, NC: Duke University Press.

Carrasco, D. (1990). *Religions of Mesoamerica*. New York: Harper & Row.

Castillo, A., ed. (1996). *Goddess of the Americas: Writings on the Virgin of Guadalupe*. New York: Riverhead.

Davis, K. G., and Tarango Y., eds. (2000). *Bridging Boundaries: The Pastoral Care of U.S. Hispanics*. Scranton, PA: University of Scranton Press.

Dolan, J. P., and Deck, A. F., eds. (1994). *Hispanic Catholic Culture in the U.S.: Issues and Concerns*. Notre Dame, IN: University of Notre Dame Press.

Ferré, R. (1996). *The House on the Lagoon*. New York: Plume.

Gonzalez, R. (1996). *Muy Macho: Latino Men Confront Their Manhood*. New York: Anchor.

Gossen, G. H., ed. (1997). *South and Meso-American Native Spirituality: From the Cult of the Feathered Serpent to the Theology of Liberation*. New York: Crossroad.

Hernández, C. D., ed. (1997). *Puerto Rican Voices in English*. Westport, CT: Praeger.

Horno-Delgado, A., Ortega, E., Scott, N. M., and Sternbach, N. S., eds. (1989). *Breaking Boundaries: Latina Writing and Critical Readings.* Amherst: University of Massachusetts Press.

Ikas, K. R. (2002). *Conversations with Ten Chicana Writers.* Reno: University of Nevada Press.

McClintock, A. (1995). *Imperial Leather: Race, Gender and Sexuality in the Colonial Conquest.* New York: Routledge.

Mermann-Jozwiak, E. (2000). Gritos desde la Frontera: Ana Castillo, Sandra Cisneros, and postmodernism. *MELUS* 25(2):101–118.

Rodriguez, R. E. (2000). Chicana/o fiction from resistance to contestation: the role of creation in Ana Castillo's *So Far from God. MELUS* 25(2):63–82.

Romano, S. (2004). Tlaltelolco: the grammatical-rhetorical *Indios* of colonial Mexico. *College English* 68(3):257–277.

Rosenberg, M. B., Kincaid, A. D., and Logan, K., eds. (1992). In women's hands: the changing roles of women. In *Americas: An Anthology*, pp. 173–179. New York: Oxford University Press.

Said, E. (1993). *Culture and Imperialism.* New York: Vintage.

Tarango, Y. (2000). Conclusion. In *Bridging Boundaries: The Pastoral Care of U.S. Hispanics*, ed. K. G. Davis and Y. Tarango, pp. 129–132. Scranton, PA: University of Scranton Press.

Thavis, J. (2000). Vatican report warns of religious pluralism threat. *Catholic Anchor* 2(19):1,11.

Versluis, A. (1997). *The Elements of Native American Traditions.* Boston: Element.

Warhol, R. R., and Herndl, D. P., eds. (1991, 1997). *Feminisms: An Anthology of Literary Theory and Criticism.* New Brunswick, NJ: Rutgers University Press.

Glossary

Abuela—grandmother
abuelita—little grandmother (a diminutive)
agua santa—holy water
antepasados—ancestors
¡Ay Dios!—Oh God!
¡Ay Dios mío!—Oh my God!
Blessed Mother—*see* Blessed Virgin Mary
Blessed Virgin—*see* Blessed Virgin Mary
Blessed Virgin Mary—the mother of Jesus (in orthodox Catholicism)
Bruja/o—witch
cabildo—a brotherhood or social group
campesinos—country people, simple folk
La Caridad del Cobre—Our Lady of Charity of Copper
causas—minor spirits who cause difficulties for people
Chicana/o—a mestiza/o with origins in the Mexico/United States bor-
    derlands
La Chingada—the fucked one; an insulting comparison to Doña Marina
conscientización—raised consciousness prerequisite to being *Xicanista*
coyote—a guide for people wishing to cross the U.S./Mexico border
    illegally
La Cuarenta—Number Forty, site of Trujillo's torture chambers in *In
    the Time of the Butterflies*
cuento—story
curandera/o—an herbalist healer, a medicine woman/man
Doña—title for a Spanish matron, sometimes translated as "Mrs." but
    not necessarily a marital title

237

Espiritismo—Latin American spiritism derived from Catholicism and nineteenth—century European spiritism

espiritista—a spiritist in Espiritismo

folk Catholicism—a highly variable version of Catholicism that rejects or places different emphasis on orthodox beliefs and practices. It may also include elements of other belief systems.

Guadalupe—familiar name for the Virgin of Guadalupe

hermana—sister

Las Hermanas–a U.S. Latina Catholic organization of lay women and nuns formed in 1971 to consolidate and advance its members in the hierarchy of the church

Tres Hermanas–Three Sisters

Holy Family—Jesus, Mary, and Joseph (in orthodox Catholicism)

Huitzilopochtli—Aztec war god

Huitzitzilin—hummingbird (Nahuatl)

india/o—Indian (noun or adjective)

indito—Indian (noun)

El Jefe—the ruler, the boss, the one in charge

Latin American—pertaining to Spanish-influenced lands south of the United States of America

liberation theology—the belief that the Catholic Church should protect the downtrodden even if it must oppose the government to do so

La Llorona—the wailing or crying woman who wanders by water at night, lamenting her lost children

la lucha—struggle

la lucha cotidiana—daily struggle

lo cotidiano—daily life, daily struggle

Lupe—familiar name for the Virgin of Guadalupe

luto—mourning

macho—(1) male; (2) the model male who is a strong, stoic protector, husband, father, lover, and leader; (3) [popular misuse] a violent and sexist male

machismo—the code of proper male behaviors

madonismo—U.S. Southwest peasant tradition that defines motherhood in terms beyond the physical

madre—mother

¡madre de Dios!—Mother of God!

mala influencia—evil influence, a cause of soul sickness

La Malinche—Marina, the Indian woman taken by Cortés as a mistress and interpreter

marianismo—the code of imitating the Blessed Virgin Mary

Mariposas—Butterflies, the code name for the rebel Mirabal sisters in *In the Time of the Butterflies*

Mary—*see* Blessed Virgin Mary

Medellín, Colombia—1968 meeting place where the Latin American bishops interpreted the dictates of Vatican II as they applied to the Church in Latin America

mesa blanca—white table or altar kept by an espiritista

mestiza/o—an individual with a mixed ethnic heritage

mestizaje—the condition of being of mixed blood

Mexica—ancient Mesoamerican tribe of modern-day Mexico

Mexican—pertaining to the independent country of Mexico

la Migra—border police; immigration agents

milagro—miracle

Moctezuma—Montezuma, Aztec ruler of Tenochtitlan at the time of the Conquest

mojados—illegal aliens, "wetbacks"

Muerte—death

mujer—woman

Mujerista Theology—a belief that religion should be responsive to the daily lived experience of the common Latina. Justice and reconciliation are two of its important goals.

mulato/o—of mixed Spanish and African blood

muy Católica—very devoutly Catholic

Nuyorican—a Puerto Rican American living in New York City

el olvido—the forgetting of cultural roots

orisha—a saint in the Santería religion

padre—Father, a title for a Catholic priest

partera—midwife

popular Catholicism—*see* folk Catholicism

promesa—a promise; an act of self-sacrifice

prueba—a test

puta—whore

quinceañera—a celebration of a Latina's fifteenth birthday

religión popular—popular religion; *see* folk Catholicism

salon—a gathering of intellectuals, so called because they met in the drawing rooms of French aristocrats (French, 18th century)

santera/o—(1) Santería spirit medium; (2) carver of holy statues

Santería—Latin American spiritism derived from Catholicism and African spiritism

Señora—title for a married woman

las siguientes siete generaciones—the following seven generations

Sor—Sister, a title for a Mother Superior in an order of nuns

el ser mujer—womanhood

sufrida—a woman who believes earthly suffering to be a duty and an honor

syncretism—the side-by-side practice of different and possibly contradictory customs

Tenochtitlan—Aztec city in the area now occupied by Mexico City

testimonio—a quasi-autobiographical work that relates the general experience of a group of people but tells it from the point of view of one person

traditio—an official Catholic tradition that dictated both doctrines and practices

tradition—reformable practices of Catholicism

Tradition—unchanging doctrines of the Catholic religion

tres—three

U.S. Latina/o—(n.) A woman/man of Latin American descent living in the United States of America

U.S. Latino—(adj.) descriptor for factors common to men and women alike, such as the larger culture with its many components

Vatican II—the Second Vatican Council of bishops which met in Rome in 1962 to examine the future direction of the Catholic Church

velorio—a candlelight wake

virgen—virgin (*see* Blessed Virgin Mary)

virgencita—little virgin, a diminutive (*see* Blessed Virgin Mary)

Voodoo—a chiefly Haitian religion derived from African spiritism

Xicanista—a socially and politically aware Chicana feminist

Acknowledgments

Julia Alvarez. From *In the Time of the Butterflies*. Copyright © 1994 by Julia Alvarez. Originally published by Algonquin Books of Chapel Hill and republished by Plume, an imprint of Penguin Group (USA) Inc. Reprinted by permission of Susan Bergholz Literary Services, New York. All rights reserved.

Julia Alvarez. From *The Other Side/El Otro Lado*. Copyright © 1995 by Julia Alvarez. Published by Plume, an imprint of Penguin Group (USA) Inc. Reprinted by permission of Susan Bergholz Literary Services, New York. All rights reserved.

Julia Alvarez. From *Something to Declare*. Copyright © 1998 by Julia Alvarez. Originally published by Algonquin Books of Chapel Hill and republished by Plume, an imprint of Penguin Group (USA) Inc. Reprinted by permission of Susan Bergholz Literary Services, New York. All rights reserved.

Julia Alvarez. From *¡Yo!* Copyright © 1997 by Julia Alvarez. Originally published by Algonquin Books of Chapel Hill and republished by Plume, an imprint of Penguin Group (USA) Inc. Reprinted by permission of Susan Bergholz Literary Services, New York. All rights reserved.

Ana Castillo. From "el ser mujer" in *My Father Was a Toltec and Selected Poems*. Copyright © 1995 by Ana Castillo. Published by Vintage/Anchor, an imprint of Random House, Inc., and originally published by West End Press. Reprinted by permission of Susan Bergholz Literary Services, New York. All rights reserved.

Ana Castillo. From *So Far from God*. Copyright © 1993 by Ana Castillo. Published by Plume, an imprint of Penguin Group (USA) Inc. Reprinted by permission of the publisher.

Denise Chávez. From "Heat and Rain" in *Breaking Boundaries: Latina Writing and Critical Readings*, ed. Asunción Horno-Delgado, et al. and published by University of Massachusetts Press, Copyright © 1989. Reprinted by permission of the publisher.

Denise Chávez. From *Novena Narrativas y Ofrendas Nuevomexicanas*. Copyright © 1987 by Denise Chávez. Reprinted by permission in *Goddess of the Americas/La Diosa de las Americas: Writings on the Virgin de Guadalupe*, ed. Ana Castillo, and published by Riverhead Books. Reprinted here by permission of the author.

Sandra Cisneros. From "Guadalupe the Sex Goddess." Copyright © 1996 by Sandra Cisneros. Reprinted by permission in *Goddess of the Americas/La Diosa de las Americas: Writings on the Virgin de Guadalupe*, ed. Ana Castillo, and published by Riverhead Books. Reprinted here by permission of Susan Bergholz Literary Services, New York. All rights reserved.

Sandra Cisneros. From "Loose Woman" in *Loose Woman*. Copyright © 1994 by Sandra Cisneros. Originally published by Alfred A. Knopf, Inc. and republished by Vintage, an imprint of Random House, Inc. Reprinted by permission of Susan Bergholz Literary Services, New York. All rights reserved.

Sandra Cisneros. From *Woman Hollering Creek and Other Stories*. Copyright © 1991 by Sandra Cisneros. Originally published by Random House, Inc. and republished by Vintage, an imprint of Random House, Inc. Reprinted by permission of Susan Bergholz Literary Services, New York. All rights reserved.

Confraternity of Christian Doctrine. From "Psalm 27" in *The New American Bible*. Copyright © 1970 by Confraternity of Christian Doctrine. Published by Catholic Bible Publishers. Reprinted by permission of Confraternity of Christian Doctrine.

Kenneth G. Davis. From "Introduction." Originally appeared in *Listening: A Journal of Religion and Culture* (1997). Reprinted with permission in *Bridging Boundaries: The Pastoral Care of U.S. Hispanics*, ed. Kenneth G. Davis and Yolanda Tarango and published by University of Scranton Press, Copyright © 2000. Reprinted here by permission of University of Scranton Press.

Kenneth G. Davis. From "Still Gringo after All These Years." Originally appeared in *Quarterly Review: A Journal of Theological Resources for Ministry*. Reprinted with permission in *Bridging Boundaries: The*

Pastoral Care of U.S. Hispanics, ed. Kenneth G. Davis and Yolanda Tarango and published by University of Scranton Press, Copyright © 2000. Reprinted here by permission of University of Scranton Press.

Cristina García. From *The Agüero Sisters*. Copyright © 1997 by Cristina García. Published by Ballantine, an imprint of Random House, Inc. Reprinted by permission of the publisher.

Cristina García. From *Dreaming in Cuban*. Copyright © 1992 by Cristina García. Published by Ballantine, an imprint of Random House, Inc. Reprinted by permission of the publisher.

Ada María Isasi-Díaz. From "Preface" in *Bridging Boundaries: The Pastoral Care of U.S. Hispanics*, ed. Kenneth G. Davis and Yolanda Tarango. University of Scranton Press, Copyright © 2000. Reprinted by permission of the author and the publisher.

Ada María Isasi-Díaz and Yolanda Tarango. From *Hispanic Women: Prophetic Voice in the Church*. Copyright © 1988 by Ada María Isasi-Díaz and Yolanda Tarango. Published by Fortress Press, 1992. Reprinted by permission of Ada María Isasi-Díaz.

Graciela Limón. From *Song of the Hummingbird*. Copyright © 1996 by Graciela Limón. Published by Arte Público Press-University of Houston. Reprinted by permission of the publisher.

Pat Mora. From *House of Houses*. Copyright © 1997 by Pat Mora. Published by Beacon Press, Boston. Reprinted by permission of the publisher.

Cherríe Moraga. From "el mito Azteca." Copyright © 1993 by Cherríe Moraga. Reprinted from *The Last Generation* (South End Press) by permission in *Goddess of the Americas/La Diosa de las Americas: Writings on the Virgin de Guadalupe*, ed. Ana Castillo and published by Riverhead Books. Reprinted here by permission of South End Press.

Judith Ortiz Cofer. From "The Latin Deli: An Ars Poetica." Originally published in *The Americas Review* and republished with permission by Arte Público Press-University of Houston, Copyright © 1991. Reprinted by permission of Arte Público.

Judith Ortiz Cofer. From "Latin Women Pray" in *Terms of Survival*. Copyright © 1995 by Judith Ortiz Cofer. Published by Arte Público Press-University of Houston. Reprinted by permission of the publisher.

Judith Ortiz Cofer. From *The Line of the Sun*. Copyright © 1989 by Judith Ortiz Cofer. Published by University of Georgia Press. Reprinted by permission of the publisher.

Judith Ortiz Cofer. From *Silent Dancing: A Partial Remembrance of a Puerto Rican Childhood*. Copyright © 1990 by Judith Ortiz Cofer. Published by Arte Público Press-University of Houston. Reprinted by permission of the publisher.

Esmeralda Santiago. From *Almost a Woman*. Copyright © 1998 by Esmeralda Santiago. Published by Vintage, an imprint of Random House, Inc. Reprinted by permission of the publisher.

Helena María Viramontes. From *The Moths and Other Stories*. Copyright © 1995 by Helena María Viramontes. Published by Arte Público Press-University of Houston. Reprinted by permission of the publisher.

Helena María Viramontes. From "Nopalitos" in *Breaking Boundaries: Latina Writing and Critical Readings*, ed. Asunción Horno-Delgado, et al. and published by University of Massachusetts Press, Copyright © 1989. Reprinted by permission of the publisher.

Helena María Viramontes. From *Under the Feet of Jesus*. Copyright © 1996 by Helena María Viramontes. Published by Plume, an imprint of Penguin Group (USA) Inc. Reprinted by permission of the publisher.

Index